The Quest
for Anonymity

The Quest for Anonymity

The Novels of George Eliot

Henry Alley

DELAWARE

Newark: University of Delaware Press
London: Associated University Presses

Associated University Presses
440 Forsgate Drive
Cranbury, NJ 08512

Associated University Presses
16 Barter Street
London WC1A 2AH, England

Associated University Presses
P.O. Box 338, Port Credit
Mississauga, Ontario
Canada L5G 4L8

The paper used in this publication meets the requirements
of the American National Standard for Permanence of Paper
for Printed Library Materials Z39.48–1984.

Library of Congress Cataloging-in-Publication Data

Alley, Henry, 1945–
    The quest for anonymity : the novels of George Eliot / Henry
Alley.
    Includes bibliographical references (p.   ) and index.
    ISBN 0-87413-621-0 (alk. paper)
    1. Eliot, George, 1819–1880—Ethics. 2. Women and literature—
England—History—19th century. 3. Didactic fiction, English—
History and criticism. 4. Social ethics in literature. 5. Self-
denial in literature. 6. Heroes in literature. 7. Quests in
literature. I. Title.
PR4692.E8A45   1997
823'.8—dc21   96-29628
                                                       CIP

PRINTED IN THE UNITED STATES OF AMERICA

For my Mother,
Johnnie C. Greer

Contents

Acknowledgments

I would like to thank James McConkey for his guidance in my graduate study of George Eliot, as well as James R. Kincaid, Bernard Lightman, and Elizabeth Campbell for reading early drafts of the manuscript and offering numerous suggestions. I would also like to acknowledge the Research Council of the University of Idaho and the Office of Research and Sponsored Programs at the University of Oregon for summer funding in important years of the writing process, as well as to thank *Midwest Quarterly, Victorians Institute Journal, Rocky Mountain Review of Language and Literature, Greyfriar: Siena Studies in Literature* and *Cithara* for publishing early forms of chapters of this book. The Northwest British Studies Conference has, also, been faithful and inspiring in its reception of my various papers on Eliot over the years, and their audience has been another essential component in the formation of the book. Finally, I would like to thank my students, who, over the course of twenty-five years, have found George Eliot to be such an endless source of excitement, debate, and illumination in their lives, and who have passed their energy on to me. To them I also dedicate this study.

The Quest
for Anonymity

Introduction: "George Eliot" and the Road to Emmaus

IN what Eliot described as "that most beautiful passage in Luke's Gospel—the appearance of Jesus to the disciples at Emmaus," Christ appears anonymously; after the crucifixion, he is the stranger on the road who tests his disciples' faith and powers of detection. Writing to her friend Sara Sophia Hennell, Eliot, at the age of twenty-seven, went on to exclaim, "How universal in its significance! The soul that has hopefully followed its form—its impersonation of the highest and best—all in despondency—its thoughts all refuted, its dreams all dissipated. Then comes another Jesus—another, but the same—the same highest and best, only chastened, crucified instead of triumphant—and the soul learns that this is the true way to conquest and glory—And then there is the burning of the heart which assures that 'This was the Lord!' that this is the inspiration from above—the true Comforter that leads into truth" (*Letters* 2: 228).

For Eliot, in the eight books of fiction that were to follow, this frequently is the critical moment: when the heart "burns" in the presence of the yet undisclosed hero or heroine, one who is apparently vanquished but becomes truly victorious once the recognition finally arrives. The acknowledgment has required faith, kept pure by the anonymity of the subject and the event. The subject—the hero whose presence "burns" the onlooker—is uplifted, since his or her motivation has been directed to the greatness of the task at hand, rather than to the personal glory that the choral figure might provide. In this sense, all of Eliot's major characters are travelers on the road to Emmaus; their true commitment, whether to themselves or to others, is continually being tested by the absence of external recognition. True heroism must always be rendered great by the equally heroic acknowledgment of the quietly burning heart; in Eliot it is never helped along by prestige—indeed, it is frequently deterred by it and even sometimes advanced by its opposites—by scandal, exile, ostracism, and obscurity.

13

In *Scenes of Clerical Life,* Janet Dempster, who becomes the "living memorial" to Mr. Tryan, embodies this moment most clearly. When she overhears the minister praying with Sally, the narrator observes, "the most brilliant deed of virtue could not have inclined Janet's good-will towards Mr. Tryan so much as this fellowship in suffering, and the softening thought was in her eyes when he appeared in the doorway, pale, weary, and depressed" (ch. 12, 331). The hero has prayed unaware of Janet's silent audience, and thus anonymous heroism emerges from a private moment. Like Christ, Mr. Tryan is resurrected from his "pale, weary, and depressed" state through the point of view of another, who is also resurrected from despondency.

A magnified version of this same pattern may be found in *Middlemarch.* Although the effect of Dorothea's life was "not widely visible," the narrator, in enlisting the reader to supply the appropriate silent audience, concludes by saying that "the effect of her being on those around her was incalculably diffusive: for the growing good of the world is partly dependent on unhistoric acts; and that things are not so ill with you and me as they might have been, is half owing to the number who lived faithfully a hidden life, and rest in unvisited tombs" (896). Dorothea begins by hoping to be a prestigious hero; she ends by attaining the greater glory of being an anonymous one. The unvisited nature of her tomb is a living monument to the purity of her faith. Although her life ends in anonymity, it does not end in oblivion. The overall impact of Eliot's vast novel, then, is not ironic but subtly and finally elegaic; by extension, all of Middlemarch rises from the ashes of what was thought to be irreparably forgotten, a past which also includes the coordinate hero, Lydgate, whom Dorothea, in paralleling Janet's role as well, has recognized.

In *The Essence of Christianity,* a work whose translation belongs to the same year as Eliot's letter, Feuerbach, in his chapter "The Mystery of the Resurrection," writes that the "resurrection of Christ is therefore the satisfied desire of man for an immediate certainty of his personal existence after death,—personal immortality as a sensible, indubitable fact" (ch. 14, 135). Although Eliot could not meet this need by writing directly of the biblical Christ and his Passion and Ascension, she could meet it by populating her metaphorical road to Emmaus with people whose presence would better the world with invisible good. The process of psychologically detecting this betterment would supply the analogue to "the burning heart"—or better, the resurrecting heart—in the witnessing characters, in the narrator, and in the reader as well.

Heroism emerges through disclosure, rather than grandly executed action, and since the revelation requires discerning effort
on the part of those watching, both observer and observed are
celebrated. Janet becomes heroic when she becomes a living memorial to Mr. Tryan's obscure quest. The older Adam Bede finally
achieves the heroic stature he sought as a younger man by re-
membering the unacknowledged heroism of Mr. Irwine, who
himself had an "unwearying tenderness for obscure and monotonous suffering" (ch. 5, 59). Character becomes recollection and
resurrection.

As the storyteller who wished to invoke a new deity for the age,
Eliot set herself the task of separating acts of goodness from their
acknowledgment and then acknowledging them anyway within
the witnessing minds of other characters and upon the silent
screen of the narrative itself. This paradoxical perspective—of recognizing what goes unrecognized—is perhaps best illustrated by
her pivotal novel, *Felix Holt*. Quite early and quite typically, it
becomes apparent that the hero of the story is not the hero of the
title at all, but the nondescript parson, Rufus Lyon. As he works
in his study, Eliot's narrator pauses and observes:

> If a cynical sprite were present, riding on one of the motes in that
> dusty room, he may have made himself merry at the illusions of the
> little minister who brought so much conscience to bear on the produc-
> tion of so slight an effect. I confess to smiling myself, being sceptical
> as to the effect of ardent appeals and nice distinctions on gentlemen
> who are got up, both inside and out, as candidates in the style of the
> period; but I never smiled at Mr. Lyon's trustful energy without falling
> to penitence and veneration immediately after. For what we call illu-
> sions are often, in truth, a wider vision of past and present realities—
> a willing movement of a man's soul with the larger sweep of the world's
> forces—a movement towards a more assured end than the chances of
> a single life. We see human heroism broken into units and say, this
> unit did little—might as well not have been. But in this way we might
> break up a great army into units; in this way we might break the
> sunlight into fragments, and think that this and the other might be
> cheaply parted with. Let us rather raise a monument to the soldiers
> whose brave hearts only kept the ranks unbroken, and met death—a
> monument to the faithful who were not famous, and who are precious
> as the continuity of the sunbeams is precious, though some of them
> fall unseen and on barrenness. (ch. 16, 276–77)

As is frequently the case in the later novels, the reader passes,
in one paragraph, from superior smiles to veneration, a process
perhaps best described as irony backfiring on itself or, as we shall

see later, the reaffirming of a heroic voice. We are finding that our hearts are burning anyway and that we are granting Mr. Lyon his "personal immortality" in relation to all the other legions of anonymous heroes. The reader is not allowed to ride the "dusty mote" of the cynical sprite for long; Mr. Lyon's obscure efforts are suddenly given the same respect as those works which might immediately win our esteem and attention—with this addition, that Mr. Lyon's efforts, in all their anonymity, require greater faith, both on his part as well as ours. In terms of the dramatic context of the novel, then, Esther's condescensions toward her father acquire a decided tension at this point, since she seems to share, at least to some degree, the perspective of the cynical sprite. Thus, even without her being present, the heroine's pathway is laid out before us at this early stage; her growth will be gauged largely by her ability to throw off the Byronic heroes of her reading and come to appreciate her father in all his hidden grandeur—an education which is itself heroic and which eventually links reader and narrator with the principal characters, who happen to be parent and child.

In a broader sense, parenthood, for Eliot, whether symbolic or literal, constitutes perhaps the greatest example of anonymous heroism. A living memorial is the child or disciple or witness who lives on to embody the "great" bequeathal of the unsung hero or heroine. We might consider Eppie, the child of Silas, Esther, the child of Rufus, Janet, the "child" of Tryan, and Lillo, the "child" of Romola. In all these cases, the concluding visions suggest how true heroism seeks generative life anonymously, without nominative prestige, prestige and its pursuit being, for Eliot, frequently a kind of living death.

We might necessarily add, too, that many of the parent-child relationships often do not belong to any specific family tree; rather, they are relationships, like Silas's and Eppie's, of informal and spiritual adoption. The reason is quite clear: the parents do their good works in a state of anonymity, and the lack of acknowledgment—in this case, of having a namesake—tests the true spirit of the devotion. Eliot's books in some respects take the perspective of adoption agencies; they are more concerned with the kind of parenting that comes from love rather than from blood lineage and surnames. Very tellingly, Esther does not arrive at a full conversion, in recognizing her father's value, until she has realized that he is not her natural parent after all but instead someone who had the externally thankless task of loving and nurturing her for her own sake.

The anonymous heroes of Eliot's making, whether they are characters, narrators, or readers, have distinct characteristics, which might be best understood by invoking the classical and Renaissance hero or heroine who precedes and the modernist hero or heroine who follows. Eliot herself moved easily between literary figures, of whatever epoch, frequently acknowledging the "huge colossi" of the past as though they were movable statues in a vast personal pantheon, or better, the members of a living, word-created hotel. She also had no problem with ironically or sympathetically invoking later scientists, poets, and writers to shadow or color over the earlier historical period of which she was writing. This allusive easiness, which might be called "joyous anachronism," is present not only in her novels, with their numerous epigraphs and surprising allusions, but also in her notebooks and journals where, for example, her reading for *Middlemarch* alone would include such entries as Aristotle, Aristophanes, Lucretius, Milton, Goethe's *Wilhelm Meister,* Ben Jonson, M'Lennan's "The Worship of Animals and Plants," Drayton's "Nymphidia," the major works of Sir Thomas Browne, and William Smith's *Dictionary of Greek and Roman Biography and Mythology.*

Thus, we cannot fully understand Lydgate without the surprise of seeing Hamlet placed beside him, as though he were an invited but unexpected guest. Indeed, Eliot's creative process, reflected by her art, seems to be best symbolized by the hodgepodge of Piero di Cosimo's studio, with its "heterogeneous still life" (ch. 18, 245) or by the engraving-lined walls of Mrs. Meyrick's erudite parlor or in fact by the murmuring and tumbling allusions in Mr. Brooke's mind itself. The very idea of her keeping a "Quarry" for a novel like *Middlemarch* suggests an unearthing of both gems and sediment, and again, as in Mr. Brooke's mind, no one knows what sort of extraordinary combination is going to turn up next.

Thus, it would seem best in a critical treatment of Eliot to allow ourselves the latitude of what goes on time and time again in her novels—a contextualizing via a broadly interpreted comparative literature. In her recent study, Gillian Beer writes that "the 'imaginative' for her [George Eliot] means the mind's primary power of 'swift images' which register desire's entry into consciousness" (194), and I would add that part of the excitement of reading her work comes from the sudden, frequently pictorial and sometimes jaunty allusions which link the ancient with the current, the English with the "foreign"—an excitement which parallels the sudden experience of desire in her characters—in particular, when their hearts "burn" with recognition.

The thrust of this study will also be one of comparative literature, because in Eliot, "heroism" is almost always being defined
or defied in relation to models of the past, as the direction and
spirit of her own associative and creative processes would suggest.
In looking, in particular, at what I see as Eliot's most central subject, we might first begin by saying that many of her models for
anonymous heroism are derived originally from Greek tragedy,
the principal figure being Prometheus. In Eliot's view, this early
hero is central, because he is presented as taking a chance on
mankind without the promise of benefit from anyone, whether
god or human. In *Daniel Deronda*, the narrator makes Eliot's archetype very clear, insisting, even, that the reader contemplate
Prometheus at exactly his most anonymous and therefore most
heroic moment:

> There be who hold that the deeper tragedy were a Prometheus Bound
> not *after* but *before* he had well got the celestial fire into the νάρθηζ
> whereby it might be conveyed to mortals: thrust by Kratos and Bix of
> instituted methods into a solitude of despised ideas, fastened in
> throbbing helplessness by the fatal pressure of poverty and disease—
> a solitude where many pass by, but none regard. (ch. 38, 527)

In her "Notes on the Spanish Gypsy and Tragedy in General," Eliot
also writes that, from the Greek point of view, "the Prometheus
represents the ineffectual struggle to redeem the small and miserable race of man, against the stronger adverse ordinances that
govern the frame of things with a triumphant power" (Cross 3:
34), but she goes on to defend his tragic example by saying that
human serenity does not arrive through rational thought but by
a more spiritual process:

> Love, pity, constituting sympathy, and generous joy with regard to
> the lot of our fellow-men, comes in,—has been growing since the
> beginning,—enormously enhanced by wider vision of results, by an
> imagination actively interested in the lot of mankind generally; and
> these feelings become piety,—i.e., loving, willing submission, and he-
> roic Promethean effort towards high possibilities, which may result
> from our individual life. (3: 36)

In Eliot's imagination, and certainly throughout her novels, love
and apparent ineffectuality are interlinked, since the first is
brought about through the intense challenge of the second, when
all motivation for positive action seems gone. Heroism, unseen
heroism, results when an inner faith causes the woman or man to

trust in "the wider vision of results," even when individual success seems lost. Thus, in an earlier epigraph to a chapter in *Daniel Deronda,* it is no surprise that the narrator refers to "the cry of Prometheus" as having "a greater energy than the sea and sky he invokes and the deity he defies," since his cry, and not the apparent result, is the point. It is no surprise, either, that the same epigraph charges that the "narrator of human actions," like "the astronomer [who] threads the darkness," should trace cries like those of Prometheus back to "the hidden pathways of feeling and thought which lead up to every moment of action, and to those moments of intense suffering which take the quality of action," thus defining the novelist as, in fact, the scribe, the bard, of anonymous heroism, because "men, like planets, have both a visible and an invisible history" (ch. 16, 202).

Eliot also modeled her anonymous heroes on the chorus of Greek tragedy and in the principal witness figures of its dramatis personae. One might consider, for example, that Antigone is a heroine even prior to her own tragedy, when she provides the appropriate purgation of pity and fear by observing and affirming her father's plight in *Oedipus at Colonus.* She, in her own way, becomes Oedipus by acknowledging him, and, on a more subtle track, Oedipus rises in stature by embracing and acquiring the more tender qualities of the Theban princess. Like Tom and Maggie of Eliot's work to follow, together they form the completed psyche, and thus they add the component of androgyny to the Emmaus experience. Most important, however, if we focus on Antigone alone, we can see, at the end of the *Colonus,* a young woman much like Dorothea, whose greatness partly resides, as was suggested earlier, in making another soul great (in this case, Lydgate), through her sustained memory of him and through her female acquisition of who he is as a man. It is no accident that the Sophoclean heroine is named also in the final paragraph of Eliot's proclaimed masterpiece, and although the narrator quickly acknowledges that the mythical medium is forever gone, the narrator also ushers in a new generation of Antigones to fill in for the old and thus creates, even at the end, a sense of that particular, varied world, or better, culture of the novel.

It is also true that Eliot draws on the model of *The Aeneid* and its followers when shaping the central anonymous experiences of her characters. In the epic that has had one of the most sustained impacts on the imagination of the Western world and which incorporated, in narrative form, much of the influence of classical tragedy, Aeneas passes from a state of egoism into a rebirth of communal dedication, supplanting the old Hellenic egoism of his foil, Turnus. In this transformation, he also arrives at an acceptance of death, not only as it applies to himself, but to others as well. This pattern Eliot was to absorb. But as opposed to Aeneas, Eliot's heroes do not gain Rome anyway, anymore than they gain the celebrations of a Theban chorus, and the gains they make have nothing to do with the vanquishment of others, as commemorated, ultimately, in some Elysian Fields. The Elysian Fields, if there are any, are in the community of travelers on the road to Emmaus, who all acknowledge, frequently in silence, one another's anonymous feats of goodness. These unsung acts must be sufficient unto themselves, so far as one's sense of satisfaction and self-esteem are concerned. No mean feat, since even a character as inwardly gifted as Aeneas was still given empire and fame as external reward and incentive. Eliot thus sets her obscure characters a hard task, and, as Elizabeth Ermarth concludes in her recent study, "To find the anonymity of the effort depressing implies a taste for World-Historical Action, or for Remarkable Genius, that George Eliot sees as another form of special pleading to justify inactivity or shabby achievement" (134).

For other models of this sort of courage, Eliot also went on to Milton, her "demigod" and Virgil's great descendant. It was important, of course, that Eliot develop a heroism that would embrace and yet transcend both the classical and Christian traditions. Milton's "Lycidas" and its elegaic crisis of fame versus identity supply a major source, but more dramatically, Milton's *Paradise Lost* offers Adam, Eve (see Wittreich, McColley), and Christ as the heroes and heroine of his epic, all of whom vanquish the great embodiment of selfish enterprise, Satan, who finds his prototype in the equally expelled Turnus. As the prologue to book 9 of *Paradise Lost* makes clear, we are no longer in a world where valor "in battles feigned" is prized; rather, it is the psychological victory that matters. For new virtues, we must have new heroes. Thus Achilles, Odysseus, and even Aeneas are turned aside, for the perfect hero in heaven and the reborn hero and heroine—at least by book 12—on earth. At this conclusion, Adam sums up the advice he has been given by the archangel Michael, as if, at least in part, he were reciting Eliot's Promethean code, saying he has learned to be "merciful over all his [God's] works, with good/ still overcoming evil, and by small/ accomplishing great things" (12: 565–7).

Eliot therefore takes her anonymous heroes further than Aeneas and also draws on other works of Renaissance literature—

in particular those of Shakespeare—to deepen the psychological resonance of her model. Hamlet, who is compared to Aeneas in the second act of the central tragedy, is offered the possibility of honorable action and, by the end, to some extent achieves it, although without the grandeur of a Roman conquest. Mainly he asks that Horatio live on to tell his story, and so Horatio does, starting with the assembled Elsinore court, in the final lines. Some lessening, then, of the fame associated with heroism has occurred, and Eliot was to develop this sense of diminishment when, embodying the tradition, she was to compare not only Lydgate with Hamlet, but Gwendolen Harleth as well. (See Alley, "Gwendolen Harleth: George Eliot's Modernization of Hamlet.") Her main point is that these young people suffer but lack even Hamlet's compensations of partial adulation, as preceded by grandly executed soliloquies. Thus the exquisite silences of their invisible trials become dramatized instead, and their personal Horatios—Dorothea and Daniel—are moved more to center stage so that the anonymity of the heroism may be accentuated.

As Dorothea Brooke, Tertius Lydgate, Gwendolen Harleth, and Daniel Deronda might suggest, Eliot's consciousness of her subject bloomed slowly, and for primarily this reason, my study will examine the works of book-length fiction in the order in which they appeared. David Carroll, in his recent *George Eliot and the Conflict of Interpretations,* a study which follows a similar scheme, notes that "George Eliot saw her career as a novelist both as a unity and as a series of distinct stages. As she wrote to John Blackwood in 1861 over the publication of *Silas Marner:* 'My chief reason for wishing to publish the story now, is, that I like my writings to appear in the order in which they are written, because they belong to successive mental phases'" (23). It has been often noted that her individual novels gather an extraordinary momentum as they go along, paralleling the novelist's own rhythm of increasingly accelerated composition. The same may be said of Eliot's canon as a whole—that, somewhere along about *Felix Holt,* the concept of "human heroism broken into units" emerged not only into the narrative commentary but into the very shaping of Rufus Lyon's character. Later Eliot, in writing of her experimentations with a story called "Miss Brooke," would say that "it is a subject which has been recorded among my possible themes ever since I began to write fiction, but will probably take new shapes in the development" (Cross 3: 97). For Eliot, the pursuit of her subject over her literary career became itself a kind of quest as she developed it in the form of more and more elaborate characters and placed it more and more at the center of her narrative dramas.

The subject of anonymous heroism has been so prominent that many other critics, of course, have touched on it since the "Renaissance" of Eliot scholarship, which began in the 1950s with Gordon S. Haight's pioneering research. However, no single study has dealt with it consistently or as a key to the complex and cumulative mysteries of her art. This book, in fact, represents a twenty-five-year quest to define and illustrate what has been to me so elusive and subtle in her fiction, yet so central. Gradually I began to discover that the best way of paying tribute to George Eliot was to focus on the way her characters deal with and heroically transcend receiving no apparent tribute at all. At last I concluded that no other subject in Eliot ramifies out so largely, so as to embrace her esthetics, her belief in fiction as moral exploration, her sense of character composition, her evocation of classical tradition, her understanding of male-female relations, her dramatization of political commitment and disillusionment, her development of narrative technique, her modulation of comic, epic, and tragic genres, her analysis of family, her conception of psychological androgyny, her affirmation of the healing properties of literature, her approach to vocation, her approach to the Woman Question, and even her vision of her own biography and her need to adopt her famously anonymous pen name.

It seems also that Eliot criticism is ready for another study which once more takes the novels in the order in which they were written and which provides a consistent theme that embraces many topics, acknowledging both "post-modern" and what came before, and avoiding the assumption that new theories render all else obsolete. In the past twenty years, once critics and biographers such as Haight, Leavis, Hardy, Harvey, Paris, and Thale had worked to reestablish Eliot as a great, if not the greatest, English novelist, the necessarily more specialized work of such people as Witemeyer, Graver, and Bonaparte soon followed, paralleled by studies modeled on deconstructionist or feminist theory. The result has been a huge and sometimes intimidating critical canon, which stresses the novelist's extraordinary and diverse appeal as well as her timely topicality. But it is important that readers look at her work close up again, become reacquainted with the patterns of her scenes and character dynamics, hear once more the music of her sentences in the context of the full scholarship. In this vein, three more general studies have appeared in the past ten years, updating their precedents of the 1950s and 1960s, following on the heels of the more specialized interlude of the 1970s and 1980s, and turning attention once again to the reading of Eliot on more broadly defined moral and esthetic foundations.

These three new *George Eliots*, with their widely different readings and biographical interpretations, have initiated a necessary rebalancing, and I am grateful to Jennifer Uglow, Elizabeth Deeds Ermarth, and Gillian Beer for recreating, in the spirit of Eliot paradoxes, an old frontier, where my study nicely fits. I am also grateful to them for writing in a concise but frequently poetically sensitive language that serves as an excellent means of illuminating the similar properties of Eliot's style. To draw on Eliot's own "Notes on Form in Art," which she made just before she was about to embark on *Middlemarch*, we can say that rhythm—whether of individual words, sentences, or psychic changes—formed the very center of her art, and in keeping with my more immediate critical precedents, I have also tried to do justice to the beauties of her language and histories, by trying to suggest, via quotation and commentary, how very dynamic and frequently surprising her characters, images, and allusions are.

In a similar vein, I have tried to restore the importance of reading Eliot in relation to what she would have defined as the classics, since she saw them not as decorative embroidery but instead, in the spirit of her precedents, Shakespeare and Milton, and her literary heirs, Woolf and Joyce, as the very source of literary life for her own newly developing characters, as well as a pattern, evolved from the inflected beauties of both Greek and Latin, for advancing her elegant and lucid prose. I have also tried to suggest all the immense scholarship which has come before, with emphasis not only on the monographs but the article literature as well, which, it has frequently seemed to me, has been a much overlooked treasure house, somewhat in the spirit of Eliot's "human heroism broken in units" or even, in some cases, her anonymously heroic "unvisited tombs."

The biographical scholarship I have also tried to take into account, and it might be appropriate here to conclude, briefly, with the concept of anonymous heroism as it applied to the life of Marian Evans, since one cannot even write the name "George Eliot" without referring to it. And certainly the thought that first comes to mind is that "George Eliot" was anything but anonymous, having received fame and even worship during her own lifetime. In the same breath, however, we must add that the historical Marian Evans was sensitively and sometimes distressingly aware of this very disparity—between her major subject and her own experi-

ence. Thirteen years after writing her letter to Sara Sophia Hennell, that is, the very year *Adam Bede* appeared, Eliot revealled to
her friend that "I was the author of Adam Bede and Clerical
Scenes, and they seemed overwhelmed with surprize. This experience has enlightened me a good deal as to the ignorance in which
we all live of each other" (Cross 2: 85). The dropping of her
anonymity was immediately followed by a difficult moment, three
days later, when Eliot criticized one of Sara's own manuscripts
and Sara was clearly hurt. "I see now," Sara wrote to her, "that I
have lost the only reader in whom I felt confident in having secure
sympathy with the *subject* (not with *me*) whom I most gratefully
believe—believed in—that she has floated beyond me in another
sphere, and I remain gazing at the glory into which she has departed, wistfully and very lonely" (*Letters* 3: 95–96). Quite characteristically, Eliot apologized immediately, confessing that she "had
blundered, as most of us do, from too much egoism and too little
sympathy" (*Letters* 3: 90). It seems fair to conclude that this was
the moment when Eliot felt that her friend had become an anonymous hero just when prestige was over taking her own life. In
other words, Eliot had stepped off the road to Emmaus just when
her friend had stepped on, and in terms of her letter thirteen years
earlier, she had become superficially "triumphant" whereas her
friend, whose sensitivity was painfully like her own, had been
admirably "crucified." Clearly she was uncomfortable in the midst
of her friend's vulnerability when her own star was ascending, at
the time when the real identity of "George Eliot" was becoming
the best-kept secret in England. The distress of this realization is
underscored by an earlier part of the letter where Eliot concludes
that "we are quite unable to represent ourselves truly—why
should we complain that our friends see a false image?"

How was Marian Evans to manage the burden of her growing
fame when it sought to deprive her of what she perhaps valued
the most—that is, the faith of a life whose effects were not widely
visible? It is apparent throughout her letters, journals, and notebooks, as well as the manifold accounts of her life, that she passionately sought all the ingredients of an anonymous heroism for
herself as well as her characters—acceptance of her own mortality,
affirmation of communal achievement through literal and symbolic parenthood, and an intense and androgynous identification
with both sexes, an identification that would lead, analogously, to
a magnanimous ability to identify with all points of view.

One answer, of course, comes in the form of George Henry

Lewes and his famous protection of his partner from all the ill effects of being a celebrity. But a more satisfactory answer is found if we say that after the days of *Adam Bede* and all the discomforts which attended the excitement, she perhaps derived the formula of "George Eliot" as a means of maintaining and developing all the precious components of anonymous heroism, even though its initial purpose of maintaining secrecy had well fallen away. It seems she became content with not "representing herself" as she really was—at least to the outer world—so that the faith of her inner life might be preserved. Another recent study, Alison Booth's *Greatness Engendered: George Eliot and Virginia Woolf,* connects Woolf's "narrative ideal of androgynous unself-consciousness" with Eliot's "narrative ideal of selfless objectivity" (78), or what George Levine has earlier called her "constructed, selfless self" ("Hypothesis," 19). While Booth sees these ideals as releases from the narrative problems of being identified as a woman novelist, I would add that for Eliot, in particular, the "selflessness" was an escape from ego, and therefore an opportunity to achieve her own brand of heroism that itself identifies heroism and beauty.

Although her books would bear her prestigious pen name, "George Eliot," Marian Evans could never be lulled into self-importance and therefore self-exile from the road to Emmaus. Marian Lewes could go on and become a "Mutter" (Haight, *Biography,* 332) to the young Charles Lewes, the year after her first novel would appear and participate in the anonymous heroism of parenthood. And above all, the male pen name would allow her to identify with both male and female characters, to enter, without ceremony, the parlor and the workshop both, disclosing the private histories that would cross gender lines, and show her dramatis personae embroiled in the same heroically anonymous activity. Perhaps divining this, she would write to Blackwood, on the very brink of her career as a writer of fiction, that "whatever may be the success of my stories, I shall be resolute in preserving my *incognito,* having observed that a *nom de plume* secures all the advantages without the disagreeables of reputation" (*Letters* 2: 292). For Eliot, it seems clear that she must live and thrive in exactly the arena where her own protagonists struggled and grew.

To shed further light on this relation between "incognito" and artistic and anonymous heroism, Jennifer Uglow, in her commentary on *Middlemarch,* offers an extraordinary insight into the justly celebrated chapter 81, where Dorothea and Rosamond "clasped each other as if they had been in a shipwreck," in a reference to the Cross memoir of his departed and famous spouse:

"she told me that in all her best writing there was a 'not herself' which took possession of her, and that she felt her own personality to be merely the instrument through which this spirit, as it were, was acting. Particularly she dwelt on this in regard to the scene in 'Middlemarch' between Dorothea and Rosamund" (Cross 3: 306). Uglow emphasizes Eliot's "mysterious loss" (252) of self, and, I would add, this unburdening via the muse would constitute, perfectly, that experience of anonymous heroism which Eliot so sought as a release from her own fame and her own ego. The Cross passage also perfectly illustrates the paradox of Eliot being filled at just the moment when Eliot was least herself—in this case, filled with the two sides of her psyche, Rosamond and Dorothea, egoist and seer. The women's hearts burn for each other; Eliot's heart burns for them; and Cross supplies the final acknowledgment for his wife, now apparently lost to death but restored through the recollection of this moment of creation, so indicative of her genius, and so indicative of anonymous heroism.

1

Scenes of Clerical Life and the
Art of Indirect Idealization

Eᴌɪᴏᴛ's ultimate goal—morally, esthetically—was to free the individual ego from the suffering of reflecting upon itself. Her fiction, which we have seen her describing as a series of evolving psychological phases, achieves this liberation through strongly argued models of balance and through the kinds of recognitions linked to anonymous heroism. If mental anguish is to be escaped through the contemplation of others, it is not satisfactory to rejoice in one's own monuments alone. Therefore it would follow that Eliot's cumulative effort would clarify what it means to achieve on the level of quiet and anonymous bequeathal. In her recent study, Gillian Beer emphasizes the "the extent to which silent writing and reading gave dramatic expression to her [George Eliot's] particular psychic position" (10) and suggests the corollary between the novelist's own subdued creative act and the private reading experience of becoming another person. Through the dynamic visualizations embodied in her characters, the reader becomes liberated; imaginatively, we break out of our egos and experience personalities and a world where the concept of single-minded achievement is challenged.

Beer also speaks of how Eliot "dramatised the private and dwelt in the unachieving, even while the scope of her fiction reclaimed the broadest extent of social inquiry and of critical insight into the workings of class, gender, age, power, and need" (10). The scope and the dramatization of "the unachieving" do not exist in opposition; rather, as we shall see, the scope provides the means to understanding and appreciating what is only apparently unproductive; to be anonymous is not to be insignificant.

Eliot discovered that if this perspective is to be reached, time must either be speeded up or slowed down. As we are, we can only live in the "present" and therefore can only suffer from the imprisonment of believing that what we do is bound by our birth and death. As we read Eliot, however, her novels become a large means of entering such a time frame which shows how what we do today might bear tenable and communal fruit sometime beyond our interment in an unvisited tomb. This is one of the major comforts of anonymity. Coordinately, her books are our major means of making us an additional gender, through an identification with a Dorothea, a Lydgate, or both.

The escape from pain and the subsequent experience of anonymity, then, constitute a paradoxical and healing process. On the one hand, one's ego shrinks; on the other, it expands. Just as one loses by becoming a reader, so does one gain. When the reader becomes Dorothea, he becomes both larger and smaller by becoming the woman he never could be; when she becomes Lydgate, she becomes both larger and smaller in the same way. Similarly, the moment we become the larger consciousness of *Middlemarch,* our egos both expand and contract. We are bound by a short period of eighteen months; yet we are led to see our lives and the lives of others within the entire Western tradition. Applied to Eliot's characters, the paradox can be seen in the various tragic and epic states of Adam, Maggie, Romola, Tom, Mr. Irwine, Felix, Esther, Lydgate, Dorothea, Gwendolen, and Daniel. There is a fall from mental euphoria, frequently derived from a secure and private world of study or reflection; there is a subsequent littleness which "crowds" in and enlarges the reaches of their souls. In engaging in this process, many of Eliot's protagonists, as suggested earlier, show their antecedents in the witness figures of classical and Renaissance tragedy, for they are the ones who must live on to tell someone else's story and therefore bring some restoration of order to the kingdom created. Antigone, in *Oedipus at Colonus,* both grows and diminishes in her sense of importance as she undergoes the *pathos.* On the one hand, she becomes her father and therefore is larger by being both princess and king. On the other, she is less in that she must read her individual destiny within the context of the House of Thebes.

We might, then, begin by considering Eliot's first book-length work of fiction, *Scenes of Clerical Life,* as an argument for the consistency of Eliot's vision of the anonymous hero—and her or his escape from pain. In light of many schools of Eliot criticism, *Scenes of Clerical Life* has been perceived either as the advent of an *oeuvre* dedicated to keeping heroes out, or as a picturesque phase, given to quiet *pathos,* which Eliot later transcended. Barbara Hardy, in developing the second approach, writes, "The humble character who is unusual in tragedy (less because of his social class than because of his limited emotional capacity) gradually makes way for the character with sensibility and intelligence, until in *Middlemarch* and *Daniel Deronda* she creates tragic figures who share and express their author's vision of their *catharsis*" (*Novels,* 14). Equally influential has been U. C. Knoepflmacher's conclusion in *George Eliot's Early Novels: The Limits of Realism:* "The norms that she had set for herself in 'Amos Barton' were ultimately repudiated when she aggrandized Deronda into an 'ideal or exceptional character' of Carlylean proportions" (36).

Eliot's fiction is, however, many times more consistent than these views would suggest. The distance that we must travel from "Amos Barton" to *Daniel Deronda* is, primarily, one of technical and spatial complexity—an indication that George Eliot was learning about her major theme as she continued to write. Just the same, to idealize her principal characters, to create a spirit of reverence for their apparently prosaic struggles remains constant throughout the spectrum of her book-length fiction, from her humble parish clergymen to her remote Jewish prophets. All are "martyrs of obscure circumstance" whose destinies the reader and narrator are meant to retrieve. As Gillian Beer writes, "In these first works, *Scenes* and *Adam Bede,* George Eliot is developing the central theme of her work: that commonplace life is heroic, requires no raising to be remarkable, but does require a special quality of attention if its significance is to be truly observed" (74).

When Eliot began writing fiction, she was well aware that the old-style hero, the hero of epics, romances, and fashionable novels, was no longer a living being for the intelligent readership of her day. The task she set herself, then, was to find new ways of reaching the sympathies of her audience by inventing new narrative devices and a new kind of protagonist, one who could stand in the tradition of Ulysses, Aeneas, Antigone, and Hermione and yet command the admiration of her contemporary public. For her, the task of modern fiction was to heighten one's perception to such a point that the inner lives of her characters would make them heroic; this is the "special attention" that Beer mentions. Thus, in this first book of fiction, she writes:

> I should imagine that neither Luther nor John Bunyan, for example, would have satisfied the modern demand for an ideal hero, who believes nothing but what is true, feels nothing but what is exalted and does nothing but what is graceful. The real heroes, of God's making, are quite different: they have their natural heritage of love and conscience which they drew in with their mother's milk; they know one

or two of those deep spiritual truths which are only to be won by long wrestling with their own sins and their sorrows. ("Janet's Repentance," ch. 8, 321)

And in *Daniel Deronda*, she writes:

Such is the irony of earthly mixtures, that the heroes have not always had carpets and tea-cups of their own; and, seen through the open window by the mackerel vendor, may have been invited with some hopefulness to pay three hundred per cent in the form of fourpence. (*Daniel Deronda*, ch. 43, 606)

Eliot assumes that, prior to opening her novels, the reader has polarized the grand world of historic fame—the world of Bunyan and Luther—with the mundane worlds of Shepperton, Treby, Hayslope, Middlemarch, and London. By the time the book is closed, the reader has been carefully moved toward perceiving the linkages, partly through the spirit of "joyous anachronism" mentioned earlier, and also by acknowledgment of the unavoidable imperfections of the Great, which the narrator has been careful to point out, as well as by appreciation of the psychic struggles of those heroes who belong to the imperfect medium of the everyday and the present day. Such a sometimes arduous process of detection demands, of course, heroism of the reader.

If we advance this large paradigm for all of Eliot's book-length fiction and say that it develops with increasing intricacy throughout her life's work, then we might find it helpful to examine some major critical assumptions about her esthetic contemplation of a hero. In the earlier stages of Eliot criticism, it was stated that from *Scenes of Clerical Life* on forward, Eliot was a proponent of Ruskin's "realism" and therefore a writer largely concerned with art of the photographic sort. Earlier critics like Mario Praz also assumed that Eliot began her fiction career as a polemicist against idealization, and, proceeding from the famous passage on Dutch painting, many were quick to note the absence of angels in all of her work—or the failure or the inconsistency of such idealizations if they do appear. The appropriate answer, however, was found in Hugh Witemeyer's *George Eliot and the Visual Arts*, as well other critical studies appearing in the last twenty years. In reexamining the passage from *Adam Bede*, he writes: "She is pleading for catholicity of taste and sympathy, but not for a leveling of artistic subject matter. Eliot's narrator has strong prejudices about the limitations of the Dutch school, as does Ruskin, whose qualified defense of

Dutch art in *Modern Painters* underlies chapter 17 of *Adam Bede*" (25–26).

Therefore, Eliot must not be placed in the company of those artists who render observable "reality" slavishly but rather in those who idealized it. This company of poets, philosophers, and painters extends all the way back to the Neoplatonic tradition of Plotinus, Proclus, Cicero, Junius, and manifests itself, in a more familiar mode, in the work of Sir Joshua Reynolds, a painter whose presence plays such an argumentative part in the *Scenes*.[1] In his *Discourses on Art,* Reynolds writes:

> The wish of the genuine painter must be more extensive: instead of endeavouring to amuse mankind with the minute neatness of his imitations, he must endeavor to improve them by the grandeur of his idea; instead of seeking praise, by deceiving the superficial sense of the spectator, he must strive for fame, by captivating the imagination.
>
> The principle now laid down that the perfection of this art does not consist in mere imitation is far from being singular. It is, indeed, supported by the general opinion of the enlightened part of mankind. The poets, orators, and rhetoricians of antiquity are continually enforcing this position; that all the arts receive their perfection from an ideal beauty, superior to what is to be found in individual nature. They are ever referring to the practice of the painters and sculptors of their times, particularly Phidias. (42)

Under these esthetic assumptions, the possibilities of developing an anonymous hero are expanded in a variety of ways. If idealization springs from an attitude developed within the reader, rather than from some absolute moral code, then heroism can be created upon a bridge between the author's and the reader's minds. Eliot, who was known to praise Reynolds, seems to follow this advice when drawing this portrait of Lady Cheverel in "Mr. Gilfil's Love-Story":

> She is nearly fifty, but her complexion is still fresh and beautiful, with the beauty of an auburn blond; her proud pouting lips, and her head thrown a little backward as she walks, gives an expression of *hauteur* which is not contradicted by the cold grey eye. The tucked-in kerchief, rising full over the low tight bodice of her blue dress, sets off the majestic form of her bust, and she treads the lawn as if she were one of Sir Joshua Reynolds's stately ladies, who had suddenly stepped from her frame to enjoy the evening cool. (ch. 2, 133)

As in many of Eliot's narrative portraits, some of the details suggest mundane faults as well as attractions, but the overall effect of the description is one of stateliness; the overall impression of the scene, with Caterina included in the landscape, is one of the idyll, not the dingy or middlebrow snapshot. The reader is most noticeably called upon to create the scene with the narrator, not only through her or his imagination of a memory but also through her or his recollections of an artifact. Lady Cheverel is made as much of canvas as she is of flesh and blood. In this novella as well as in her other fiction, Eliot, when introducing a character, resembles more a painter undraping a portrait—who is calling upon the audience to help with the cloth—rather than a photographer offering a slice of life, and thus the reader is asked to participate in the artistic process of formulating a personality, which, for Eliot and Reynolds alike, is an act of heroic appreciation.

In keeping with these aims, Eliot's first short novel, "Amos Barton," presents us with a man who is an unlikely heroic candidate and yet a character who, through the transforming vision of the narrator and reader, becomes a full claimant to our sympathy and, at last, our veneration. As Alexandra Norton points out, Eliot takes great pains to emphasize the "created" nature of her narrator, thereby distancing herself from her project and accentuating "the wider relevance of the recollected experience he describes" (218). At the beginning of the work, the mimesis is clearly one of represented memory, rather than represented fact. Although the narrator wants to tell us what really happened, he rejoices in the subjectivity of his narrative and his own interferences—devices that do much to change our response to what would have been a pathetic tale about a nondescript parson. Almost from the start, the reader is put on the defensive, is informed that he or she is most likely "a miserable town-bred reader" (ch. 1, 45), so that very soon we realize the narrator is not only a nostalgic historian of his own memories but a defender of the life he is describing.[2]

Even in the passage most frequently cited as Eliot's "whole programme"[3] for presenting the dull and average, we can find the strategy which plans to change precisely that impression:

The Rev. Amos Barton, whose sad fortunes I have undertaken to relate was, you perceive, in no respect an ideal or exceptional character; and perhaps I am doing a bold thing to bespeak your sympathy on behalf of a man who was so very far from remarkable,—a man whose virtues were not heroic, and who had no undetected crime within his breast; who had not the slightest mystery hanging about him, but was palpably and unmistakably commonplace;—who was not even in love, but had had that complaint favourably many years ago. "An utterly unin-

teresting character!" I think I hear a lady reader exclaim—Mrs. Farthingale, for example, who prefers the ideal in fiction: to whom tragedy
means ermine tippets, adultery, and murder; and comedy, the adventures of some personage, who is quite a "character." (ch. 5, 80)

Eliot's narrator is working by reverses. Amos Barton does not
emerge as commonplace or uninteresting; Mrs. Farthingale does.
If "idealism" is glittering grandeur and intrigue, then indeed Mr.
Barton is unideal. The reader's response is, of course, to separate
himself or herself from such categorical assumptions and wonder
in what way the protagonist is truly exceptional, truly extraordinary, and the answer lies in the hero's connection with "the tragedy and the comedy, lying in the experience of a human soul that
looks out through dull grey eyes, and that speaks in a voice of quite
ordinary tones" (81). Heroism, after all, is a mental construction.
Barton is not idealized in the way Mrs. Farthingale would have
him; he is neither glamorous nor perfect, yet in another way he
is exceptional. A miscast vocational interest, a partial moral blindness, combined with an unfair assessment from the outside world,
underlie the pathos of his misfortunes—misfortunes that must
remain distinguished from those of Mrs. Farthingale's romantic
cads—and Barton, suffering and enduring through them, proves
to be "heroic" in that his lot symbolizes, in a heightened way, what
all of us know but few experience so directly.

Of course, in having addressed poor Mrs. Farthingale in this
way, the narrator shows her the road to redemption, through the
highly formed experience of the hero and the narrator. Tellingly,
the invocation of a "well-wadded" reader anticipates chapter 17 of
Adam Bede, where the narrator again second-guesses a stereotypical response, and the author seems to be having fun with expectations concerning gender. Mrs. Farthingale is patronized as a
woman, much the way Hetty is in the narration of her story. However, the apparent subordination of women is underminded, not
only by the resolution of the stories themselves but by the clear
artifactuality of "George Eliot" himself/herself, for whom conde-
scension is merely a charade to gain the presumably compassionate reader's attention. How very sophisticated this observed arm-
in-arm movement can become will be seen in *The Mill on the
Floss*. As for now, the reader, if male, must avoid Mrs. Farthingale,
whether he likes it or not, and identify with Amos Barton, who is
already closely tied to two women, Milly and the Countess. The
reader, if female, has already become Amos Barton or has strongly

identified with the male narrator, whose role and level of erudition and experience is always changing.

Eliot is asking much of these readers. To be wafted into escape is too easy. To be interested or even engaged is not enough. The reader, during the course of the narration, must make an imaginative contribution. One must see the *agon* behind the dull grey eyes, must learn to excuse what society would peremptorily condemn, and above all the past and present must be linked, so that Barton can step into the world of Bunyan and Luther, not because his historic importance was as great as theirs but because in the eyes of the Unseen Pity—to quote from *The Mill on the Floss*—there is no significant difference between the suffering the world acknowledges and what continues on as "unwept tragedy." Barton's sorrows, like those of the Great, are representative, and this is the important point. Thus through this redirection of sympathies, redemption is held out for the "miserable town-bred reader" just as it is for Mrs. Farthingale.

This initial presentation of the clergyman does much to alter the commonly held view that the novella ends in simple *pathos* and lacks the fear and catharsis associated with a more heroic characterization.[4] If Barton's suffering is universal, rather than merely quaint and picturesque, then it must be assessed and venerated, not only outside the story (by the reader) but within (by a chosen witness figure). Mr. Cleves provides that function, similar to the chorus of Greek tragedy or the restorative figures of Shakespeare's fifth acts. From his initial portrait in chapter 6, on through to the final scenes where he buries Milly and comforts Barton, Mr. Cleves is seen as an idealized character, one capable of heroic perception—the ability, in Eliot's world, to value what the narrator and the reader have learned to value, that is, heroism in its anonymous forms. Cleves begins by defending Barton to the tribunal-like Seven ["Depend upon it . . . there is some simple explanation of the whole affair, if we only happened to know it" (96)] and then later offers "the painful thrill of life recovering warmth to the poor benumbed heart of the stricken man" (ch. 9, 109). As reader and healer, Mr. Cleves saves us and Amos Barton from the frustrations of an ironic plot. Linking both Greek scholarship and the role of healing, in a way that seems particularly characteristic of Eliot, Cleves shows us how the protagonist's dignity may be best recovered, while offering direct aid to his fellow creature. Thus, compassion closes over death itself, and—when we turn from the witness figure to the hero himself—we find that

Barton is also able to look into his own destiny, involving the past as well as the future:

> but now he re-lived all their life together, with that terrible keenness of memory and imagination which bereavement gives, and he felt as if his very love needed a pardon for its poverty and selfishness. (ch. 9, 111)

Cleves's impact has been felt, and Barton is beginning to share in the reader's sympathetic experience. In a typically pathetic vignette with its attendant unheroic hero, all is closed off with the dimming of the deathbed scene. In this story, its tougher and more cognizant hero ends with the catharsis that follows understanding, both within himself and within the context of a plot that creates a similar effect in the reader. We are in a world closer to that of Lear than Joyce's Mr. Duffy or the less reflecting sufferers of Chekov's vision. As Alexandra Norton also points out, not just Amos Barton but Milly Barton herself, the occasion for the entire tragedy, is herself an idealized, larger-than-life character (219), along with the nemesis Countess.

When we turn to "Mr. Gilfil's Love Story," the shadow of Sir Joshua Reynolds and the Reynolds-like portraitures does much to sustain and unite the various lines of plot, and the sustained grandeur of the setting also prepares us for the high-frequency emotions that control the center of the story. Barbara Hardy has spoken of the Cheverel episodes as an "inset," bracketed by ironic treatments of the Shepperton society (*Novels*, 21).[5] The principal irony, however, is not social but psychological—Mr. Gilfil was capable of romance and even greatness of mind, even though he is awkward and eccentric "now."

It is as if, from the very beginning, the short novel promises a change of perspective in the reader rather than suspense, romance, or anything else. In the first part of the story, Gilfil's "slipshod chat and homely manners" are compared to "weather-stains on a fine old block of marble, allowing you still to see here and there the fineness of the grain, and the delicacy of the original tint" (ch. 1, 127). Later this detection becomes polemical: "I, at least, hardly ever look at a bent old man, or a wizened old woman, but I see also, with my mind's eye, that Past of which they are the shrunken remnant" (128). The reader, of course, does not initially share this vision and interest, having just been presented with Mr. Gilfil, but already the indirect idealization of him has begun. The narrator offers to carry us to a time when his grander qualities were more apparent, the gift being an x-ray vision, which might apply to other characters in other contexts.

The story, then, is dynamic, but not in the same way as "Amos Barton." Unlike Amos, Mr. Gilfil does not travel the edifying route from blindness to recognition but, rather, begins as pure and loving and then only grows old. If he is to be a somewhat perfect character, in the sense that he is long-suffering and sensitive from the start, then these virtuous but rather static qualities must appear only as punctuation at carefully timed moments. The staging of the central section, heightened and "melodramatic,"[6] necessarily keeps Gilfil off in the wings, until just the right moment. After Tina has precipitated the catastrophe, and the baronet lies broken, he steps in and like Mr. Cleves of the previous story and Mr. Irwine, Philip Wakem, and Daniel Deronda of the novels to come, offers compassion and heroically assesses the hidden pain of Sir Christopher's tragedy:

> It was the first time Mr. Gilfil had had an interview with him this morning, and he was struck to see how a single day and night of grief had aged the fine old man. The lines in his brow and about his mouth were deepened; his complexion looked dull and withered; there was a swollen ridge under his eyes; and the eyes themselves, that used to cast so keen a glance on the present, had a vacant expression which tells that vision is no longer a sense, but a memory. (ch. 17, 224)

We are led, at this point, to think back on the detailed description of Sir Christopher's architectural transformation of the manor, and the narrator's open defense of the baronet's carrying "something of the fervour of genius" (ch. 4, 159), which also belongs to the grandly achieving, omniscient but of course unknown narrator. The passage also harkens back to the nonironic comparisons of Gilfil to Samson (ch. 4, 162) and Caterina to Helen, Dido, Desdemona, and Juliet (160). In this heightened world, the characters are given a great elevation from which to fall. Caterina falls out of mad jealousy; Sir Christopher out of his well-intentioned design to create an Eden-like world, when the desires of others were not consulted, and thus in the consolation scene, it is not surprising that he should echo Oedipus: "I thought I saw everything and was stone-blind all the while" (225). Such heightening, however, could not have occurred unless Mr. Gilfil had been present to witness it. He is the reader within the story and a direct link between the characters and the narrator; he participates in their creation. He is thus a nearly ideal being in his early years, fated to be a sympathetic listener and intermediary in a highly flawed world. For this reason, his role in the central section is ancillary, but the story must bear his name as tribute to his anonymous heroism.

When we return to the "present" of the epilogue, it seems fitting that in the intervening time, he should have joined the ranks of "spotted"—and, we may add, anonymous—humanity, but even so we are reminded of the earlier man through the narrator's use of an epic simile: "what might have been a grand tree expanding into liberal shade, is but a whimsical misshapen trunk" (244). The story closes not with an agreement between the inner and social views of Mr. Gilfil—for there is a wide disparity; Shepperton has no real idea of the suffering he underwent—still, the major point is not even found in the fact of Shepperton's ignorance. The tripart structure, rather, brings the reader's view of apparently unheroic people into agreement with the narrator's—people who have been thrown into bold relief by the grander personages of Cheverel Manor. The reader hopefully feels the full force of the simile, perceiving the selfless, loving Gilfil to be as alive as the eccentric and sometimes irascible old man: "And so the dear old Vicar, though he had something of the knotted whimsical character of the poor lopped oak, had yet been sketched out by nature as a noble tree. The heart of him was sound, the grain was of the finest" (epilogue, 244). And without him, we could not have entered the Reynolds-like world of Cheverel.

In the last short novel, "Janet's Repentance," we are presented with a character even more refined than Gilfil. In her letters, Eliot spoke plainly of Mr. Tryan as "ideal" (2: 375), and U. C. Knoepflmacher, in his *Eliot's Early Novels: The Limits of Realism*, has suggested that in the course of writing the *Scenes*, particularly the third, Eliot became increasingly interested in the "correlatives of romance and the epic" (33). In relation to Janet Dempster's view of Tryan, Bernard Paris has identified him with God (*Experiments*, 99), and Joseph Wiesenfarth has called him "the Good Shepherd" (*Mythmaking*, 72)—not only as he is perceived by Janet but by the reader as well.

It should be no surprise, then, that Tryan shares more with the selfless prophet Mordecai than he does with some of the rustic subordinates of *Adam Bede* and *The Mill on the Floss*. He is a voice crying in the wilderness that the title character must learn to hear. His body is wasted from the trials of the spirit, but, as Eliot says of him, "[he] was not cast in the mould of the gratuitous martyr" (ch. 8, 310). Like Mordecai, Tryan is also testimony to the fact "that the heroes have not always had carpets and tea-cups of their own," but in learning to disregard their shabbiness, as

well as the apparent narrowness of their enthusiasm, the reader—
as well as Janet and later Deronda—escapes the more superficial view:

> So it was with Mr. Tryan: and any one looking at him with the bird's
> eye glance of a critic might perhaps say that he made the mistake of
> identifying Christianity with a too narrow doctrinal system. . . .
>   But I am not poised at that lofty height. I am on the level and in
> the press with him, as he struggles his way along the stony road,
> through the crowd of unloving fellow-men. (ch. 10, 322)

The passage anticipates the declaratory defense of Mr. Lyon
quoted in the Introduction to this study and also anticipates the
famous qualification of the Fielding tradition in chapter 17 of *Middlemarch,* where the narrator also insists on the closer and ultimately more sympathetic view. The heroism of Tryan or Mordecai
or Dorothea or Mr. Lyon will never become apparent to us from
a lofty height. The idealization is of a special sort, since it demands
parallel qualities from both narrator and reader and an equal willingness to engage in a creative act.

As in *Middlemarch* and *Daniel Deronda,* the character who plays
choral figure to the hero is also a protagonist, and it is Janet's
conversion (as it is Deronda's, but in a different way) that helps
bring us around to the narrator's full view of human possibility,
while working to define what, in Eliot, constitutes heroism. The
balance of male and female is achieved by two protagonists who
are both on stage; Amos Barton and Mrs. Farthingale become Mr.
Tryan and Janet. As the two previous stories have suggested, the
new anonymous hero, like Eliot's various narrators, works less in
chivalric sweeps than in meaningful words, balanced with silences, in selfless action that makes no claim to the invidious
egoism of self-aggrandizement or even self-denial. To refer back
again to what was mentioned in the Introduction, Janet, in over-
hearing Tryan's consolation of Sally, undergoes the first phase of
her conversion by admiring and honoring his honest declaration
of his own weaknesses:

> The most brilliant deed of virtue could not have inclined Janet's good-
> will towards Mr. Tryan so much as this fellowship in suffering, and
> the softening thought was in her eyes when he appeared in the door-
> way, pale, weary, and depressed. (ch. 12, 331)

Clearly this is a world where "brilliant deeds of virtue" have
vanished along with the old-time chivalry, but the possibility of

heroism and the "fervour of genius" remain. A Tryan, a Mr. Irwine, a Romola, a Gwendolen will act bravely and brilliantly at important moments, but the stress is placed not so much on what they do as on their faith in the unseen honor that imbues both their thoughts and actions. This is the heroism of anonymity. It is for this reason that it is not ultimately important that Romola never lives to bring Savanarola's legacy to historic fruition or that Dorothea's life spends "itself in channels which had no great name on the earth." Similarly, the mutual confession of chapter 18 of the short novel is the simple but profound display of honesty that supplants flashy dramatic action. Thus, paradoxically, the characters are idealized, since it is through their acknowledged weaknesses and obscurity that the author invites our veneration. The same will hold true for Dorothea and Lydgate (ch. 76) and Gwendolen and Deronda (ch. 69) at the novels' momentous fusions of separately developing plots.

Once completed, Janet's conversion and repentance underscore the final element in Eliot's examination of heroism. For Tryan also, there is no glittering memorial that leagues of worshippers will visit. Eliot even goes on to suggest that there is, in fact, a connection between the heroic quality of Tryan's achievement and the anonymity assigned to its ultimate effects. The work of the new hero does not die with the hero himself or herself; it is carried forward by a witness figure whose personal investment, like the reader's, may be larger, because the legacy's value is not perceived by the wide world. Elizabeth Ermarth has pointed out that "the idea that nothing is lost, as she [George Eliot] wrote a friend, 'is one of my favorite altars where I oftenest go to contemplate and to seek for invigorating motive' (*Letters* 3: 316)" (134). In the last chapter, then, the narrator speaks of "a simple gravestone in Milby Churchyard" (412), which is truly "a meagre memorial," when considered alongside the living memorial embodied in Janet Dempster, who is at last described as "rescued from self-despair." As a living memorial, she anticipates Dorothea, who, after seeing Lydgate to his fictional grave, anticipates the reader, who sees her to her elegaic internment in the last sentence of the finale.

Thus the ultimate test of human greatness is in the embodied actions of men and women, who outlive the anonymous heroes but also become anonymous heroes themselves. In the presumably mundane worlds of Shepperton and Milby, these characters, under the transfiguring vision of the compassionate narrator, help create the growing good of the world, which exists wherever the reader travels in Eliot—in Hayslope, Middlemarch, London, or the broad world itself.

2

Heroic Perception in *Adam Bede*

Since *Adam Bede* is known not only as Eliot's first novel but also as her esthetic manifesto, we might best begin by looking at some of her assumptions concerning art and characterization. For Eliot, character was a form of art and therefore could be "called higher or lower only on the same principle as that on which we apply these words to organisms; viz. in proportion to the complexity of the parts bound up into one indissoluble whole" (*Pinney*, 435). We might conclude from this assessment, then, that she sought to create complex characters—or better, a complex response toward them—not out of some strictly moral devotion to "realism" but more out of a desire to create a contemplation of "wholeness" which would have in it a special edification. Later, in the same private essay, "Notes on Form in Art," she adds in a postscript, "In the later development of poetic fable the αναγνωρισις tends to consist in the discernment of a previously unrecognized *character,* & this may also form the περιπατεια, according to Aristotle's notion that in the highest form the two coincide" (Pinney, 436). The ultimate goal, then, for Eliot's higher art would be to bring about a newly recognized character through the formation of a reversal and bring about a contemplation of the character in his or her wholeness.

Early in Eliot's days as a writer of fiction, she discovered she could develop a variety of forms of this process, not just once, as Sophocles does in his *Oedipus,* but again and again by enlisting the reader, narrator, and characters to discover a protagonist—or any other character—anew. Rather than depending entirely on dramatic turnabouts of plot and psychology, Eliot's narrators would provide a diversity of angles from which the characters could be seen. At the various moments in the text, the protagonist becomes a hero; he or she is recognized in all of his or her complex beauty—complex because the former impression is united into composition with the newer one. Later on, the narrator of *Daniel*

Deronda will speak of the "iridescence" of Gwendolen's character. This new light allows not only the heroine's heroism to be seen, but the anonymous heroism of the reader and narrator as well—presences who are quietly observing, recognizing someone who is also heroic but is still beneath the notice of the outer world.

Mimesis, for Eliot, is visualization, and in her famous chapter on art in *Adam Bede*, she raises a credo which promises "to give a faithful account of men and things as they have mirrored themselves in my mind" (ch. 17, 150). As J. Hillis Miller has pointed out, however, we are indeed on slippery ground if we take this as a manifesto for photographic truth, since mirroring is in the mind, not a mechanical device, and we are working with words (*Ethics*, 65) not paint or film. Indeed, the ultimate language Eliot celebrates is not the language of the workshop but, more broadly, the figurative language of poetry. "I turn, without shrinking," the narrator says, "from cloud-borne angels, from prophets, sibyls, and heroic warriors, to an old woman bending over her flower-pot, or eating her solitary dinner, while the noonday light, softened perhaps by a screen of leaves, falls on her mob-cap, and just touches the rim of her spinning-wheel, and her stone jug, and all those cheap common things which are the precious necessaries of life to her" (152). This is no snapshot, and it would not be, even if we had grimmer particulars. Even when choosing her homely subject, the narrator wants to get all the lighting right, so that what is mirrored from her mind to ours is a portrait idealized by the verbal stage set and the literary corollary to artistic perspective, and so that it will provide as many angles of perspective as possible, such as we would expect of a "higher" or more complex form of art.

If mimesis is a particular form of visualization, then we are in a world much more flexible than one of journalistic veracity. The narrator, who is an unabashed artistic construction "himself," turns from angels and warriors not so much because they are less real but because they do not offer the same challenges to the reader's complex powers of "visualization" and anagnorisis, as translated to fiction. A portrait of Aeneas comes "ready-made"—to borrow a phrase from another of Eliot's famous essays. He is a character already in activity, who offers little or no "recognition" value; the esthetic impression promises to be flat. Therefore, while the artistic pose in chapter 17 is somewhat journalistic, it appears as otherwise elsewhere in the narrative. For example, in the very first sentence of the novel, the narrator presents himself as a sorcerer or transformer, who will create a world out of a drop of ink, and who himself will grow out of it.

Perceiving mimesis as journalistic truth still goes on—as the chapter on *Scenes of Clerical Life* would suggest, even to this day, not only in the study of Eliot but in references to the whole Aristotelian tradition. Mimesis is simply much more flexible and artifactual than many commentators would have it. Jacques Derrida, for example, asks, "Is not the most naive form of representation *mimesis*?" For life, he concludes, "is the nonrepresentable origin of representation" (*Writing,* 234), assuming that mimesis attempts to represent life in the first place. However, both Aristotle and Eliot insist otherwise. Mimesis, according to them, is not a record of the outer world or life, as in *Life* magazine, but a process of visualization that occurs somewhere between the mind of the artist and his or her audience. It is not surprising, then, that Derrida, like Nietzsche before him, would then go on to attack the highly artifactual experience of tragic catharsis, using what might be called an esthetics of journalese. In insisting that the theater actually takes its cues from the street rather than the life of the mind, he, also like Artaud, can celebrate a resistance to the ordering properties of mimesis as "an affirmation of life" (234)—a concept which itself is highly naive, and in Eliot's case, at least, entirely foreign to the esthetic experience of "higher" art. In Eliot, the artist, not the camera, is predominant.

Further, in her private essay "Notes on Form in Art," Eliot says directly that "in Poetry—which has this superiority over all the other arts, that its medium, language, is the least imitative, & is in the most complex relation with what it expresses—Form begins in the choice of rhythms & images as signs of a mental state" (435). We would want to emphasize, then, that in fiction, particularly Eliot's, those rhythms and images impinge upon the audience in a way much less visually fixed than in a painting, poem, or even play, and thus there is greater room for translation. Far from being a limitation, this "superiority" allows greater recognition on the part of the reader because he or she is doing more of the work in making the "visual" impression "real." It is no surprise, consequently, that most of Eliot's heroes are heroes of reflection and that the process of their becoming heroic involves some transcendence of a former self or the contemplation of that transcendence in others: a process that demands a highly sophisticated form of mimetic thinking on the part of reader and narrator. To illustrate, we might borrow again from Eliot's last novel and look at the "portrait" of Gwendolen Harleth offered late in her moral history, the one which perhaps gave Henry James his cue for the "composition" of Isabel Archer:

> Mrs. Grandcourt was handsomer than Gwendolen Harleth: her grace and expression were informed by a greater variety of inward experience, giving new play to the facial muscles, new attitudes in movement and repose; her whole person and air had the nameless something which often makes a woman more interesting after marriage than before, less confident that all things are according to her opinion and yet with less of deer-like shyness—more fully a human being. (ch. 54, 741)

Although the subject of this portrait is apparently more "pleasing" and "beautiful," the narrative slant here grows out of the credo that surrounded the old woman in the mob-cap in *Adam Bede*. The form of the work of art depends on the displacement of our expectations and on our power of recall. Gwendolen is not what she was—in other words, a "spoiled child"; the old woman is not what she seems—in other words, every other peasant woman whom we have thought to be beneath our notice. If the narrator is offering a mirror of her mind, then it is a dynamic one, developing apparently "still-life" portraits which are themselves miniature Aristotelian dramas involving recognition and reversal, or recognition through reversal, as the major components of the artistically complex "character." They are more fully human beings.

In this sense, Eliot's modern-day cinematic corollary would not be a Soviet documentary but more the highly wrought films of Ingmar Bergman, who, in the instance of *Cries and Whispers*, directed Sven Nykvist to "photograph" the soul—"to try," as the cinematographer himself reports, "to get inside the human being with my lighting" (30). Indeed, the composed unit of the character of Agnes, who is the center of the film, is brought together through the facets of her sisters' actions, and, "recognized" through Anna's opening of her diary at the film's conclusion, her character constitutes an almost exact example of what Eliot would call "higher artistic form." The impact is also the same; the audience recognizes Agnes's anonymous heroism at the moment her friend and servant Anna does, and everyone is implicated or elevated in the simultaneous action of collective portraiture.

In *Adam Bede*, there is work afoot to create, also, a special heroism, through carefully planned moments of recognition in a variety of characters. The loudest voice, which provides a good place to begin, comes in the exhortative portion of chapter 17, where the novel comes to a dead halt:

"This Rector of Broxton is little better than a pagan!" I hear one of my readers exclaim. "How much more edifying it would have been if you had made him give Arthur some truly spiritual advice. You might have put into his mouth the most beautiful things—quite as good as reading a sermon."

Certainly I could, if I held it the highest vocation of the novelist to represent things as they never have been and never will be. (150)

As in *Scenes of Clerical Life*, Eliot's object is to second-guess the presumably urbane reader, who sustains unrealistic expectations and, by a process of reverse psychology, to make the man in question—in this case, Mr. Irwine—more heroic than ever. Adam will be developed and educated so that he can supply the appropriate anagnorisis that will change his mentor's image.

The stance of *Adam Bede*, then, will be somewhat defensive, and the reader of Eliot's first novel will be brought to stages of understanding and admiration step by step and, at times, argument by argument, because, first, the setting, while picturesque, is remote in time and space and, second, the author assumes more resistance of sympathy in her readership. While W. J. Harvey finds such a voice to be "infuriating",[1] tone and spirit are entirely consistent with Eliot's rather boldfaced plan.

The tone, the stance, shares, in fact, much with the voice of *Moby Dick*, whose Ishmael must speak defensively of the *Pequod*'s motley crew:

If, then, to meanest mariners, and renegades and castaways, I shall hereafter ascribe high qualities, though dark; weave round them tragic graces; if even the most mournful, perchance the most abased, among them all, shall at times lift himself to the exalted mounts; if I shall touch that workman's arm with some ethereal light; if I shall spread a rainbow over his disastrous set of sun; then against all mortal critics bear me out in it, thou just Spirit of Equality, which hast spread one royal mantle of humanity over all my kind! (ch. 26, 212)

The task in *Adam Bede*, however, remains tougher than in *Moby Dick*, since Melville, after this open declaration, introduces a series of Shakespearean scenes (one of them an actual playlet) that, once and for all, establishes the regality of those presumably low people, unequivocally answering the question of what form we are in; we are in the heightened poetic world of tragedy.

In *Adam Bede*, however, we have flaws, paradoxical grandeur, but no consistent genre which would place Mr. Irwine at its center. Certainly it has its moments of tragedy—so many that some critics are inclined to label the entire novel as such.[2] If we do, however, immediately we are on difficult ground, since, in one way or another, all the traditional expectations are defied. Indeed there is a "fall," but as Murray Krieger puts it, it is a "cushioned" one (*The Classic Vision*, 197). There is *hubris* but it never serves as any sort of single-minded impetus to the catastrophe. We have pity, fear, and the tragic recognition necessary for catharsis, but in the final third of the novel, Hetty's "tragedy,"[3] after being so prominent, is simply pushed, once again, to the background. In her study *Will and Destiny: Morality and Tragedy in George Eliot*, Felicia Bonaparte has called Hetty's plight an instance of "fatal innocence" (180), yet clearly because of Hetty's overall subordinate role in the novel, her story—if it can be called tragic—is one of the many strands of the form, not the predominant one which outlines the complete form itself.

Eliot's refusal to do as Melville does, that is, create a consistently tragic stage, suggests that she has other ideas for her Mr. Irwine and her title hero. At first she suggests some possibilities. Adam has all the trappings of a tragic protagonist. He is a physical ideal and he is a man of impulse and action. He stands out from the rest of the workmen, and his overweening pride, especially as it is prefigured in his treatment of his father, certainly marks him out for the grandeur of tragedy. But Eliot is leading us elsewhere; her modern hero is not a person of impulse but of meditation and mediation. He is grand not in the physical sense but in the spiritual. This is why chapter 17 is crucial. In it, she rejects a completely tragic form in one dramatic gesture. The narrator is, essentially, turning the expectations of the reader upside down, and, in his loudest polemical voice, is positing Irwine as the major target of admiration. As if this change were not enough, Adam is then aged by many decades—that is, ushered to the background— and as witness figure, is speaking a warm defense of Irwine as well. At this point, it becomes clear that the aged Adam has become like Irwine, and therefore, even before we are a third of the way into the book, the younger Adam's moral destination or, better, model, has been defined. The recognition or anagnorisis thought to be at the end of the road changes our impressions now.

The plot that surrounds Mr. Irwine—the one that opens and closes the novel—is ameliorative, an emphatic alternative to the tragic story of Hetty and the nearly tragic story of Adam. Although catastrophe occurs in his world, "nature repairs" at least some of "her ravages" (*Mill*, 457), and although proud people are toppled, many of them endure beyond the Fall and are presented reorder-

ing their lives or the lives of others. The open-ended epilogue
underscores this vision; we do not see life ending; rather, whatever
good that was gained is being passed on to subsequent generations—and most often by the hands of the protagonists themselves. The anonymous heroism has been bequeathed. In this last
task, Irwine's role is critical. He is the fixed model for heroism,
while Adam is its active seeker.

As for the readership, the polemical narrator is right in assuming resistance. Irwine can only become a moral blueprint for
Adam—after an argument and after careful preparation. The
preparation begins early. In the portrait chapter, "The Rector," the
idealization is direct; he is associated with warmth, light, generosity, clarity, and affectionate memory:

> It is very pleasant to see some men turn round; pleasant as a sudden
> rush of warm air in winter, or the flash of firelight in the chill dusk. Mr.
> Irwine was one of those men. He bore the same sort of resemblance to
> his mother that our loving memory of a friend's face often bears to
> the face itself: the lines were all the more generous, the smile brighter,
> the expression heartier. If the outline had been less finely cut, his
> face might have been called jolly; but that was not the right word for
> its mixture of bonhommie and distinction. (ch.5, 49–50)

In the context of Eliot's esthetics, Irwine is a work of art himself;
he is a part of nature, changed and yet clarified by memory. Also,
he is defined not just by masculine characteristics but by feminine
characteristics as well. In contrast, when Arthur Donnithorne enters the room, no such meticulous or modulated portrait is offered.
The narrator asks us to imagine any "tawny-whiskered, brown-
locked, clear-complexioned young Englishman" (53), and Arthur
remains—in counterpart—as vague and conventionally masculine
as his morals.

The strategy of the chapter is to bring us into the rectory almost
as spies, to observe and discover that the private and public Mr.
Irwine is what he seems—and more. Just after the confrontation
with Joshua, the narrator pivots and takes us from the outward
view into Mr. Irwine's mind:

> for his was one of those large-hearted, sweet-blooded natures that
> never know a narrow or a grudging thought; epicurean, if you will,
> with no enthusiasm, no self-scourging sense of duty; but yet, as you
> have seen, of a sufficiently subtle moral fibre to have an unwearying
> tenderness for obscure and monotonous suffering. (59)

Mr. Irwine is the first character in Eliot's novels to possess heroic perception in its full form, and he will head a whole series of characters, extending all the way to Deronda, whose major quest matches the narrator's and the reader's—the perception of greatness in others, through the veil of obscure pain and tragedy. Because he does not live a tragedy, he attains that enduring heroism that can perceive it in others on a global scale. In writing of the same passage, Christopher Herbert, in his "Preachers and the Schemes of Nature in Adam Bede," notes that "the force of the concluding phrase is very great, for it embodies nothing less than George Eliot's conception of the truly godlike in mankind. . . . He is capable of true moral heroism, in other words" (418), and in focusing on the same phrase, Krieger writes that "Eliot joins his 'subtle moral fibre' with her own" (200). In order to appreciate the Rector, we must literally adopt his point of view, his sympathy with hidden pain, for his lot is bound up with his silent, long-suffering care for his sisters and his solicitude over his mother's decided deficit of concern. Like Tryan, he is heroic not because of his "brilliant deeds" but because he has "more insight into men's characters than interest in their opinions" (60). And like Mr. Cleves of "Amos Barton," his understanding of psychic life is signaled by his facility in Greek literature and by his communication of sympathy in silent pressures of the hand—in Mr. Irwine's case, at his sister's bedside. In fact, it is very telling that all of these men are characterized, at least in some part, in terms of motherhood, and in terms, therefore, of their alienation from the tribunals of certain rigid men. As we shall see in *The Mill on the Floss*, the strain of ego frequently causes Eliot's characters to cling to one character type, but anonymity releases them into diversity. If Mr. Irwine no longer cares about the expectations of a categorical society or how he is recognized, why can he not be a mother to his sisters?

At the conclusion of the chapter, the narrator, still polemical, echoes chapter 10 of "Janet's Repentance" and chapter 43 of *Daniel Deronda* by turning aside the distant "mackerel-vendor's" view. Scrutinized indifferently or categorically, Mr. Irwine is worthy of our blame, not our admiration, and once more the reader is elevated into sharing the vision of the artist, which demands a firm grasp of particulars. Gillian Beer, in fact, writes of the importance of detail in the novel and says that within Eliot's plan, "the writing should *work*, through description, through analysis, through rumination" (60). In the case of Mr. Irwine, detail serves as the key to his mind—and therefore the mind of the narrator. He notices clues that lead to inner truth, and the same process of noticing, stemming from the narrator, causes us to appreciate him. With Mr. Irwine as loadstone, we are equipped, then, to cull out the details which will give the other characters their luminescence.

The next major scene that the Rector plays is, of course, the one which prompts the narrator's loudest defense—Irwine's fatal suppression of advice in the "Links" chapter. Although this hitherto idealized character is shown to be culpable, the encounter with Arthur also does much, then, to develop Irwine's strengths. It is part of the heroic perceiver's ability to see "links" between history, past and present, to know the applicability and inapplicability of past examples, both literary and historical. Like Farebrother, Irwine has no difficulty showing how literature may bear upon the present; in this case, Aeschylus's chorus serves as a warning. When Arthur tries to slip out of the implications, positing the man "who struggles against a temptation into which he falls at last" (140), Mr. Irwine, in a very nontypically masculine fashion, refuses to accept the Faustian excuse and presses him harder: "I pity him in proportion to his struggles, for they foreshadow the inward suffering which is the worst form of Nemesis. Consequences are unpitying" (147). Like the enlightened minister he is, Irwine is successful in clarifying the morality of his example. Still, he is "too delicate" to force Arthur into confession, and although a horrified Faust—staring on a demented and destroyed Gretchen—is perhaps adumbrated in their dialogue, Irwine is too used to seeing Arthur as the "clear-complexioned young Englishman" to see him as anything else—until the consequences themselves arrive.[4] Thus, the narrator must defend his hero, since the "seer," while the master of many clues, does not succeed with all of them.

The sum result of the rather startling chapter 17 is the accumulation of three separate masculine voices of authority: the Rector's, the older Adam's, and the omniscient male narrator's. In a novel where Eliot slyly has her "masculine" narrative adopt a sexist attitude towards her female subjects and then ironically turns the tone back on the speaker ("Ah, what a prize the man gets who wins a sweet bride like Hetty!" [ch. 14, 130]), Irwine offers an alternative view which refuses to see women—or men, for that matter—as objects, since the wages of dehumanizing others are always "unpitying." It is as if the much-discussed ruse of the male persona serves as a foil for the more preferred sympathy of speakers who are active in the text and plot. Irwine—and later in life, Adam—is the person whose ties with anonymous tragedy develop a compassion with both sides of the human race. He is the least spiritually parochial of all the characters, and this breadth of vision is turned back, by the omniscient narrator himself, upon his principal touchstone.

With the light of chapter 17 radiating outward through the novel, other major characters acquire a different shape as well. Adam cannot be seen as simply headstrong or stiff because the reader knows that eventually he will become a workman's version of Mr. Irwine. Hetty cannot be tagged as the statuesque Mary Magdalen of the novel because the "details" of her plight, when appreciated, eclipse the vehemency of the apparently moralistic male narrator. Dinah, too, cannot be easily dismissed under one heading, since her role as rescuer illuminates more her own potential than it does some grand result. Her power, like Irwine's, must be acknowledged first as a "seed-growth"; it is a full thrust of loving attention towards the obscure which itself never quite reaches its full fruition. The overall effect, stemming from Mr. Irwine's character, is highly democratizing; our "unwearying tenderness for obscure and monotonous suffering" makes anonymous heroes of the lost populace of the novel, and our hearts "burn" as, in recollection, they stand shoulder-to-shoulder with one another.

A particularly brilliant example of this indirect effect comes in the momentous "In the Prison" chapter. What could be further away, one would wonder, from the influence of Mr. Irwine and the careful design of chapter 17 than this extraordinary exchange between the female counterparts of the novel? Yet chapter 17 is like a lighthouse beacon flashing through Hetty's confession and Dinah's quiet attendance to it. Hetty's tale is fraught with detail, and when we hear, for example, of her extraordinary response to the moon just before she abandons her child, we fix on the visual clues to her plight and psychology in exactly the way we were told in the manifesto chapter:

> . . . for there came the moon—O, Dinah, it frightened me when it first looked at me out o' the clouds—it never looked so before: and I turned out of the road into the field, for I was afraid o' meeting anybody with the moon shining on me. (ch. 45, 379)

Our response to her is being governed by our previous one to the old woman and her flower pot, and thus we are in accord with Mr. Irwine's "unwearing tenderness for obscure and monotonous suffering"; in this case, it arises and flashes, beaconlike, lighting up all the details of Hetty's speech. In this radiant context, Dinah cannot be just Dinah Morris, but must be seen, as well, as her namesake goddess, Diana, who does indeed go with the moon. Likewise, Hetty cannot be just Hetty, but the larger-than-life tragic heroine, who speaks at last for herself and brings light at last to the reader, who could not, until now, penetrate the shadow of the misguided and draconian court of law that condemned her.

The full thrust of chapter 17, then, with its frequently misunderstood esthetics, does much to widen the modern implications of Irwine's heroism rather than saying, as many critics have, that for "George Eliot" heroism no longer exists at all. It is only "the heroic warriors" (152) that the narrator eschews, not the men and women of psychological depth. If Eliot can clear the decks, so to speak, and disclaim what Mrs. Farthingale of the *Scenes* would expect, then it will be possible for a new ideal to emerge.[5] The chapter must be particularly argumentative, not only because it must say that Irwine is heroic even though flawed but also because it must say that Irwine's brand of heroism is one which belongs to a new age, in which moral grandeur has to be discovered before it can be seen.

In the context of the book's second crisis, it is more useful to talk of the role Irwine plays in relation to the sorrows of others rather than his own *agon per se*. Some critics would question the prominence of his role in this part of the novel, saying that he only becomes morally creditable once the beneficent side of nature has returned to Hayslope.[6] However, his eye for detail imbues the characterization of every member of the huge cast of dramatis personae. He offers a kind of agonized Olympian perspective, which draws Adam, Dinah, Arthur, and Hetty into bold relief. In chapter 27, Adam and Arthur act out the old-style heroic conflict—the fistfight over the lady—and in chapter 39, Adam and Irwine and their respective codes are brought together in dramatic contrast—Adam, fatigued by his frenzied pursuit of Hetty, and Irwine, anguished by his contemplation of the letters. In the conversation that ensues, Irwine, in role as mitigator, gives, by contrast, the pathos of the overactive characters a kind of bold face. First, it is necessary for him to own up to his own mistake, to speculate over what might have happened—"if he himself had been less fastidious about intruding on another man's secrets" (341). Next he must acquaint Adam with the facts, while all the while meeting his initial aim, "to suppress agitation" (340). Meanwhile, Adam seems to hasten the drama all the more, responding violently, on "the Eve of the Trial," and demanding, of Mr. Irwine, the wisdom which knows that it would be futile "to utter soothing words at present" (343). Such a contrasting detachment is parallel to the reflection of Dorothea, who, when attempting to soothe the anguished Lydgate, knows that there was "a point on which even sympathy might make a wound" (ch. 76, 824). As a final "action," Mr. Irwine staves off Adam's impulse to fetch back Arthur and, through a reminder of his duty, convinces him to go to Stoniton as "the best means of counteracting the violence of suffering in these first hours" (344). Surrounded by pieces of ruined nature, Irwine has enough insight to understand and placate even those totally unlike himself—men of immediate, fiery impulse. As Elizabeth Ermarth writes, "the novel demonstrates the truth of Mr. Irwine's observations to Adam and to Arthur that people cannot isolate themselves" (76), and the lack of isolation causes a very complex character grouping.

Joseph Wiesenfarth has traced Mr. Irwine's perspicacity to his knowledge of Aeschylus and the lessons that the Greek tragedies teach (*Eliot's Mythmaking*, 83). Mr. Irwine, like another rarity, Mr. Farebrother, has come to the novel with his experience behind him; therefore it is not surprising that this link between past and present, Aeschylus and the world of Stoniton and Hayslope, should be made effectively. His prevention of Adam's tragedy also brings out his intricate vision of guilt and innocence, and in presenting it to Adam, Mr. Irwine comes to represent the new laws of the modern hero, as opposed to the old ones of the vengeful "knight." The greatest deception that the old laws create is the sense of the errant knight's individual importance and the containability of his actions:

> There is no sort of wrong deed of which a man can bear the punishment alone; you can't isolate yourself, and say that the evil which is in you shall not spread. Men's lives are as thoroughly blended with each other as the air they breathe: evil spreads as necessarily as disease. (355; ch. 41)

Better than the polemical and mock-sexist narrator, Mr. Irwine voices what the novel has been dramatizing in all its narrative strands. As a result of what the Rector says, in this chapter and "The Tidings," and as a result of his own suffering, Adam is thus reborn through the "baptism" of chapter 42, and begins to exchange the old laws for the new.[7] But it must be stressed again that it is Irwine's eye for detail that is so operative here, disclosing not only obscure and monotonous suffering but its sources as well.

With the arrival of the trial and its troubling aftermath, Mr. Irwine's declaration of the wide complexity of crime and punishment comes into startling contrast with the makeshift treatment of Hetty after the trial:

> We find it impossible to avoid mistakes even in determining who has committed a single act, and the problem of how far a man is to be held responsible for the unforeseen consequences of his own deed, is one that might well make us tremble to look into it. (ch. 41, 354)

It is as though once Hetty has been "rescued," the general scurrying among the other characters, so evident since chapter 17, still continues. Arthur seeks exile, Adam seeks a new wife, Dinah agonizes over her sense of vocation, and then quests for the love of her life, Hetty is transported towards her punishment and there finds death. Makeshift justice goes on, Eliot seems to say, even though characters like Mr. Irwine have the broader vision. Here the rush to find a resting spot, via marriage, children, and death, "seals the picture," as Gillian Beer writes, "with a layer of varnish" (73). In contradistinction stands Mr. Irwine's role as a moral physician, as one who insists on leaving off with so much agitation. As in the earlier sections, his actions are less emphatic, less seen, and more anonymous than Adam's, Arthur's, or even Dinah's, so it is easy to underestimate his contribution to the restorative forces. Yet his design is the one which keeps Adam and the Poysers in Hayslope so that the sacred and nurturing bond between past and present may be maintained. His insight into suffering is not only familiar with punitive consequences but with the process of rebuilding as well. All of this is prefigured earlier when the Poysers are threatened with being thrown off their land by the Squire, and, with characteristic balance of restraint and calm, the Rector prepares to defend them—"But if he should give them notice at Lady Day, Arthur and I must move heaven and earth to mollify him" (ch. 33, 295).

Irwine's perception is also instrumental in removing Arthur from Hayslope and is there as a nurturing force, when it is appropriate for his return. Adam's shared concern, expressed in the epilogue, is a significant and final linking of the novel's hero with its protagonist; Adam has come around to adopting the Rector's blend of restraint and appreciative sympathy. In "Another Meeting in the Wood," the contrasting symmetry emphasizes that the old heroics have died and that Adam has adopted new laws. In the final pages, we witness a community taking care of its broken inhabitants, rather than exiling scapegoats, because it is united again under the care of Mr. Irwine, who presides at the wedding as well as oversees Arthur's final reformation. As K. M. Newton notes, Mr. Irwine's pastoral function is shown in his encouraging the "sharing of certain implied values"—thus the society is ultimately "organic" (87). But it is even better shown in the way his example has changed Adam. Surely what was said of Mr. Irwine earlier could now be said of Adam—who will live on to speak of the Rector with "affectionate veneration"—that he owns "a sufficiently subtle moral fibre to have an unwearying tenderness for obscure and monotonous suffering." And thus our visualization of Adam becomes that of Mr. Irwine, once we have recognized him. Hero and protagonist will eventually conjoin.

Chapter 17 of *Adam Bede* works to achieve this blend, with the added strength of showing the alternative hero finally coming to terms with the values prized by his mentor. But even more important, the mentoring vision of Mr. Irwine gives the reader that anonymous heroism that elevates all the characters in their dynamic moments of continuous recognition.

3

The Narrative One-Room Schoolhouse of
The Mill on the Floss

INCOMPLETION is a primary theme throughout *The Mill on the Floss*, in which two young lives are cut off before fruition, where the tragedy of a "kingly" miller almost but never quite reaches a majestic finality, where a young and sensitive lover almost wins a young woman, but is held back because of his compunctions and his inability to satisfy completely all of her needs. Even the major representative of the novel's cosmic forces, Nature, never quite sustains the humanity that the personification promises. "Nature repairs her ravages—but not all" (457), the narrator concludes, in a novel whose most controversial moment reawakens self-perception in both hero and heroine, only to have them engulfed in the terrible flood.

Many critics have pointed out that the book is a *bildungsroman* of a dual sort,[1] but its central interest lies in the incompletenesses and imbalances of education, both in the broad, psychological sense of the word, and the stricter, more academic sense. Tom Tulliver's growth is a growth into narrowness; Maggie's, after various starts, is a growth into overheightened susceptibility; Philip's, while showing more scholarly promise than the rest, is again a study of sensitivity that advances too far, eventually immobilizing him. Underlying and structuring these fragmentary or deficient educations is not only Eliot's theory of academic reform,[2] but more importantly, her definition of education in the broad sense: a perception of the continuity between past and present, once the major differences have been acknowledged; an extension, therefore, of the sympathies and an active assertion of "patience, discrimination, impartiality" (435, book 7, 2) that can distinguish between the deadening claims of the past and its vital ones. One would be tempted to say that, in view of the dramatic texture of the novel, Eliot works by implication and reversal alone; never does she demonstrate her principles positively. And yet if we consider the case of the reader—the long list of addresses and cautionary notes to him or her, as well as the way his or her memory is carefully manipulated and redirected—we can discover a carefully wrought educative plan, whereby one's imagination and sympathies are brought to flourish within the necessary bounds of detachment, in the sustaining, complete way denied to the characters. The result is the attainment of the wider view, the heroic perception of *Adam Bede,* all achieved within what I would call the one-room schoolhouse of *The Mill on the Floss,* where the anonymous narrator sits and chats with the anonymous reader.

The education of Tom Tulliver is a good starting point, since Eliot's treatment provides nearly an exact balance of dramatic realization (Tom's languishing under Mr. Stelling's regimen) and "correcting" asides from the narrator. In this context, Mr. Stelling represents a variety of sins, the most prominent being his enforcement of a "natural" approach:

> Perhaps it was because teaching came naturally to Mr. Stelling, that he set about it with that uniformity of method and independence of circumstances, which distinguish the actions of animals understood to be under the immediate teaching of nature. Mr. Broderip's amiable beaver, as that charming naturalist tells us, busied himself as earnestly in constructing a dam, in a room up three pair of stairs in London, as if he had been laying his foundation in a stream or lake in Upper Canada. . . . With the same unerring instinct, Mr. Stelling set to work at his natural method of instilling the Eton Grammar and Euclid into the mind of Tom Tulliver. (122–23, book 2, 1)

Throughout the "School Time" section, the narrator turns Mr. Stelling's "natural" theories in on themselves, in much the same way as she criticizes all appeals to an idealized concept of nature. This criticism is also apparent in *Adam Bede* when Hetty is characterized. Eliot is quite careful to show that the connection between nature and culture—like that between past and present—is a "shifting" and highly complex one, and anyone who can draw an easy link or equation makes himself or herself susceptible to the grimmest of ironies. J. Hillis Miller, in the spirited "The Two Rhetorics: George Eliot's Bestiary," shows how this passage demonstrates the limits and traps of metaphor, by, in effect, trapping itself (*Writing,* 105–112). The narrator, while striking a comic attitude, nevertheless insists that education, a product of culture, cannot be compared with justice to the planting and harvesting of a crop (124, book 2, 1), and if it is, then boys like Tom Tulliver will always be victimized. Stelling is, therefore, like the automatic beaver, because he fails to survey—and apppreciate—the context of his proposed structures, in this case, the context of Tom's mind. Eliot also stresses, of course, the persistent fact of irrelevancy in Tom's schooling, but over and above this is the irony that Stelling, in insisting on a classical regimen and the deadening and inappropriate natural metaphor that goes with it, obscures and finally denies Tom's true talents:

> Tom had never found any difficulty in discerning a pointer from a setter, when once he had been told the distinction, and his perceptive powers were not at all deficient. I fancy they were quite as strong as those of the Rev. Mr. Stelling; for Tom could predict with accuracy what number of horses were cantering behind him, he could throw a stone right into the centre of a given ripple, he could guess to a fraction how many lengths of his stick it would take to reach across the playground, and could draw almost perfect squares on his slate without any measurement. But Mr. Stelling took no note of these things. (123–24, book 2, 1)

A network of victimization has led up to Tom's mental imprisonment, just as a network of victimization will follow. It was originally Mr. Riley who recommended the school to Tom's father; it was Tom's father who, out of hubris and yet good intentions, finally delivered his son over to Mr. Stelling; it was Mr. Stelling who, because of special domestic and personal circumstances, allowed himself to fall short of true enlightenment quite early in life. As is true in *Adam Bede*, the blame is everywhere and nowhere. Along each step of the way, the narrator has been careful to offer a defense of each man, entreating the reader not to be too critical when education is "a delicate and difficult business" (149). Thus, at a very early point in the novel, Eliot places the burden on the reader to become wise in these matters, since the complexities are far too great for the limited minds of the characters, while also firmly suggesting that she is a better teacher than any of these patriarchal determiners of Tom's fate.

The second chain of victimization does not begin, as one might expect, with Edward Tulliver's downfall, but, rather, with Tom's early psychological crisis. Still in school and suffering perpetual humiliation, he perceives himself to have "something of the girl's susceptibility" (125, book 2, 1) or, as it is more directly put, Tom "had never been so much like a girl in his life before" (154). Young and poorly enlightened, he flees from the dangers of this emerging sensitiveness by first proving his "masculine" superiority to Maggie. With this Mr. Stelling readily concurs, and as Mary Jacobus has pointed out in "The Question of Language: Men of Maxims and *The Mill on the Floss*," this gentleman "proves an excellent schoolmaster to his latent misogyny" (214). Later, Tom lords his physical superiority over the even more sensitive Philip, who, as a foil, frees him from those very qualities Tom first saw in himself. Therefore, when the downfall finally arrives, Tom leaps, with astonishing gusto, into a grown man's role, pushing down the promise of his imagination and sympathy and fulfilling all the sexist demands of the Dodsons that he prove he is a man. As Gillian Beer writes, "On Tom falls the full weight of required manliness, sealing him into a pig-headed dutifulness and burdening him too young with certainty" (104). Tom's education, then, is anything but natural, since under the pressures of various choices and circumstances, his nature hardens by acquiring a practical remoteness. This self-inflicted "maturity" is in some respects admirable, since, in view of his parents' childlike behavior, the salvation of the Tulliver household rests with him. Eliot, however, always reminds us that permanent damage has been done and that part of Tom's psyche has been killed in the final stage of his thwarted education.

In his new, unseasonably severe form, Tom replicates, in many ways, the personality of Mr. Stelling, whose outlook is given to "boring in a straight line" (149, book 2, 4). Tom's actions toward Maggie begin to parallel his teacher's previous well-meaning tortures, the most painful being his assertion of copybook morality. "Your duty was clear enough" (360, book 6, 5), he tells her, having learned of her encouragement of Philip, and from that point on, her anguish remains almost unbroken. When the narrator clearly counters this assertion with "The great problem of the shifting relation between passion and duty is clear to no man who is capable of apprehending it" (435, book 7, 2), the two, separately developing lines of education are made entirely clear; by book 7, in the one-room narrative schoolhouse, the reader should have reached that plateau of understanding that proved too lofty for Tom. Consistent with this dual system, Eliot then excuses Tom's behavior, just as she did Riley's, Tulliver's, and Stelling's, reminding the reader once more that the real mental work rests with him or her:

Tom, like every one of us, was imprisoned within the limits of his own nature, and his education had simply glided over him, leaving a slight deposit of polish: if you are inclined to be severe on his severity, remember that the responsibility of tolerance lies with those who have the wider vision. (523, book 7, 3)

Presumably we readers have the "wider vision" not only because our academic lives have gone deeper, but also because we have had the full benefit of a three-volume novel whose principal educative purpose has been to extend our sympathies through the displayed continuities and disparities between past and present, and to provide the counterbalancing detachment as well. The message, while subtle, is as clear as though the narrator had written it on a blackboard. In a sense, then, Tom is the applicant who, for financial reasons, was turned away from the school where we won admission.

The theme of Tom's incompleteness, so well sustained throughout, finds its poetic manifestation in the moments of the conclusive flood. To those who object to "Tom's recognition"[3] [it was such a new revelation to his spirit, of the depths in life, that had lain beyond his vision"] (455, book 7, 5) and to the sudden death that follows, one may answer that Tom, in being wrenched to the level of the reader's perception, serves as an appropriate and final reminder of what the reader should have attained.[4] That Tom will never live to carry out his instantaneous enlightenment is only consistent with Eliot's continual placement of the burden upon the reader, not the characters. And in an important way, the premature death of his earlier education is recapitulated by the symbolism of the flood. His violent death by the hand of Nature is only consistent with the qualities ascribed to that force—half mechanism, half personification—that never harmonized with his life and education in the first place. Tom first languished under Mr. Stelling's mixed natural metaphors only to emerge into a psychological deadness. His literal and untimely death in a natural context serves, then, to emphasize the unseasonability of his end in a psychological one.

Maggie's death is, in some ways, more difficult to explain, and in order to do so, one must go back to the beginnings of her education, exploring the even more difficult relation between past and present. One might say that just as the easy Stelling link between nature and education thwarts Tom's development, so Maggie's own hurried connection between past and present— Thomas à Kempis and her own immediate life—thwarts hers. Among other pressures, her desire to live in a more remote world of the historical imagination results, paradoxically, in a kind of temporary amnesia, whereby she forgets the commitments of her personal past and allows Stephen to control her.

In a sense, Maggie's lively historical imagination represents half of an important paradox Eliot develops throughout the novel, the continuity and discontinuity between past and present. For example, Eliot's early analysis (book 1, 12) of St. Ogg's insists that "the giant forces that used to shake the earth are forever laid to sleep" (106), yet the complementary prologue of book 4, chapter 1, asserts that tragedy still exists from age to age. Indeed, for every distinction the novel finds between past and present, a similarity can be found:

> While Maggie's life-struggles had lain almost entirely within her own soul, one shadowy army fighting another, and the slain shadows for ever rising again, Tom was engaged in a dustier, noisier warfare, grappling with more substantial obstacles, and gaining more definite conquests. So it has been since the days of Hecuba, and of Hector, Tamer of horses: inside the gates, the women with streaming hair and uplifted hands offering prayers, watching the world's combat from afar, filling their long, empty days with memories and fears: outside, the men, in fierce struggle with things divine and human, quenching memory in the stronger light of purpose, losing the sense of dread and even of wounds in the hurrying ardour of action. (269)

Maggie's education involves a world where past and present are entirely fluid, and therefore it affirms an important part of the truth—but only part. Her sensitivity proves advanced enough to discover a central coexistence; however, her dwelling on this insight causes her to deny the complexity of another, and this blindness is one of the forces that brings her education to an untimely conclusion. Her perception is not refined enough to acknowledge the distinctions that Eliot and the reader acknowledge, and in "absorbing" the voice from the medieval past without qualification, she makes an error much like the one analyzed and portrayed in *The Faerie Queene*, where books are taken in without assimilation. Maggie's much discussed susceptibility to music[5] is another way of indiscriminately entering a remote world which yet romantically informs the present. Whereas Tom finds any abstract or remote realm to be sterile and useless, precisely because he cannot perceive, and is not encouraged to perceive, its bearing on the present day, Maggie can embroider all of these worlds, whether in *The History of the Devil*, *Philoctetes*, or the music of Haydn, with living particulars.

During Maggie's early visit to Mr. Stelling's school, Eliot begins by developing the positive aspect of the heroine's talent, showing that, in view of the continuity between past and present, the precocious girl asks all of the right questions. Without the ready imagination that Maggie exemplifies, no real education in Eliot's system can occur; it would simply be a Stelling- or Casaubon-like embalmment of knowledge.

> ... and she had asked Mr. Stelling so many questions about the Roman empire, and whether there really ever was a man who said in Latin, "I would not buy it for a farthing or a rotten nut," or whether that had only been turned into Latin, that Tom had actually come to a dim understanding of the fact that there had been people upon the earth who were so fortunate as to know Latin without learning it through the medium of the Eton Grammar. (134, book 2, 1)

Very little is made of Maggie's formal education, and yet the "School Time" section analyzes her emerging intelligence and sensibility with the same care as it does Tom's. While the abstractions of language seem "hideously symbolized" to him (124, book 2, 1), Maggie sees them as "mysterious . . . snatched from an unknown context,—like strange horns of beasts, and leaves of unknown plants" (131). Although her intellectual curiosity already carries an escapist tinge, Maggie, in being attracted toward the Latin, shows a fundamental love of order as well as mystery. In many ways she is like the young Tertius Lydgate, who in making a connection between Latin and English ("valves" and *valvae*) has a sudden awareness of a highly complex system (ch. 15, 173). Characteristically, Maggie's first interview with Philip, the boy who loves Greek as well as Latin, is a literary one, she inquiring "if Philoctetes had a sister" (163, book 2, 6). For Maggie and Philip both, literature and history provide a world of rich escape, where their "keen sensitiveness" (163) can remain protected. Because each is immersed in coexistent realms of books and immediate reality, their conversations, even those at the earliest stage, move easily between present and past, or better, between their own worn lives and the embroidery of literary allusions. During the second scene in the Red Deeps, Philip can look at Maggie and see her as "a tall Hamadryad, dark and strong and noble" (285, book 5, 3), and during the third interview, they can discuss the characters of Madame de Staël and Sir Walter Scott as if they lived within a short radius of St. Ogg's (290–91, book 5, 4).

The thwarting of Maggie's education and the arrival of its untimely end are, as in the case of Tom, both sudden and complex events. Although Maggie grows into larger and larger sensitiveness, through a ready sympathy with the double contexts of past and present, her inability to discriminate between the two becomes an increasing danger. After her father's downfall, she concludes that "the world outside the books was not a happy one" (208, book 3, 5), and characteristically, when she tries to brighten up the Tulliver circumstances by making a light allusion (207), Tom turns on her severely. As the earlier Homeric passage has made plain, the family's bankruptcy has polarized brother and sister, one turning to thought, the other to unreflecting action. By the center of the book, Tom and Maggie become, with the breaks in their development, complementary imbalances. Tom, in having his opportunities for self-study denied and finally cut off, becomes hard and practical: he is all distantness. Maggie, in having her lively imagination pushed toward escape, turns oversensitized and inactive; she is all sympathy. Although she longs to give her tenderness full expression, Tom and later Mr. Tulliver (243, book 4, 2) remove themselves from this love, so that like the newly married Dorothea Casaubon, Maggie finds herself in "a moral imprisonment" (ch. 28, 307), where thought becomes divorced from action:

> This time of utmost need was come to Maggie, with her short span of thirteen years. To the usual precocity of the girl, she added that early experience of struggle, of conflict between the inward impulse and outward fact, which is the lot of every imaginative and passionate nature; and the years since she hammered the nails into her wooden Fetish among the worm-eaten shelves of the attic, had been filled with so eager a life in the triple world of Reality, Books, and Waking Dreams, that Maggie was strangely old for her years in everything except in her entire want of prudence and self-command which were the qualities that made Tom manly in the midst of his intellectual boyishness. (241–42, book 4, 2).

In many ways, the polarization between Tom and Maggie, between distantness and sympathy, strengthens the conventionally male-female polarization of action and thought. Eliot, of course, suggests that things could and should be otherwise and shows Maggie and Tom turning old before their time—that is, before all aspects of a well-ordered psyche can emerge. Taken together, the two characters represent the fusion of sympathy and distantness that the reader should achieve, an outlook entirely appropriate in a novel whose path results from the extremes in the protagonists. In precipitating her sad destiny, Maggie, feeling an increasing need to express her emotion, rushes, like Dorothea, into an easy solution that will turn "all her small allowance of knowledge into principles, fusing her actions into their mould" (ch. 20, 225). But also like the younger Dorothea, who follows the outmoded example of St. Theresa, Maggie draws too hasty a link between past and present by blindly following the words of Thomas à Kempis. She mistakes self-denial for anonymity. Thus, in opening *The Imitation of Christ* and "with all the hurry of an imaginaton that could never rest in the present . . . forming plans of self-humiliation and entire devotedness" (255, book 4, 2), Maggie violates one of Eliot's major tenets and loses the distinction between what is living in the past and what is dead. "She had not perceived—how could she until she had lived longer?—the inmost truth of the old monk's outpourings" (255).

This failure creates, of course, a severe relapse, leading to the discovery that the voice from the past brought a merely "negative peace: the battle of her life, it seemed, was not to be decided in that short and easy way" (336, book 6, 3). Unlike Dorothea, who has an epic-scale education given to her, Maggie never comes to believe in the value of her own anguish, because the Unseen Pity, invoked at the novel's conclusion, never becomes a clear cosmic faith, one which is advanced by an understanding of the preciously regarded "obscure and monotonous suffering." Barbara Guth has noted how the flaw in Maggie's doctrine of self-renunciation "is that it stresses so completely the insignificance of individual happiness" (358). A sense of affirmed anonymity, however, in the face of the world's disorders would have caused a true feeling of linkage with them and perhaps the coordinate ability to take the conventionally masculine route and resort to action. As it is, the "easy" path of misapplying the past only serves to make Maggie more conventionally female and paralyzed.

How the disorder of her life is finally resolved has been a source of relentless controversy, largely fueled by Eliot herself, who anxiously admitted that "the *epische Breite* into which I was beguiled by love of my subject in the first two volumes, caused a want of proportionate fullness in the treatment of the third, which I shall always regret" (*Letters* 3: 317). This is to miscalculate, however, how very fragmented—how irreparably incomplete—Tom and Maggie are by the end of book 5 and to encourage a tragic reading of the final part of the novel, a reading which a later letter was also to take for granted. However, the dramatized imbalances of education and the thwarting of the soul are entirely different from the plan suggested by the letters. By book 6, no tragic potential waits to be unraveled. The most the novel can do is suggest what could have existed had circumstances and decisions been different. Maggie cannot prove tragic by doing such things as defiantly carrying on with her life or throwing herself into the river (Hardy, *Critical Essays*, 50), since such acts would demand an awareness reserved for the reader and the narrator herself. The greatest objection to the novel's ending is that we are cheated of the action that would demonstrate epiphany—that is, one that would round out the enlightenment from within and place Maggie on a high level of recognition. But, as we have seen, the education of Maggie—and Tom—Tulliver has contained no such promise. In the remaining two books, Eliot the author, knowing better than her self-critic, offers, among other effects, a final orchestration, through event and metaphor, of incompleteness.

At the beginning of the third volume, we find a passive Maggie, most consistently portrayed in attitudes of tableau which underscore the irony that her quest for immediate action has only paralyzed her further. Clearly, Maggie's keen sympathy causes her to live too many imaginative lives, to adopt too many points of view, so that her powers of decision-making are lost. As Philip predicted, her self-imposed asceticism has given way to her "volcanic" (257, book 4, 3) youth, with the additional irony that while he was her initial liberator, his exhortations have only cleared the way for Stephen Guest. The ready sympathy which moved Maggie with such ease between past and present in her childhood now takes her into the sexual fantasies of song that surround Stephen. Although Maggie can admit that her past indiscriminations have now led to her present-day excesses (362, book 6, 7), she remains immobile, since her most dominant trait of responsiveness acknowledges all possibilities. The reader knows that Philip's claim has the ultimate authority; however, his needs, along with Stephen's temptations and Tom's irrational demands, all impinge on her with equal force and validity. At the crucial moment, Philip, reflecting her psychic condition, bows out of the romantic struggle, "his irritable, susceptible nerves" (405, book 6, 13) leading him away from decisive action, since all has been spent on imaginative conflict, and thus Maggie is left free to submit to Stephen, the narrator significantly using the passive voice when "Maggie felt that she was being led down the garden among the roses, being helped with firm tender care into the boat" (407, book 6, 13).

The anguishing bond between Maggie's highly active historical imagination and her fatally indiscriminate powers of sympathy becomes even clearer when she awakens to the consequences of her error and remembers her allusive dream:

She was in a boat on the wide water with Stephen, and in the gathering darkness something like a star appeared, that grew and grew till they saw it was the Virgin seated in St. Ogg's boat, and it came nearer and nearer, till they saw the Virgin was Lucy and the boatman was Philip—no, not Philip, but her brother, who rowed past without looking at her; and she rose to stretch out her arms and call to him, and their own boat turned over with the movement, and they began to sink, till with one spasm of dread she seemed to awake, and find she was a child again in the parlour at evening twilight, and Tom was not really angry. (413, book 6, 14).

Characteristically, Maggie's imagination creates a ready cohesion between the legendary world of St. Ogg's and the actual one, and in this double context, all priorities of sympathy are cast out; everyone holds the major role, with Philip changing into Tom in the perpetual spiritual metamorphosis and indecision of her waking moral life. Significantly, these illuminations are lost on the disoriented and suddenly conscious Maggie, whose memory is a frequent source of confusion for her. However, the message to the reader is clear: the St. Ogg's story does apply to Maggie's dilemma and to her second error of misguided loyalty. Philip is the appropriate analogue to the generous boatman; he does strive to serve her heart's need. Tom, of course, does not, but because of the childhood experiences with which the dream closes, Maggie blindly holds on to the belief that he will change, come to love her again, and thus all is lost.

The impasse at the novel's end is undeniable. Even though James thinks Stephen would have been the right choice for Maggie ("Novels," 52), he could hardly be so, not only because of Lucy but also because of his own incompatibility with Maggie's imagination and intelligence. Philip—although morally the right choice, had Maggie the strength to choose—is imprisoned by those very weaknesses which paralyze her. His final letter of unrequited love shows he still perceives her with the same self-effacement of their former conversations ["perhaps I feel about you as the artist does about the scene over which his soul has brooded with love" (439, book 7, 3)], and, tellingly, he ends waiting for her to send word rather than acting himself. Thus, the frustration—that is, the outcome of the two thwarted educations—is complete, and Eliot, left with the final scenes, decides to work by contrast: to start the novel over in the metaphorical sense and to suggest what Maggie and Tom could have reached had their educations been fulfilled.[6]

The flood, then, forces their personalities into a momentary totalness, so that, by contrast, the pity and fear of what went wrong may be accentuated. The flood instantly breaks down the polarity of thought and action which has separated brother and sister, thereby making the renewal of the affinity between them most believable. Maggie suddenly attains heroism of action, Tom heroism of thought. This role reversal demonstrates, most movingly, quite the opposite of what some critics perceive in the novel's conclusion. There is no false finality, but, rather, only a sense of what could have been: an infinality. Maggie and Tom have lived in a world far too complex for them, and their failure to perceive the subtle links between past and present as well as true and false commitment means they cannot go on living; they lack the fabric of coexistence which, in Eliot, serves as the staff of life. They must die after their brief fulfillments, and when they go down clasping each other, they symbolize the completed psyche: "in their death they were not divided." If, in life they had not been divided, they would have perceived each other as analogues to their own suffering and would have advanced to that state beyond their own egos where one's sufferings are acknowledged within the context of the world's collective tragedies: that is, a state of anonymity. As it is, paradoxically, their grave is the full self, in embryo.

Thus, we have the pity and fear of a tragedy without the sustained self-perception, whether in hero or in attendant chorus, that creates catharsis. As critics have insisted, the solution to the dilemma is entirely external. If Maggie is to be compared with Hamlet, we have no soliloquies from the heroine or any speeches from an analogous Horatio which would bring us meditative peace. However, to expect these, as some have, is to commit Maggie's error of confusing past forms with present ones. As we have seen, there are two entirely different levels of solution, the reader's and the characters'. If, consistent with classical tradition, it is the chorus who must demonstrate the appropriate balance of sympathy and distantness and who must remember past details accurately and apply them with relevance to the present, then it is the educated reader who, in *The Mill on the Floss,* must serve this function, entering the one-room schoolhouse and filling in where no character could. Since there is no Horatio or Edgar to recall the hero's story, the reader must serve as the choral figure in a cluster of incomplete tragedies which have all but the final recognition scene. And as chorus, the reader will neither oversympathize nor overjudge, will neither dismiss the past nor romanticize it. All fine lines will be drawn and insisted on the narrative chalkboard, in the course of the reader's "proper" education.

A number of critics have pointed to the narrator's more orga-
nized presence in *The Mill on the Floss*, with Graham Martin
speaking of an "Intourist Guide" (Smith, 37) and Carl Malmgren
speaking of one who is "perceptive and loquacious," who serves
as both "guide and teacher" and who "takes advantage of all the
narrational devices available to the authorial narrator" (480).[7] As
in *Adam Bede*, we have a speaker who is exhortative and lessoning,
but his or her lesson plans, in this case, have a more pronounced
and subtle strategy to them. At the opening of the novel, the narrator gives us a lesson in memory without our initially knowing
what it is. We are invited into a conventional though luminous
landscape and then are suddenly "snapped out" of it by our being
presented with the narrator dozing in his or her chair. The lesson
to be learned is—the powers of personal recollection are so strong
we can actually live on multiple planes of reality. In addition, we
are reminded that, in memory, we can become both the little girl
who has been placed in the landscape as well as the coachman—
another multiple reality. We are already acquiring the balance
that, together, Maggie and Tom represent. In conjunction with
this lesson plan, the narrator, for the first time in Eliot's fiction,
keeps his or her gender unidentified—neither is "her" bonnet
blown off the bridge nor is "his" cigar seen burning in the ashtray
when he awakens. Perhaps this transition was made, perfectly, via
The Lifted Veil, which intervenes between *Adam Bede* and *The
Mill on the Floss*, with Eliot moving from an equation between
her pseudonym and her narrator to an actual imaginary speaker—
one who is androgynous and more sketched in as a character. In
just the few opening pages of *The Mill on the Floss*, we have
learned to identify with someone who is both androgynous and
anonymous—this final quality being an addition to the Latimer-
like speaker. We have viewed a scene without anyone acknowledging us and thus have participated in "the gross sum of obscure
vitality" (238, book 4, 1), and we have exercised our powers of
memory such that we have learned to become others. Our school-
mistress or schoolmaster remains anonymous and appropriately
fades in corporality as the second chapter nears, because we, as
readers and pupils are in the same state. The invisible, one-room
schoolhouse can only be effective if "like" instructs "like."

Eliot is entirely consistent in following her educative plan, providing, to the letter of her definition, the didactic experience which
Tom and Maggie missed, and making us, the readers, into anonymous heroes. We have been, of course, instructed, via the extremes of brother and sister, in the positive values of sympathy

and distantness, as well as in the dual continuity and discontinuity of past and present, upon which the emotional balance is dependent. The narrator continually sways the reader in two directions, exhorting him or her to sympathize with experiences or areas of life that might seem remote: childhood, the lower class, a distant time period. Yet we are also reminded that the areas are indeed remote, the narrator even going so far as to admit, "I share with you this sense of oppressive narrowness" (238, book 4, 1), so that the necessary esthetic distantness is maintained. Although our patronizing of a *bildungsroman* set in the provinces is often anticipated and chastised (35, book 1, 5; 156, book 2, 4), our sympathy is not pushed so far that we make Maggie's mistake of leaping indiscriminately into another world. To take the reader's education to the second power, Eliot has every intention of keeping *The Mill on the Floss* from being another "voice from the past"; it will build on its own distinctions.

These distinctions are particularly alive in those passages which pivot on classical allusion, and in an as yet uncollected Eliot review of Thomas Keightley's *Life, Opinions, and Writings of John Milton*, we can see that she agrees with the Miltonic concept that pupils should be educated in the lesser classics before going on to the Greats: "Too early an intimacy with the highest, in any department," she writes, "deadens the sensibility and robs the mature mind of its proper enjoyments. A child who has been taken to see the Alps at ten years of age is pitiable; he will never know the rush of thought and feeling which would have made the sight an epoch for his manhood" (603–4). Such a principle not only sheds light on the Stelling-like approach to deadening Tom's sensibility before it can mature; it also explains why Eliot reserves the true disclosure of these texts for the mature reader, who can manage an assignment like "read Sophocles. Note the differences and similarities." We can stand on the Alps and have the wider view.

Such literary instruction can arrive, for example, through a medley of comic and ironic effects:

In order to see Mr. and Mrs. Glegg at home, we must enter the town of St. Ogg's—that venerable town with the red-fluted roofs and the broad warehouse gables, where the black ships unlade themselves of their burthens from the far north, and carry away, in exchange, the precious island products, the well-crushed cheese and the soft fleeces, which my refined readers have doubtless become acquainted with through the medium of the best pastorals. (103, book 1, 12)

As in *Scenes of Clerical Life*, the classical postscript provides some laughter at the reader's expense, since his or her patronizing attitude is itself patronized; the narrator openly ridicules the fashionable sedentary habits that presumably dominate the reader's life and extols, by implication, the hard labor of "that venerable town." At the same time, however, Eliot also holds the picture of St. Ogg's at arm's length, since, in conjuring up an alternative, Arcadian world, she accentuates the grimness of workaday life—in particular, the kind of life that the Gleggs represent. The vision from the peaks of the classical Alps works in a variety of ways. As Jennifer Uglow points out:

> The wider network of allusions to geology, natural history, music, Greek Tragedy, the eighteenth-century novel, the poetry of Wordsworth or of Goethe offer a wealth of alternative visions and remind us at the same time of the limited view of the world of St. Ogg's. (132).

This resulting balance of sympathy and detachment is sustained in later passages: those that contain mock-heroic allusions (as in the "mud" episode), allusions whose power ultimately depends on the comic distance between past and present; and those that show a Homeric continuity between past and present, or demonstrate a past that is laughably similar to the present, with Hamlet, for example, becoming comically testy with his still-living father-in-law.

In addition to these more comic or ironic areas, the most directly tragic story in the novel, the downfall of Edward Tulliver, also sustains this careful balancing. The narrator insists that the miller is both like Oedipus (117, book 1, 13) and unlike him (173–74, book 3, 1); his fall has thunderous repercussions for all concerned, and yet his ultimate death mysteriously lacks that self-enlightenment that would make him a full-scale Lear or Oedipus. Thus, we can perceive Mr. Tulliver only if we perceive both continuity and discontinuity, apply both sympathy and detachment, by recalling the past with a firmly controlled imagination:

> And Mr. Tulliver, you perceive, though nothing more than a superior miller and maltster, was as proud and obstinate as if he had been a very lofty personage, in whom such dispositions might be a source of that conspicuous, far-echoing tragedy, which sweeps the stage in regal robes and makes the dullest chronicler sublime. The pride and obstinacy of millers, and other insignificant people, whom you pass unnoticingly on the road every day, have their tragedy, too; but it is of that unwept, hidden sort, that goes on from generation to generation, and

leaves no record—such tragedy, perhaps, as lies in the conflicts of young souls, hungry for joy. (173, book 3, 1)

As mentioned before, it is as though Eliot has made a double assignment to her reader pupils: "read Sophocles and study everyday millers from the past English countryside. Note the differences and similarities." Thus, for the reader, sympathy, through a ready entry into the past, is thereby enforced, and thus Maggie's initial talent is fostered, encouraged, even while the imposition on someone like Tom is avoided. Maggie's excesses do not enter in, since the reader, on the second level, is also reminded of the particulars of St. Ogg's life; its proportionate smallness must be admitted. Tulliver, "you perceive," is "nothing more than a superior miller and maltster," and thus the reminder holds our sympathy in check, in balance—the reader does not soar too far into the past.

Such refining of the reader's powers of memory, through a meticulous adjustment of rhetorical distancing, occurs, in some form, in all the allusive passages that web the novel. And the effect is not merely rhetorical in the decorative sense but has immediate bearing on the drama at hand. Forced into their premature adulthood, both Maggie and Tom become fatally blind to the claims of memory. Tom, losing touch with the warmth of his childhood, "forgets" the sympathy that he pledged to Maggie and ruthlessly banishes Philip from her presence. Maggie, on the other hand, also finds it impossible to keep to her pledges of personal remembrance. Retreating first into Thomas à Kempis and later into the ecstasy of arias and songs, she loses touch, suffers a temporary amnesia, whereby "memory was excluded" (407, book 6, 13), when she is led by Stephen to the fatal boat. Such a loss, however, never exists for the reader, since allusions to the past, with their built-in discontinuities, always serve to clarify moral responsibility rather than obscure it. In chapter 12 of book 1, for example, the narrator describes the town of St. Ogg's as a vital coexistence of past and present; it "carries," we are told, "the traces of its long growth and history like a millenial tree" (104). Later on, this comparison acquires even greater force, in a passage that recalls the Red Deeps:

For Philip, who a little while ago was associated continually in Maggie's mind with the sense that Tom might reproach her with some justice, had now, in this short space, become a sort of outward conscience to her, that she might fly to for rescue and strength. Her tranquil, tender affection for Philip, with its root deep down in her childhood, and its memories of long quiet talk confirming by distinct successive impressions the first instinctive bias—the fact that in him the appeal was more strongly to her pity and womanly devotedness than to her vanity or other egoistic excitability of her nature, seemed now to make a sort of sacred place. (359, book 6, 7)

As a result, when the reader comes to that moment when "memory was excluded" for Maggie, just the opposite is occurring for him or her, for the whole weight of the novel, all motifs of memory, including the major symbol of the "millenial tree," are brought to bear upon that single sentence.

Within the context of the reader's educated memory, the arrival of death in the novel, so disturbingly barren on first reading—for example in such statements as "poor Tulliver's dimly-lighted soul had for ever ceased to be vexed with the painful riddle of this world" (315, book 5, 7) and "The next instant the boat was no longer seen upon the water—and the huge mass was hurrying on in hideous triumph" (456, book 7, 5)—acquire a new resonance. When Maggie enters the biblical deluge, the reader must acknowledge the allusion while at the same time perceiving the difference; there is no covenant for Maggie, because she has lived in the dreams like the one she is enacting. The covenant of thought and action, nature and culture, past and present, resulting from the complex interplay of memory, is denied to both Maggie and her brother. Significantly, the trees, symbolizing the recollection of the past and its nourishing hold upon the present, are also uprooted by the flood, only to be preserved in memory by the solitary Philip, who recalls the Red Deeps at Maggie's graveside. But while the allusions point up a lack of covenants, they also show a presence and serve as a kind of a valedictory address given as one steps from the one-room schoolhouse. There is a covenant provided for the reader, and under its laws he or she will serve as both anonymous chorus and student.

4

Silas Marner and the Anonymous Heroism of Parenthood

Since Henry James, critics have seen *Silas Marner* as the culmination of a phase.[1] At the same time, however, it signals the beginning of Eliot's closer examination of how traditionally masculine and feminine traits might be successfully combined and how such a combination might lead to the proper raising of children who, in turn, would also acquire the balance. In the fiction that precedes *Silas Marner*, George Eliot dramatizes intense conflicts between the sexes, between husband and wife, brother and sister, lover and lover. The corollary to this struggle is an effort, on the part of the protagonists, to develop, side by side, both male and female characteristics within themselves; feminine susceptibility must be complemented by male detachment. But in all cases, the tradition of heroic chivalry, with its attendant evils of predominance and subordination, is exchanged for a newer, more freeing vision. There are precursors to Silas, in Mr. Irwine of *Adam Bede,* with his quiet attendance to his family and his flock, Mr. Tryan of *Scenes of Clerical Life,* and in Philip Wakem, who "nursed," as U. C. Knoepflmacher puts it, "Maggie's internal conflicts" (*George Eliot's Early Novels,* 228).

Maggie's struggles alone dramatize the desire to defy convention and acquire that worldliness normally reserved for polite gentlemen. Eliot offers no sustained resolution until, paradoxically, we reach the even remoter world of Raveloe, where Silas must become both mother and father to Eppie, and embody, as a character, the education that in *The Mill on the Floss* was reserved for the reader alone. In this sense, *Silas Marner* could be called an idyll, in exactly the way Freidrich von Schiller defined the form, one which holds all in a "dynamic calm" (146) and yet "display[s] that pastoral innocence even in creatures of civilization and under all the conditions of the most active and vigorous life" (153). In the spirit of the pastoral, *Silas Marner* charms away tensions that, in the more conventionally realistic works, would have led to tragic consequences[2], and the novel also prepares the way for the larger inner solutions which the four works of Eliot's later phase were to explore.

Implicitly and with an understatedness that has been frequently praised, *Silas Marner* shows how the enlightened raising of children—a part of the "active and vigorous life"—crucially depends on the balancing of male and female within the parent. In this case, the competent father is the man who can be both protective and sympathetic, who can know the value of the single-minded masculine world which provides one's bread and yet can withstand the challenges of being "moithered" (180)[3] in the female world of sustenance and care. Conversely, the antihero is the displaced father, the man, who, for one reason or another, fails to heed the call to develop his nurturing powers. For thematic emphasis, Eliot makes this foil the natural father, in contrast to the true father who has acquired the role through patient performance and love. In achieving the wider vision, which leads, ultimately, to anonymous heroism, one father succeeds and the other fails. Jennifer Uglow, when writing of this challenge, says that "the two men are therefore tested by the way they respond to an inarticulate plea in the shock of the moment" (154).

In *Silas Marner*, the covenant between apparent opposites[4] is made obtainable to those who are willing to be humble and teachable. This is true not only of the covenant between man and woman but also between past and present, individual and society—and the man and woman within the self. The iconographic symbol of Oedipus and Antigone at Colonus, which, as mentioned earlier, perhaps best explains this kind of union, also unites the three-novel sequence of *The Mill on the Floss, Silas Marner,* and *Romola*. Each presents a father who loses power and must endure his daughter's guidance—an experience which, paradoxically, strengthens him and makes him a new sort of parent. Such a yielding and such a renewal of energy are critical to our understanding of both the biographical Marian Evans, who saw the nursing of her father as a "worship for mortals" (*Letters* 1: 284) and the literary George Eliot, who offers an ideal of parental balance. In her novels, it is only through such a symbiosis of dependency and independence that the child herself can grow into power. In writing to Blackwood concerning the proofing of *Silas Marner* (3: 398), Eliot was particularly vehement about "quite the worst error," a one-letter misprint in Eppie's vehement retort to Godfrey: "And it'd be poor work for me to put on things, and ride in a gig, and sit in a place at church as 'ud make them as I'm fond of think me unfitting company for 'em. What could *I* care for then?" (234). The printer had put in "them" just before the question mark— which shifted the whole meaning away to the finer "things." What the one letter correction meant was exactly this: if Eppie could not care for the covenant that she and Silas-Aaron-Dolly embod- ied, she would not have the power to care for anything.

While a number of critics have pointed out the balance of male and female as an ideal in the novel, we have yet to see, closely and in a most explicit way, how Eliot introduces the concept of anonymity, as obtained through this bridging of the genders, which is in turn symbolic of Silas's reentry into the community as a whole. At the opening of the novel proper, Silas is seen as traditionally masculine and bound, by work, to his loom. As he grows through the child, however, he learns to see himself as a mother as well and as an anonymous contributor to the world as a whole.

Surely this transformation does not occur overnight. Prior to his coming to Raveloe, Silas is presented as a reformulation of Philip Wakem, struggling to preserve a sensibility that is more feminine than masculine. Paralleling the Philip-Tom friendship, Silas's ado- ration of William Dane (William Waif in the original manuscript) gives way to "strong," "masculine" defensiveness once the initial trust is broken.[5] It is as though Silas perceived William as the waif who needed both love and worship, and then underwent a kind of dreadful disillusionment of motherhood. Unlike Philip, however, Silas is given time to recover and to recover the lost side of himself. After secluding himself away, Silas learns to trust men once more, once he has discovered that his reputation is less im- portant than his anonymous dedication to what he holds dear.

The dramatic metamorphosis occurs through Silas's recollec- tions of his mother and sister. The William Dane crisis, combined with the zeal of Lantern Yard, causes him, initially, to discard his mother's "bequest" (57) of healing herbal knowledge and dedicate his life to the invulnerable loom. When Eppie suddenly appears on his hearth, however, we witness a return to the "remedial"[6] memories of his mother and what he knew of her in his sister:

> Could this be his little sister come back to him in a dream—his little sister whom he had carried about in his arms for a year before she died, when he was a small boy without shoes or stockings? (168)

Thus, *Silas Marner* is not simply the story of a withered man whose wounded sensibility is restored through love of a child but

the story of an incomplete man, one as incomplete as Philip Wakem or Tom Tulliver, whose female self is reawakened through
the raising of a daughter. It is important to note, as David Carroll
does (*Silas Marner,* 153), that Eppie enters through "the chasm
in his consciousness" (ch. 12, 167). Thus Silas undergoes a complete loss of self before embracing the female part of himself. This
change, symbolized by the catalepsy, shows Silas letting go of his
egoistic concerns and welcoming not only Eppie but his little sister, who passed away, and who was the only one, most likely, who
appreciated and acknowledged his heroic tenderness. The memory of boyhood returns to Silas with the point that whatever credit
he received for his efforts as a brother, came from an unseen
Good, one closely linked with Dolly's higher "Them." The two
"chasms of consciousness" which preceded this inner revolution
have, of course, been the perfect preparation. Silas had to lose his
good standing at Lantern Yard as well as his Raveloe treasure
trove before he could secure the anonymous heroism which would
secure Eppie.

Eppie, then, must be named for Silas's mother and sister, since
she draws together those memories of womanly care and healing
that are to be the wellspring of the life of the present and are to
be the models for this special form of parenthood. If Hepzibah
means "my delight in her," surely Silas is delighting in the new
fullness of his psyche as well as in Eppie herself and in a world
no longer connected with trophies and recognition.

Once Silas begins attending to Eppie and his mind starts "growing into memory," he also recalls his mother's lore and looks "for
the once familiar herbs again" (ch. 14, 185).[7] The search is made
possible also because Silas has given up his own resentment over
the Salley Oates incident, an incident that had involved, once
again, a concern with reputation and external recognition. With
his new goals of motherhood and anonymous heroism, he is able
to transcend a sulky disposition and move on to the very thing
that symbolizes an enlightened pity and therefore his own regen-
eration. Jennifer Uglow writes that "they [the herbs] become part
of his own healing, knitting together his broken spirit and soothing his wounded memory" (152).

Silas's psychic change is heightened, or better, facilitated, by
the frequently noted fairytale quality of the Raveloe society. Often
in Eliot, modernization can be seen to hasten the tensions between
man and woman—as if to move through time were to advance
further and further from an Edenic sexual harmony. Thus Raveloe, although remote and out of date, encourages Silas not only

in his adoption of Eppie but also in his pursuit of the dual roles that must come with it. We are in an ideal world where the past easily connects with the present and the ways of woman harmonize with the ways of man, even in the halves of a single nature. On the other side of the universe is St. Ogg's, where all exists in division. Maggie cannot connect the world of the fabled past with her present and therefore cannot unite conflicting characteristics within herself. Although Silas makes some of the same errors as Maggie, as well as those of Tom and Philip, redemption arrives for him—and speedily—because in Raveloe, the past is always restorative, and its bearing upon the present is readily felt:

> The thoughts were strange to him now, like old friendships impossible to revive; and yet he had a dreamy feeling that this child was somehow a message come to him from that far-off life: it stirred fibres that had never been moved in Raveloe—old quiverings of tenderness—old impressions of awe at the presentiment of some Power presiding over his life; for him imagination had not yet extricated itself from the sense of mystery in the child's sudden presence, and had formed no conjectures of ordinary natural means by which the event could have been brought about. (ch. 12, 168)

Unlike many of Eliot's protagonists, Silas finds the powers of memory to be completely at his disposal as he reenters society. The past returns with ease and leads directly to a sense of rightness and devotion. Just as Raveloe, with its powerful traditions, has no trouble connecting the past with the present, so Silas, in belonging to its charmed context, can reach, almost effortlessly, that part of his personal history which he most requires. As Silas recovers his old affections for his mother and sister, as well as his compassionate religious zeal, he becomes the tender boy "without shoes or stockings" again, and therefore, motherlike, can press Eppie to him "and almost unconsciously [offer] hushing tenderness" (168). He is no longer "himself" because he has lost his identity to a universal parenthood, and because of this change, his anxiety over whether the old "Silas" will survive on his gold disappears. He is on his own way to achieving anonymous heroism because he has embraced a faith in the unseen. The moment of change is altogether convincing since we are in a novel of charmed psychological transformation, where error, though still possible, can be rectified or bypassed at the right moment.

At the same time, however, Silas's growth into a special brand of "motherhood"[8] does not loosen his hold on the world of masculine work, and it is as if Eliot wishes to emphasize the point that her protagonist stays simultaneously in both worlds. As Gillian Beer writes, "Silas is a weaver, deliberately set *across* the stereotype of the woman weaving" (126, emphasis hers). The subsequent conflict is small, however, since, in Raveloe, as opposed to St. Ogg's, harmony is also possible between traditionally male and female duties. In doing what is surprising for a man, Silas elicits the sympathy of the community:

> Silas Marner's determination to keep the "tramp's child" was matter of hardly less surprise and iterated talk in the village than the robbery of his money. That softening of feeling towards him which dated from his misfortune, that merging of suspicion and dislike in a rather contemptuous pity for him as lone and crazy, was now accompanied with a more active sympathy, especially amongst the women. (ch. 14, 178)

The mothers' representative is, of course, Dolly Winthrop, but in an important way, she takes Raveloe's eccentricity one step further in denying the supposedly impassable gulf between masculine labor and childrearing. Although some critics might argue that mother figures are conspicuously missing from the novel— and therefore Eliot is once again concentrating solely on the transformed male, while ignoring the psychically balanced woman— Dolly should be seen as a distinct reply. She also is an anonymous hero because she acknowledges the delicacy and the challenge of the tasks facing Silas. Frequently she encourages and often embodies the many strong "masculine" attributes which enable Silas to earn his bread while raising Eppie at the same time. Like Mr. Irwine of *Adam Bede*, she suggests a heroic perception and breadth of vision which the other characters must quest for until the novel is finished. Thus, it makes sense that she is, in some ways, the commander, advisor, and teacher of the protagonist. In the dialogue of chapter 14, while the difficulties of combining childrearing with the pursuit of one's trade are always acknowledged, compromises are found: the rather alarming prospect of leashing Eppie to the loom so as to keep her from hurting herself is balanced by Dolly's proposal of "my little chair, and some bits o' red rag and things for her to play wi'; an' she'll sit and chatter to 'em as if they was alive" (181). This exchange between Dolly and Silas, along with the solution of prospective conflict in roles, foreshadows, crucially, the novel's ultimate harmonizing of both male and female and also shows a mutual celebration of what no exterior point of view could appreciate.

During Silas's subsequent raising of Eppie, the difficult balance between severity and permissiveness, so elusive to the parent is, once again, achievable. Eppie is not spoiled because psychology serves the idyllic laws of the pastoral. Eppie can grow into perfection, even while her doting father lacks the will of the conventional male to discipline her. Because Eppie is loved, with a father's true, balanced love, she can grow into the best of children:

> Perfect love has a breath of poetry which can exalt the relations of the least-instructed human beings; and this breath of poetry had surrounded Eppie from the time she had followed the bright gleam that had beckoned her to Silas' hearth; so that it is not surprising if, in other things besides her delicate prettiness, she was not quite a common village maiden, but had a touch of refinement and fervour which came from no other teaching than that of tenderly nurtured unvitiated feeling. (ch. 16, 206)

Thus, even though "Eppie was reared without punishment" (189), there is to be no ensuing nemesis, as there is in the history of Gwendolen Harleth, since in Raveloe, making the child the center of attention cannot lead to problems. It is poetry that dominates the life of Silas and his adopted daughter.

Surely Eliot had this in mind when writing her often-quoted letter concerning the composition of the novel. "I have felt," she wrote, "all through as if the story would have lent itself best to metrical rather than prose fiction, especially in all that relates to the psychology of Silas" (*Letters* 3: 382). Not only is the psychological transformation of Silas a charmed process, as in a verse romance or idyll, but so are the effects: love, even doting love, is beneficent without qualification. In the "Notes on Form in Art," which was quoted earlier, Eliot speaks of "rhythms & images" forming a "natural history of mind" (435). Here the meter of the changing idyllic landscape lays before us the unique and dynamic process of Silas's male and female mind, as well as its quest toward the anonymous heroism of parenthood. Healing is made visible and believable through a dense imagery and rhythmic sentences that invoke a protected but poetically heightened world—in this case, in a prose context. We will see this again when Eliot adapts another German poet and playwright—Goethe—to the healing medium of the novel *Middlemarch*.

Although Silas's case seems to be the special one, the one reserved for a "legendary" world rather than a realistic one, Eliot is quite consistent in fulfilling Schiller's call for a work that could be idealized and yet apply to the actual world of the reader.[9] The strategy is multiple; it is achieved first through a series of direct editorial links, between Silas's experience and the experience of "modernday" people; it is achieved, by extension, through the negative example of Godfrey Cass. Also the peculiarity of Silas's case presents a balance. He belongs and yet does not belong, and he is given a variety of suggested identities, with which the reader might possibly identify; he is compared to an artist, a storyteller,[10] and a scholar. The resulting bridge[11] means that Raveloe itself has a more realistic presence than, say, Sidney's Arcadia or even Austen's Highbury. David Carroll, in writing of *Silas Marner*'s double nature as both tale and novel, captures again this tenuous balance, saying that "the reader is constantly being reminded that amidst the fictional complexity there is a simple story with its own narrative logic" (*George Eliot and the Conflict of Interpretations*, 141), so that both magic and narrative explanation of the fictional "reality" are accepted.

Silas's example, of course, becomes most applicable to the reader's experience when he tries to become both mother and father to Eppie. By contrast, Godfrey Cass heightens the achievement, when he proves unable to follow his more vulnerable instincts. Unlike Silas, who has distinct memories of a mother and sister to guide him, Godfrey has only "an essentially domestic nature" (ch. 3, 81)—which another family, the Lammeters, must work to save. Thus, at the crucial[12] moment, Godfrey condemns and isolates himself, making Silas's sympathetic response all the more desirable—much more so than the original scheme proposed by Eliot, the isolated "metrical" treatment, devoid of contrast, would have done. Like Arthur Donnithorne and Adam Bede in his initial phases, Godfrey stands as the rejected heroic model. He has all the trappings of a "big muscular frame" (76), but, consistent with Eliot's sustained irony, he is not yielding enough to rise to the level of true heroism, and he is too concerned with what reputation will bring in order to come close to anything like true parenthood.

With the force of a musical recapitulation, chapter 19 holds important links with the opening of the book, dramatizing Silas initially in crisis "when the keenness of the susceptibility makes external stimulus intolerable" (225). Silas then defeats the crisis and defends his right of parenthood in a combined effort to keep his dual sensibility whole and yet counter Godfrey with "a touch of parental fierceness" (231). Godfrey, for his part, clings to his code of proprietorship and represents, quite predictably, the Letter of the Law. It is quite clear that he has started to pursue the title of "father" in a mechanical and conventionally masculine attempt to head off the anonymity of dying without an identified heir. If the child is father to the man, then in Wordsworthian terms, this scene shows Godfrey to be morally illegitimate.[13]

In the heated debate between the father-by-blood and the father-by-love, we expect Silas to be more awkward and less articulate than he is, and we are pleasantly surprised to find the true parent winning even on Godfrey's argumentative territory. The full force of this scene depends partly on the reader's dawning awareness of the extent of Silas's growth. Eppie surprises as well, in her moving reply to Godfrey's offer, showing herself the rightful heir to the transformed Silas, a protector of his anonymous heroism, in full line with the role that Dolly Winthrop has served all along: "And he took care of me and loved me from the first" (234). In making this affirmation directly to her legal father, she proves, more than could any shy country maiden, to be a true integrater also of masculine and feminine ways. Consistent with the power shift that Eliot was careful to assure in correcting the galley proofs, Eppie's "What could I care for then?" prepares the way for her vision of taking care of Silas: "I've always thought of a little home where he'd sit i' the corner, and I should fend and do everything for him" (234). She will become an unrecognized hero as well. Thus, the scene allows the reader to see Eppie's character in a new light, and as Dianne Sadoff notes, when comparing Silas Marner with Felix Holt, there is a "redemption first of father, then of daughter" (72).

Because Godfrey is the shallower character, he is left to find his equilibrium in a more external way; he must turn to Nancy's feminine wisdom and higher moral nature in order to reach the balance that Silas finds within. In this sense, Silas is, morally, miles ahead of Godfrey, since he sought Dolly's tutelage first and demonstrated the full fruits of his education when the moment came to defend himself and his home. Appropriately, then, Godfrey cannot share in the joy of Eppie and Aaron's wedding, since he has been the absent father during the crucial years of her childhood and adolescence; yet even his salvation can be anticipated in the new peace he finds with Nancy, after the confrontation with Silas.

The "rainbow" at the conclusion of the novel, then, spans the polarity of male and female as it unites symbolically the other crucial opposites that Eliot has dramatized. Presumably, Aaron will live on to sustain Silas's example of the nurturing parent, when he openly declares his plan that his father-in-law live with them. Further, Aaron's being a gardener suggests, symbolically, that he has a caring hand in all matters. Of him, Silas says, "He's his mother's lad" (ch. 16, 209), defying the patriarchal tradition while, ironically, suggesting how much Aaron is like himself. Decidedly he has let go of the self who was an isolated achiever, finding his "living memorial" in another man—and woman. In providing this reconciliation along with the struggle of an ultimately triumphing "legitimate" parent, Eliot has opened up her definition of heroism. For Silas transcends the narrower examples of Dinah Morris, who attended to Hayslope and Stoniton but only with a certain limited piety, and Mr. Irwine, who was large-souled but confined to the outer reaches of the novel. Silas's heroism also transcends *The Mill on the Floss,* where heroism must occur as an implied aggregate of the best qualities of several characters, once the instructive narrator has pointed them out. In *Silas Marner,* heroism is thus discovered to be a revelation of both the male and female nature, as embodied in enlightened parenthood, which seeks no rewards. This is true not only because the old codes of chivalry are emphatically transformed, but also because true heroism exists as a harmony between man and woman within the individual soul, whether of man or woman, and the harmony may be passed on—bequeathed—not as a name but as a nurturing condition. For this reason, the penultimate scene of Eppie attending Silas to the vanished Lantern Yard must overshadow the wedding. It is indeed a reformulation of Antigone helping Oedipus "see" Colonus, but it is also, more generally, a scene of a man letting go of his hard, masculine past that, most fortunately, only temporarily excluded the woman within. He has yielded to the anonymity that has been planned for him. We begin to understand that Silas's catalepsy and "chasm[s] in consciousness" were really only a beneficent forewarning of his growth in soul. Anxiety over individual survival has yielded to faith in a collective identity, and in the tradition which Aaron and Eppie will sustain. Thus, at the end of the novel, when Silas speaks of the mysterious disappearance of Lantern Yard, he ushers in a new code when he says "I doubt it'll be dark to the last."

"Well, yes, Master Marner," said Dolly, who sat with a placid listening face, now bordered by grey hairs; "I doubt it may. It's the will o'Them above as a many things should be dark to us; but there's some things as I've never felt i'the dark about, and they're mostly what comes i' the day's work. You were hard done by that once, Master Marner, and it seems as you'll never know the rights of it; but that doesn't hinder there being a rights, Master Marner, for all it's dark to you and me."

"No," said Silas, "no; that doesn't hinder. Since the time the child was sent to me and I've come to love her as myself, I've had light enough to trusten by; and now she says she'll never leave me, I think I shall trusten till I die." (ch. 20, 241)

Surely Dolly's "Them" must acknowledge the deeds of heroism "which have no great name on earth," because they were done for their own sake—in the enlightened dark, so to speak, rather than by the light of external reward, and surely Dolly's "Them" must suggest that the Divine Ones above must be both genders.

5

Romola and the Preservation
of Household Gods

Romola's place in George Eliot's creative development has been difficult to determine, not only because of Eliot's own statements of doubt and agony (Haight, *Biography,* 351, 361–62), but also because of what seems, in her previous works of full-length fiction, to be an almost linear progression of subjects, a progression that is suddenly interrupted by a novel of distracting erudition and remote characters, many of whom are themselves scholars. The very fact that *Silas Marner* delayed the completion of the historical work even seems to suggest a certain resistance on Eliot's part. To step from merry England to late fifteenth-century Florence is to endure a cultural shock within the canon of an individual artist.

Romola is, however, continuous with the fiction before and after it, because it also embodies the emblem, already mentioned, of an aged, kingly father and proud, supporting daughter—Oedipus and Antigone. As we have seen, how a young woman nurtures age and how she may transcend a strong family hubris were more than themes to Eliot; they were a haunting, iconographic symbol—Maggie tending to the stricken Mr. Tulliver, hoping he might retract his curse; Eppie leading Silas through the unnamed town, in search of Lantern Yard; Romola reaching down a copy of Nonnus to the blind Bardo in the darkened library; and Esther, as a token of penitence, quietly brushing her father's hair. In Sophocles' *Oedipus at Colonus,* much of this father-daughter relationship is established in the short exchange, very close to the opening:

> *Oedipus.* Help me sit down; take care of the blind man.
> *Antigone.* After so long, you need not tell me, father.
> (Sophocles, Fitzgerald, 82)[1]

In the chapter "The Blind Scholar and his Daughter," it is as if Romola and Bardo had just spoken these same lines, when the narrator subsequently comments: "As Romola said this, a fine ear would have detected in her clear voice and distinct utterance, a faint suggestion of weariness struggling with habitual patience" (ch. 5, 95)—even when the issue is the referencing of an obscure text rather than a simple hand to help an aging body. For Eliot to make the scene at one with Sophocles is to delineate the way tragedy exists from "generation to generation" and from novel to novel, and to prepare the way for Piero di Cosimo, an artist who, like the narrator herself, perceives the mythological, the heroic, within the everyday. In fact, when one looks at the novel's plot structure, the world of ancient Thebes seems to be suggested as much as that of Renaissance Florence: an old blind man, of noble lineage, uses his daughter as his "eyes" and as a sensitive intermediary to the outer world. He has cursed his son, but the daughter, in her dual love, never relents in her tenderness for both. When the father and brother are dead, the story pivots when the daughter, bearing out the pride of the family name, defies the egotism and narrowness of the outer world in order to fulfill pledges to those who have died or are about to die. For Romola as for Antigone, the underworld, housing the family ghosts, often seems to require a stronger commitment than the daylight world of intriguing politicians and lovers.

The emblematic relationship between Romola and her father should not be confused, however, with Dorothea's slavish marriage to Casaubon, even though a number of critics have made that link. Romola's bond, although including that of being an amanuensis, is also one of "sacramental obligation" (ch. 27, 310), that has been born out of returned love and nurturance as well as a sense of inner and outer subordination. Although Bardo's bullying chauvinism and his even more imprisoning tenderness [which acknowledges, in a paternal but hurtful way, the capacities of Romola's "feminine mind" (ch. 5, 100)] suggest something of the nightmare Dorothea enters in *Middlemarch*,[2] Bardo's ends are critically different from Casaubon's—as is, ultimately, his treatment of the principal woman in his life. Unlike the Key to All Mythologies, the father-scholar's plans can be seen as having a public benefit, beneficently conceived—a library for the people of Florence—not just the assurance of an immortal name. Unlike Dorothea, Romola cannot, at the center of the novel, simply remove herself from the clutch of a dead hand. Her relationship to the past must be sustained and yet qualified, and it, in fact, serves as a way out of a claustrophobic marriage to the wrong younger man. Romola is more firmly in the tradition of Maggie Tulliver, who inherits positive as well as negative legacies from her once-known and living father, and she anticipates Esther Lyon, who will grow into a heroic appreciation of Rufus while he is still alive. In all these positive instances, the heroines learn to acquire certain "man-like" characteristics that further their quests.

Ironically, Romola's protection of Bardo and his memory is her first source of liberation, her means of escaping the stifling feminine world of subjection, of "Reality, Books and Waking Dreams," which incarcerated Maggie. Once Romola's father is dead, her sense of familial piety throws her into direct conflict with the serpentine Tito, the husband who would have destroyed even what small freedom she knew as a daughter. Tito's wholesale destruction of Bardo's library is a pivotal point in the life of Romola's psyche, when she must choose between coercion and truly felt commitment:

> Romola sat silent and motionless; she could not blind herself to the direction in which Tito's words pointed; he wanted to persuade her that they might get the library deposited in some monastery, or take some other ready means to rid themselves of a task, and of a tie to Florence: and she was determined never to submit her mind to his judgment on this question of duty to her father; she was inwardly prepared to encounter any sort of pain of resistance. (ch. 32, 352)

Thus, when "the pride and fierceness of the old Bardi blood had been thoroughly awaked in her for the first time" (356), there is no doubt that Romola can stand up to Tito's "masculine predominance," because she can counter him on his own ground as well as wife to husband. In a parallel manner, Silas, in adopting his mother's characteristics, acquires a "fierceness" which puts Godfrey Cass in his place.

The moment of Romola's "discrowning" herself is a response to both an inner need and a message from the grave. She is no longer content to be the feminine ornament known as Ariadne. As she hastens from Florence, she sees her father's library being carried away and feels "less that she was seeing this herself than that her father was conscious of it as he lay helpless under the imprisoning stones, where her hand could not reach his to tell him that he was not alone" (ch. 36, 386). Here she is at one with the omniscient narrator, who not only knows all points of view but also sees human anguish in a context larger than one's individual ego. That is, in becoming her father for a moment, Romola loses herself to a sense of anonymity—eventually she will rest in an unvisited tomb, but before she does, she will struggle for what she feels to be right. The same process will be true of Esther.

This act of defiance, as well as tender recollection, constitutes Romola's first step into the world of activity, to apply, enrich, and also defy the circumscribed life of stoical scholarship. Savonarola, when he meets her on the road, is Thomas à Kempis giving a reborn Maggie a true opportunity to make use of self-renunciation. Romola has all of suffering, transitional Florence before her, for "the giant forces" are very much alive. Romola can become the visible Madonna of Maggie's dreams.

This idealization, which has troubled critics from virtually the novel's publication, does not seem so unlikely or disturbing when one considers the case of the multidimensional Lydgate, who like Romola, must "come to us in our need with a more sublime beneficence than that of miracle workers" (ch. 66, 720) because his own private life is desolate. Romola's obeying Savonarola's arresting voice does not spring so much from an improbable magnanimity as it does from a desire to redirect her energies and tenderness. In essence, Savonarola tells her that if she cannot return for the sake of her husband, she can at least return for Florence. In his influential article, "'Romola' as Fable," George Levine typifies many critics when he says that Romola "fails utterly on almost every occasion to live up to the supposed Bardo-like pride" (Hardy, *Critical Essays*, 84). However, Romola, in retracing her steps, in living at an emotional distance from her husband and in transforming her valued but insular education into charitable activity, is surely asserting pride and—in Eliot's world—a pride of the most enlightened sort:

> All that ardour of her nature which could no longer spend itself in the woman's tenderness for father and husband, had transformed itself into an enthusiasm of sympathy with the general life. (ch. 44, 463)

In pursuing anonymous heroism, Romola has had excellent training, not only from Savonarola but, indirectly, from her father as well. Both father and daughter can be seen as spiritual exiles, devoted to a proud pledge of conduct within a resisting context— in Bardo's case, the scholarly world of Florence; in Romola's case, her own marriage. Like Lydgate, she wishes to take booklearning and, transcending a failing marriage, transform it into a discovery of how humanity at large can be helped and a discovery of what the "primal tissue" is—only in this case, for the heroine, it is the primal tissue of the community, the magnanimous bonds that hold human beings together.

It is important to point out that Romola, in her new role as the visible Madonna, forms a full daughterly attachment to Bernardo del Nero as well as Savonarola. She becomes ardently and ideally devoted to both; however, her very compelling humanness keeps her from seeing, as the reader does, that eventually a violent contradiction will arise. For the time being, a passionate commitment to one's "close relations" (ch. 56, 552)—which constitutes the fullest assertion of the Bardo legacy—urges her love of her godfather, just as it urges her through Florence, tending to the needy and the sick, who form, on their own, a second family, or second group of close relations. Romola never serves Savonarola in any truly political way, for that would be to bring her own prestige into the foreground. Florence only enlarges the possibilities for developing her sense of larger personal commitment. Thus, she must, in her groping, very human way, discover that when the laws of the city, even Savonarola's City of God, conflict with the higher laws, a choice must be made and one's "reverential memories" (ch. 59, 576) affirmed, since they were the source of the more communal virtues in the first place. She must ultimately side with Bernardo and, by extension, her father.

Two critics, Susan Greenstein, and, more recently, Susan Winnett, have pointed to Romola's role of anonymous heroism as a sign that she has lost her identity and freedom. Greenstein writes that "Romola, like Dorothea, achieves no more than an 'unhistoric lot'" (491), and Winnett concludes that "although her selfless, anonymous actions toward the befuddled, ailing old man [Baldasarre] and the charmingly vain and naive *contadina* are meant to demonstrate Romola's intention to subject her personal energies to the commmonweal, what these events show us is the extent to which Romola, as the novel's protagonist, is subject to the exemplary oedipal plot even when she thinks she is generating a plot of her own" (513). As in some other treatments of Eliot's heroines, the suggestion is that "unhistoricity" is a special condition or curse assigned to women alone, when, actually, in Eliot, it is the ultimate challenge to heroes and heroines alike. Some views of Romola miss this predominant fact because they unconsciously subscribe to a code of prestige that, ironically, Eliot criticizes as belonging to the old-style masculine ways of raising monuments to one's personal victories. Very interestingly, Winnett goes on to see part of Romola's plot as belonging to a legendary world, where Antigone, as her quote suggests, guides Oedipus to a world of myth, rather than the particularized one of Florence, and then asks the question, "Is there not something wrong with disappearing into the impersonality of legend in the course of the narrative of one's own life?" (514). But as we have seen in *Silas Marner,* disappearance and that transcendence of self that is anonymity are not the same thing. As Elizabeth Ermarth writes, "What comes gradually to Romola and Silas is a kind of resignation that is the opposite of losing the self. By acknowledging the difference between themselves and others, by accepting the gaps between their desires and their abilities, they both validate their individual experience and locate it in relation to others" (100).

At the start of her second, or Christian, phase, Romola is outfitted with some of these assumptions—namely that no grandeur can exist for her in the historical context she lives in—"she had been brought up in learned seclusion from the interests of actual life, and been accustomed to think of heroic deeds and great principles as something antithetic to the vulgar present" (ch. 27, 311)—a quote that is reminiscent of the speculative Mrs. Farthingale of *Scenes of Clerical Life* and the bookworm readers who are exhorted in the pages of *Adam Bede* and *The Mill on the Floss.* The character of Romola comprises a new direction for Eliot, however; for we are allowed, for the first time, to identify with a romantic attitude toward the past and then grow into an appreciation of the immediate life of the text as the heroine herself becomes both anonymously heroic and committed to the life around her. Such a strategy is essential to this historical novel, where the danger of excessive remoteness and glamor is omnipresent. She is Eliot's first reader-hero who is on stage for the full time. We are to Romola as Romola is to the past legendary world of Florence. She will herself become legendary, but only after she has given up the quest for some attendant prestige.

The special veneration that Romola grows toward is clearly illustrated in the later episodes with her godfather. In many ways, he is Bardo taken to the political arena, and because of this he best mirrors the new psychic dimension she has acquired. When at last she becomes disillusioned with the government of Savonarola, she is brought, in choral fashion, to recollect all of Bernardo's virtues, at the point when he is most reviled:

> Her mind rushed back with a new attraction towards the strong world sense, the dignified prudence, the untheoretic virtues of her godfather, who was to be treated as a sort of Agag because he held that a more restricted form of government was better than the Great Council, and

because he would not pretend to forget old ties to the banished family. . . . Her affection and respect were clinging with new tenacity to
her godfather, and with him to those memories of her father which
were in the same opposition to the division of men into sheep and goats
by the easy mark of some political or religious symbol. (ch. 52, 527)

Romola has learned much from both men—integrity, reverence
for the past, and, finally, a lesson in the ways of worldly prestige.
In addition, the "Pleading" chapter brings into strong juxtaposition what we have seen at every major climax of her previous
novels, the vision of the Letter and the vision of the Spirit: Adam
and Irwine on the eve of Hetty's trial, Tom and Maggie in the Red
Deeps, Cass and Silas after the disclosure of Eppie's parentage,
and now Savonarola and Romola on the eve of another hanging.[3]
It is, of course, the ancient conflict of Creon and Antigone, but in
her fiction, Eliot is much surer about who is right than she is in
her famous essay. When Romola proves unable to move Savonarola to clemency and Bernardo is thus forced to mount the scaffold,
Cennini foresees how the execution will raise "the old Bardo blood"
in Romola, and rise it does, bringing her to a strong awareness of
her heritage: "Romola was feeling the full force of that sympathy
with the individual lot that is continually opposing itself to the
formulae by which actions and parties are judged" (ch. 60, 583).

If the individual lot cannot be sympathized with, then all communal demands become meaningless. This insight Savonarola has
lost just at the moment it has become abundantly and bitterly
clear to Romola. Ironically, however, it occurs to her when she is
no longer acting and feeling as an isolated individual but as the
visible Madonna, who transcends purely personal interests. In the
final seconds, she "rescues" Bernardo's memory through her assurance that he has become a part of her "sacramental obligation"
and that she herself will become a living memorial.

> She seized the fettered hands that were hung down again, and
> kissed them as if they had been sacred things.
> "My poor Romola," said Bernardo, in a low voice, "I have only to die
> but thou hast to live—and I shall not be there to help thee."
> "Yes," said Romola, hurriedly, "you will help me—always—because
> I shall remember you." (ch. 60, 584)

In Eliot, remembrance becomes the distinction between identity
and oblivion—not through prestige or glory, but through the individual's ability to make another a part of his or her own household
gods. To put it a different way, Romola recognizes Bernardo on

the road to Emmaus, seconds before his death, and afterwards her heart burns for him. Because of this bond, the passage echoes Lydgate's crucial statement to Dorothea: "Yet you have made a great difference in my courage by believing in me" (ch. 76, 825).

The third stage of Romola's education consists of a refining and enlarging of her capacity to remember. Severed, now, from all Florentine ties, she is ready to "drift away" to a place where her beneficence can become even more secularized and is ready, once she returns, to meet again the character who appears in the final lines of the epilogue and has formed, all along, a second moral center, Piero di Cosimo. At just those moments when Romola starts reaching beyond the Christian confines of Savonarola's government, Eliot begins reminding the reader that as an artist, Piero has also been a preserver of household gods.[4]

In light of the complicated message that Eliot wanted to develop in the epilogue, her choice of the historical Piero seems particularly apt, and one must look at him before coming to a full understanding of Romola's resting point at the end of the novel. First of all, he was and is virtually an unknown, residing in an obscurity which, typically in the Eliot cosmos, heightens our sense of his commitment to his craft rather than lessens it. If she had chosen someone truly famous, the reader would tend to take his visionary qualities in his or her stride. After all, what is the heroism of putting paint to canvas when one is a Raphael? The point is, of course, that the action of acknowledged genius would be too far removed from our own world, which is filled with self-doubt and all its opportunities for faith. This same idea will later shed light on the reader's relation to Herr Klesmer.

In addition, Piero's paintings, when divided according to their mythological versus Christian subject matter, form, at least initially, a rather violent conflict, and there is a particularly narrative quality to his work that is missing from that of some of his contemporaries—one which Eliot may have identified with.[5] It is quite possible, also, that his *Story of Silenus* paintings suggested the characters of Ariadne and Bacchus[6] or that his *Teseo e Arianna, Bacco e Arianna* (at that time erroneously credited to him) inspired in Eliot the kind of moral and originally mythological contrast so characteristic of her.[7] In the early parts of the novel, Tito plays Bacchus to Romola's Ariadne, but in his perfidy, he is much more like Theseus. More important, the obscurity of Piero's fame and the sketchiness of Vasari's account of him gave Eliot a freedom which would have been lost in the recreation of a Botticelli. She could make his artistic vision more a reformulation of her own. In this sense, she is very much like Piero of the novel (or better, he is like her), who, when assigned Tito's project based on Ovid, protests when the amount of information offered becomes too binding.

In being part of a larger context, Piero must be brought into the epilogue as a living being, because he is the novel's consistently best example of the broad humanity, freed from conventional religion, which is embodied in the narrator herself. His attitude toward Tito is at one with hers, and his perceiving Sinon in his modern-day face constitutes the hybrid of immediate observation and classical acumen that Eliot strove to convey in her own work. More specifically, his sketch of Tito serves as an interruptive, moral commentary on the outward revel the groom-to-be wishes to create, and "the painted record" becomes at one with Eliot's own puncturing sentences, once the Bacchic beauty has been conceded. As Tito himself says, "That is a subject after your own heart, Messer Piero—a revel interrupted by a ghost" (ch. 18, 247). It is a subject very much after Eliot's heart, and once one considers how many interrupted revels exist in *Romola,* the very structure of the novel seems to grow out of Piero's vision. His Masque of Time, which disrupts "The Day of the Betrothal" chapter and closes book 1, is the pictographic analogue to the narrator's own positioning of characters through time and space in order to bring about a reckoning with death and the self. Both Piero and the narrator are stage managers who usher in a dramatic Nemesis.

Piero's omniscience is further underscored by his enlightened use of classical history and literature, not only for their bright, decorative value but also, as has been suggested earlier, for their stunning and sometimes stark relevance to the present. What Eliot does as narrator in her rather shrill discussion of Aeschylus's *Eumenides* (ch. 11, 168–69), she does better through the character of her very active artist, who catalyzes the fear of Nemesis within the audience of the novel's dramatis personae. Like Mr. Cleves of "Amos Barton," Mr. Irwine of *Adam Bede,* and Mrs. Garth of *Middlemarch,* and totally unlike Bardo or Casaubon, Piero is able to read, immediately, the classical lesson beneath the minutiae of the present, and he, like Mr. Cleves, Mr. Irwine, and Mrs. Garth, is one of those rare creations in fiction who arrives morally ready-made but is, at the same time, altogether convincing. A number of recent critics have pointed out that the novel dramatizes the dual crisis—both of the Renaissance and Victorian times—which demanded that people be both liberated from the past and yet find a way of rejuvenating it. In writing of Robert

Browning's opening remarks to *The Ring and the Book*, for example, David Carroll elucidates this central concern as "signficantly, an action which avoids either the embalming of a dead past or creating something out of nothing: the former would be idolatrous, the latter sacrilegious" (*George Eliot and the Conflict of Interpretations*, 167–68). Piero di Cosimo best fulfills this mission and serves as a model for the heroine. It is no surprise, then, that his opinions of others are those of the author, although he is given a vehemence and tactlessness all his own.

For Romola, he is the best means of preserving the past that has become sacred to her, both when it is alive in her imagination and when it has become eclipsed by her commitment to Savonarolan charity. In book 2, no longer bound as her father's handmaiden, she yet seeks his portrait "as Oedipus," drawing on Piero's original vision in book 1 of the two of them as the mythic father and daughter at Colonus. The important suggestion is that Romola's perception is now approaching Piero's; she sees into people, into their strengths and faults, and forms, in her mind, a balanced and universal image. Alive, Bardo was only to serve as a model for the Theban king, a Florentine in ancient Greek costume; dead, and therefore perceived at a distance, he becomes Oedipus, with his hubris, blindness, and yet his power and love as well. Combining all of these elements, the portrait is the perfect visual corollary to Eliot's own portrait of words in "The Blind Scholar and His Daughter" and also to the tracing out of the shadowy archetypes of the father-daughter, Oedipus-Antigone groupings in the previous novels. In so doing, the portrait becomes anonymous in our eyes; we have not Romola and Bardo but Daughter and Father.

Once completed, Piero's painting crops up at certain strategic points throughout the remainder of the novel, as a special narrative signpost and as a particular means of keeping the male archetype alive in her. As Barbara Hardy writes, "In *Romola* the objects which precipitate crisis or turn action also tend toward conspicuous symbolism" (*Particularities*, 154). In chapter 31, the painting serves as an important catalyst to Romola's and Bernardo's discussion and recollection of Bardo's disappointed quest, and as a means of initiating a more lifelike image in the minds of both. Later, after Romola has fought with Tito over the library and has disengaged herself from him for the first time, she is shown to start up "as if some sudden freedom had come, and going to her father's chair where his picture was propped, [fall] on her knees before it and burst into sobs" (ch. 32, 359). When preparing to leave Tito, Romola places the portrait, along with the one of her mother, into a trunk that is to be sent to Bernardo for safe keeping, as a part of a trust of "sacred memory" (ch. 35, 390)—a direct connection with her uncle's soon-to-be-bound hands, which will be called "sacred things." Finally, the portrait is referred to by Lillo in the epilogue when he is brought to ask some of the novel's major questions.

Romola's relationship to the image of her father, as preserved by Piero, is a changing and dramatic one. The image is classical and thus reminiscent of the books they studied together. When, in book 3, Romola slips into the contradiction of supporting the Pyramid of Vanities while yet remaining her father's daughter, Piero, quite appropriately, is the one to appear and point it out:

> And I should like to know what the excellent Messer Bardo would have said to the burning of the divine poets of these Frati, who are no better an imitation of men than if they were onions with the bulbs uppermost. Look at the Petrarca sticking up beside a rouge-pot. Do the idiots pretend that the heavenly Laura was a painted harridan? And Boccaccio, now: do you mean to say, Madonna Romola . . . you have never read the stories of the immortal Messer Giovanni? (ch. 49, 501)

This is her father's arresting voice, and Romola is forced to admit that she has read Boccaccio's stories and that "there are some things in them I do not ever want to forget." We know from the early chapters that Boccaccio was sacred to her father, and although she thinks herself able to dismiss the writer for now, his work will be one of the first things she will think of, once her disillusionment with Savonarola is sealed (ch. 61, 588). We also know that Boccaccio was central to Eliot's own reading and that he was part of the list she made while researching the backgrounds of *Romola*. For the historical Piero, Boccaccio's *Genealogy of the Gods* constituted the central source for several of his mythological paintings,[8] and it is possible that Eliot speculated over this book's being his source, had he ever really taken up Oedipus and Antigone at Colonus as a subject. Whatever her specific historical knowledge, Eliot makes it clear that Bardo's library cannot be denied or burned any more than the true spirit and sympathy of Savonarola's life and work—once the egotism, the rigidity, has been removed.

The other writer who is defended, Petrarch, provides a bridge to the novel's epilogue, and here, in the last pages, he is saved from the flames of Christian fanaticism. In the epilogue we are also back with Bardo again, who, in chapter 5, quoted in visionary fashion the Petrarchan defense of reading: "Books delight our inmost selves, they speak to us, advise us, and are united to us by a kind of living and clear friendship" (ch. 5. 97, n.). Romola, in teaching Lillo Petrarch's *Rime,* is preserving the best of her father's legacy, as enriched by what she learned in the Christian phase of her life. Very tellingly, the *canzone* that Lillo is reading from speaks to a young man who may be the new hope for a restored Rome, a restored Italy. Perhaps Lillo will rise to that promise, through his godmother's careful assemblage of the best elements of the human psyche. This concept of Romola, uniter of disparate elements in the soul, is most appropriate for these final pages, for indeed here she is presented as an artist, a portrait maker belonging to the school of Naturalist Idealism[9], like Piero and Eliot. Alison Booth, in writing of this final stance in her "The Silence of Great Men: Statuesque Femininity and the Ending of *Romola,*" provides this summation:

> In her quest she has slain no dragon, founded no empire or monastic order, written no epic, but she has overseen the downfall of false patriarchs, sustained Eliot's humane ideals through a dark period, founded a kind of Protestant sisterhood in miniature, and inspired a novel. (128)

And we would have to add to this overview the fact that the final Romola has become a central portrait painter of words and a key to the way the artist can be an anonymous hero.

There are three portraits that she paints for Lillo, those of Bardo, Savonarola, and Tito, forming a triptych of her own, which recalls not so much Piero's Bacchic tabernacle as his Sketch of the Three Masks. The Stoic, the Magdalen, and the Satyr symbolize, as W. J. Sullivan has pointed out (*Victorian Newsletter,* 9), the lives of these three men, respectively; and the child in the sketch "whose cherub features rose above them with something of the supernal promise in the gaze which painters had by that time learned to give to the Divine Infant" (ch. 3, 79) represents not only the younger Romola, who has learned from each early in her life, but also, I would add, Lillo, on the eve of his being presented with their histories, as narrated by his godmother. Of Bardo, her final evaluation is, "[he] had the greatness that belongs to integrity; he chose poverty and obscurity rather than falsehood" (674–75)— which anticipates the finale of *Middlemarch,* in which the whole egoistic problem of prestige is supplanted by the anonymous legacy of goodness bequeathed by dead souls, whether originally known or not. In this way, Romola returns to her vision of her father as Promethean,[10] a portrait that is itself very Piero-like, in acknowledging the *agon,* the pride, and the heroism of the subject. It is no accident that when discussing Bardo, Lillo mentions the old portrait of him, since it is meant, once again, to stir veneration without distortion, criticism without hostility.

The same may be said of the second part of the triptych, Savonarola, who "had the greatness which belongs to a life spent in struggling against powerful wrong" (675), and therefore who represents that active spirit so fatally missing from the Bardo library. W. J. Sullivan, when he says that Romola's final state becomes that of the stoic or that of Bernardo or Piero himself, does not take into account the Frate's role as a household god (*Victorian Newsletter,* 13). Restored again, in memory, to the sphere of private life, his previous concern for the growing sympathy of men and women becomes a luminous and vital example; it is retrieved. That his private self is rarely evoked in the novel constitutes a major artistic problem,[11] but in regard to the book's developing themes, it is entirely consistent that Romola keep his day sacred, that his physical and psychic portraits be brought in, just as were Bardo's.

Tito, the last man presented in Romola's triptych, is restored to his morally neutral nature at the story's opening. The fact that then he was no perfidious Bacchus but simply an *exemplum* of raw potential is emphasized. That he became like many of Eliot's chivalric discards—Arthur Donnithorne, Stephen Guest, and Harold Transome to come, men who possess an exaggerated sense of their own gallantry—is also stressed. But the parts of him that may be preserved, his charm and magnetism, are also included in the portrait, even though he is no household god.

Petrarch's "gentle spirit" promises, then, to be a composite of the qualities that the novel has idealized and that Romola has come to teach by her own words and actions. Although there is some alluring debate as to whether Romola at last retreats herself into a static domesticity (Booth, *Famous,* 126), Jennifer Uglow best sums up the extraordinary freedom of Romola's final condition:

> In *Romola* . . . she [Eliot] takes the maternal mission away from the docile wife and mother of the evangelical family, away from the "specialised" morally superior but intellectually inferior womanhood idealised by Comte, and hands it over instead to the single, sensually aware but childless woman, an educated Madonna who, having learned from

experience, has freed herself from the domination of men and is prepared henceforth to think for herself. (174)

It is no accident that this sublime state, throughout the works of Eliot, usually occurs in her artists or those with an artistic soul. Bonnie Zimmerman has written of *Daniel Deronda* as a novel "where the androgynous hero becomes a vehicle for situating female values in a male-defined universe of Signification" (Booth, *Famous*, 160). Certainly the same may be said of Romola and her questing imagination. For the heroine to draw, in the epilogue, such accurate and balanced portraits shows how far she has come—both as a "man" and as a woman. The epilogue is itself a shrine, and a totally private one at that, which carries forward the Bardo legacy of scholarship and familial devotion and the Savonarolan tradition of service to the world at large. Piero must arrive with flowers even for the dead ascetic he dislikes, since his example and the gifts he bears serve as a second balance to the all-too-unworldly Frate, who wanted "to burn colour out of life" (ch. 49, 500). Together, Piero and Romola form the best synthesis of the pagan and Christian elements which have been warring since the novel's proem, and together they serve as the best corollary to Eliot the psychologist and artist. Just as Eliot had to pick among the various qualities of Vasari's Piero in order to construct her indirectly idealized painter, so her resultant creation, as a painter, must discriminate among the qualities of those around him in order to fashion characters of mythological resonance. It is no accident, either, as we have seen, that she chose an almost unknown Italian artist, when she had so many other famous ones to choose from, not only because she could then play on history more easily but also because she could carry her point concerning anonymous heroism with greater emphasis.

Like her creator and like Piero, Romola, in reaching the novel's conclusion, must also artistically pick and choose among the qualities of Bardo, Savonarola, and Tito in order to form her triptych of the idealized human psyche, her greatest shrine to her household gods, since, in distinctly Piero-like manner, it uses the best of each without distortion, and, without seeking acclaim, in the end transcends them all.

6

Esther and Rufus Lyon: "A More Regenerating Tenderness" in *Felix Holt*

As becomes clear when we see Romola "reconstructing" the psyche in the form of the triptych of three men, or Silas reconstructing the psyche in the form of Eppie or Dolly's "Them," the balanced soul, for Eliot, achieves anonymity, in part, through an identification with the opposite sex. Her own literary persona, of course, embraces this pattern as well, and serves as the clearest example, perhaps, of how sympathetic participation in the worlds of both men and women can lead to that appreciation of the obscure that is anonymous heroism.

Both Eliot and Virginia Woolf[1] sought to make the anonymous visible and much of their extraordinary craftsmanship can be traced to this goal. In her essay on Madame de Sablé, Eliot writes:

> Let the whole field of reality be laid open to woman as well as to man, and then that which is peculiar in her mental modification, instead of being, as it is now, a source of discord and repulsion between the sexes, will be found to be a necessary complement to the truth and beauty of life. Then we shall have that marriage of minds which alone can blend all the hues of thought and feeling in one lovely rainbow of promise for the harvest of human happiness. (Pinney, 81)

As we have seen in *Silas Marner*, and we shall see in *Middlemarch*, such an androgynous rainbow represents not only a marriage of true minds but also that loss of ego which is the very source of healing. Similarly, Woolf's *A Room of One's Own* articulates the dynamic link between anonymity and gender balance:

> Some collaboration has to take place in the mind between the woman and the man before the act of creation can be accomplished. Some marriage of opposites has to be consummated. The whole of the mind must lie wide open if we are to get the sense that the writer is commu-

nicating his experience with perfect fullness. There must be freedom and there must be peace.

We might say, then, that what is true for the artists Woolf and Eliot is also true for Eliot's—and Woolf's—principal characters. Paradoxically, "fullness" is only possible through a loss; in becoming the other sex, we are no longer psychologically provincial. Such a connection is very much alive when Woolf celebrates Austen side by side with Shakespeare:

> Here was a woman about the year 1800 writing without hate, without bitterness, without fear, without protest, without preaching. That was how Shakespeare wrote, I thought, looking at *Antony and Cleopatra;* and when people compare Shakespeare and Jane Austen, they may mean that the minds of both had consumed all impediments; and for that reason we do not know Jane Austen and we do not know Shakespeare, and for that reason Jane Austen pervades every word that she wrote, and so does Shakespeare. (71)

For both authors, this state of highly passionate and creative "non-presence" conjoins artistic goals with one's goals as a moral being in the workaday world: to know so many points of view that one is neither male nor female but both; to be so complete that one is passionately attached to a community of selves.

Such a concept of androgyny has received much criticism in recent years, partly because the term, along with "selflessness," has become associated with the male concept of objectivity and with male illusions of disinterestedness in the writing of history. Elaine Showalter writes:

> The androgynous mind is, finally, a utopian projection of the ideal artist: calm, stable, unimpeded by consciousness of sex. Woolf meant it to be a luminous and fulfilling idea; but, like other utopian projections, her vision is inhuman. Whatever else one may say of androgyny, it represents an escape from the confrontation with femaleness or maleness. Her ideal artist mystically transcends sex, or has none. One could imagine another approach to androgyny, however, through total immersion in the individual experience, with all its restrictions of sex and anger and fear and chaos. A thorough understanding of what it means, in every respect, to be a woman, could lead the artist to an understanding of what it means to be a man. This revelation would not be realized in any mystical way; it would result from daring to face and express what is unique, even if unpleasant, or taboo, or destructive, in one's own experience, and thus it would speak to the secret heart in all people. (289)

Showalter's argument is a compelling one and must be answered in a variety of ways if the experience of androgyny in Eliot is to be made clear. First, I do not believe Woolf is talking about an ideal author's autobiographical experience while composing a work; she is speaking of the esthetic impression developed by the text itself, once the ideally "androgynous" work has been written. "Mind" here then is the mind that is implied by the words and the chapters. Woolf does not insist that Austen, the woman, was free of hatred, bitterness, or fear; she only insists that these emotions, if present, did not shrink her novels into "protest." The point is exactly true for Eliot when she speaks of the ideal esthetic experience as "the extension of our sympathies" and the ideal esthetic impression as "a picture of human life such as a great artist can give" (Pinney, 270). Both Eliot and Woolf sought an artistic diversity in their fiction that would provide a sense of vividness and completeness for the reader. To write only of women's issues—or only of men's, for that matter—would be fatal not because some fearsome activistic implications might result, but because any form of single-mindedness within the text might lead to a "diagram" that, with a restricted dramatis personae, would be ultimately incomplete and tedious. The rainbow would shrink to monochrome. Thus, in the terms that Eliot's "Notes on Form in Art" define, the work would not be "high" but "low" since it would be less complex.

Both *A Room of One's Own* and Eliot's essays suggest a fear of lack of particularity and vividness such as a one-gendered mission might create—the sort of fear Eliot mentioned when she wrote to Harrison of her concern that esthetic teaching ceases to be esthetic "if it lapses anywhere from the picture to the diagram" (*Letters: 4,* 300) or when she insisted to Mrs. Peter Taylor, who had requested that she speak on "certain public topics," that she saw her role as "that of the *aesthetic,* not the doctrinal teacher" (7: 44, emphasis hers). Thus, in Eliot's and Woolf's fiction, Mrs. Dalloway is balanced by a Septimus; a Mr. Ramsay by a Mrs. Ramsay; a Lydgate by a Dorothea; a Gwendolen by a Daniel—the counterpoint existing for esthetic rather than moral reasons. Thus also, Mrs. Dalloway knows jealousy, "Othello's feeling ... as strongly as Shakespeare meant Othello to feel it" (51) and Tom Tulliver "had never been in his life so much like a girl before." Interest depends on turns in the plot which suggest gender variation, or in complex turns of the psyche themselves, suggesting the changing facets of the diamond, to which Clarissa Dalloway's essence is compared, and to which Gwendolen Harleth's "iridescence" certainly could be.

Androgyny, understood in this strictly esthetical sense, does not legislate indifference; it merely says that "great literature" creates a highly visualized impression of inclusiveness and complexity, no matter what the artist's psychological state when he or she sat down to compose. Thus anger, bitterness, and fear are not bad; they merely stand the danger of boring the reader, *if* they get translated into the picture as preaching, protest, or—to use Eliot's word—appeals. Counter to Showalter's critique, the ideal of androgyny in the two women authors comes not necessarily from a fear of passion in the authors themselves but a concern that a single-minded bias might drain the life and variety out of the human picture in their works and thus indeed block passion in the audience.

A further reply to Showalter's critique also serves as a way of illuminating the way androgyny and anonymity coexist in Eliot's characters in particular. Anonymity is not indifference anymore than androgyny is. For example, Dorothea Brooke, at the end of *Middlemarch*, has reached a state of heroism, because she has broadened her identification with a vast portion of the novel's cast of characters, many of whom have been men. Her state of being at the end of *Middlemarch* is very much like that of Shakespeare—as described, in ghostly form, by Woolf when she visited his gravesite:

> I cannot without more labour than my roadrunning mind can compass describe the queer impression of sunny impersonality. Yes, everything seemed to say, this was Shakespeare's, had he sat and walked; but you won't find me, not exactly in the flesh. He is serenely absent—present; both at once; radiating round one; yes; in the flowers, in the old hall, in the garden; but never to be pinned down. And we went to the church and there was the florid foolish bust, but what I had not reckoned for was the worn simple slab, turned the wrong way, Kind Friend for Jesus'sake forebear—again he seemed to be all air and sun smiling serenely; and yet down there one foot from me lay the little bones that had spread over the world this vast illumination. (*Writer's Diary*, 209)

"This vast illumination" could scarcely be defined as the lack of feeling; rather it could be seen as closely connected to Dorothea Brooke's passionate sympathy throughout the novel. What is the difference, one wonders, between the spirit of the world's most immortalized writer and Dorothea's "finely touched spirit," even though her tomb is unvisited and his draws millions? The effects of their beings are "incalculably diffusive," because, through the conjoining of the man and woman within their psyches and thus within the psyche of the reader, the spirit of anonymity, as conveyed by Woolf and Eliot, "brings to birth in us also the creative impulse" (E. M. Forster, "Anonymity: An Enquiry," 100). Perhaps "Judith Shakespeare" is Dorothea, had she lived into the nineteenth century, and perhaps the same woman is Woolf, had she lived into the twentieth.

One might also add that such anonymity is not the same as female resignation or sacrifice. In her recent study *Greatness Engendered: George Eliot and Virginia Woolf,* Alison Booth also links Dorothea with Judith Shakespeare but writes that "Eliot and Woolf evoked the rare 'types' of female self-sacrifice whom they considered at the same time 'common' or representative; their fictional histories mitigate the harsh fate of those sacrificed by showing the resulting incremental progress" (94). The elegaic natures of both the conclusion of *A Room of One's Own* and of *Middlemarch* certainly might cause one to think of female sacrifice, but the "growing good of the world" in Woolf and Eliot is not spelled out in loss but in gains—gains that are definitely not gender specific. Lydgate, Adam, Farebrother, Irwine, Daniel, Mordecai all participate in the same process of unsung appreciation—obtainable through the extension of their sympathies—that the heroines do. Anonymity is not limited to man or woman, just as it is not limited to station or level of education. The case in point of *Silas Marner* makes this clear, in the form of Eppie as well as Silas. Thus I do agree with Booth when she says "feminine examples of the common life are honored," but greatly disagree when she adds that they "never overcome their subordination" (129). They overcome their subordination not through social power but via the recognitions associated with anonymity, and this fact is as true of Woolf's Mrs. McNabb as it is true of Eliot's Eppie. Indeed anyone, male or female, in their novels may "rise" to obscurity and, to borrow a gesture from Mrs. McNabb, turn to "tearing the veil of [its] silence" (*To the Lighthouse,* 196).

In *Felix Holt,* our next novel to consider, we see the extension of the intimate connection between anonymity and psychological androgyny—between, that is, Eliot's special brands of heroism and psychic balance. This balance is evident first in the Lyon family, and, much later, in the Esther-Felix relationship. The blocks to appreciating this clarification of theme in Eliot perhaps come from the title hero himself, who, as Booth would see him, "represents one more unconvincing attempt . . . to portray a handsome, muscular hero of the Adam Bede sort" (*Greatness,* 142). Henry James has also written that "Felix Holt, in the work which bears his name, is little more than an occasional apparition, and indeed the novel has no hero, but only a heroine" (James, "Novels," 485), and in another article, he adds, "As a novel with a hero there is no doubt that it *is* a failure. Felix is a fragment" (James, *Felix,* 274–75).

Once the incompleteness and singlemindedness of his character are affirmed, many can then arrive at the conclusions very pointedly advanced by Bonnie Zimmerman, that Esther's psychic conversion is only a question of "Felix's mesmerizing influence" (445), that it is, simply, only another "disappointing conversion into the 'Angel in the House'" (448), who goes hand-in-hand with the muscular and stiff Felix Holt.

But one must not look for wholeness of character in Felix on his own but in the novel's central family, the Lyons, who provide his one-room schoolhouse, as it were. In *Felix Holt,* we have not a predominating theme of female subjugation but a dramatization of Eliot's belief that "there is a basis for a sublimer recognition in women and more regenerating tenderness in man" (*Letters* 4: 364). Eliot does not so much celebrate subordination in women through domesticity as she insists, once again, that true moral leadership, whether from men or women, rises out of a capacity for nurturing. Matters begin to clear infinitely the moment we focus on Esther and Rufus Lyon as the primary moral interests of the novel, rather than Felix Holt or even Mrs. Transome. Between and within the father and daughter, there is a balance of male and female, since by the end of the story, both characters share in their narrator's freedom to cross gender lines and assert their power first in the private and later the public arenas. In this way, Esther shares much with Romola in that she grows stronger out of her father's legacy, and her story also outweighs the imbalances which the other characters embody.

One notes, for example, that Felix and Mrs. Transome are, in fact, on stage relatively little of the time, and when they are, they are clearly separated players in two widely diverging plots, one epic and one tragic—both of which must be conjoined, ultimately, by narrative contortions, which, for all their pleasing surprise, speak more about story than they do about character.[2] Both Felix and Mrs. Transome exist in dramatic isolation from Treby Magna as well as from each other, and thus, in a novel that frequently legislates against isolation, it is not surprising that the narrator continually turns a wider view toward the symbiosis between Esther and her father.

We know for a fact that while writing her novels beginning with *The Mill on the Floss* and ending with *Felix Holt*, Eliot was profoundly focused on Greek tragedy. It is interesting that in this same period she began dramatizing her intense gender struggles and then began offering first subtle and then extended resolutions to them. The Oedipus-Antigone emblem, then, serves, ironically, as a blueprint for what is presently the author's most timely topic. This intense interest is indeed continuous throughout Eliot's career, since the Theban king and princess suggest the balance between male and female which the author's pseudonym also suggests. The introduction to this study has indicated that in the Colonus play, as in the author's own private and literary life, there is a power exchange, whereby the female soul acquires strength through the adoption of an initially masculine anonymity. We saw how this psychic process occurs in *Romola,* but here we have the dramatic advantage of seeing it while the father is still alive and changing. Over *Silas Marner,* we can say that *Felix Holt* not only provides a greater breadth of treatment but that it provides a non-idyllic world, initially hostile to male and female balance,[3] which demands that the stages of transformation be developed rather than magically charmed. In addition, we are allowed to witness the psychic metamorphosis within the daughter as well as the father. Over *The Mill on the Floss,* we can say that the novel sees changes in a nonidyllic world as developments rather than cataclysmic upheavals. To put it more simply, *Felix Holt* has all the realism of *The Mill on the Floss* and all the resolution of *Silas Marner,* and, as the Introduction to this book has suggested, the novel provides the first full articulation of the author's most prominent subject.

The articulation comes in the form of Rufus Lyon. As early as chapter 4 in the novel, one has the feeling that the Eliot canon is at last fully staging what it means by anonymous heroism. Up to this point, rarely has a character been so decidedly an expression of her admiration and yet presented with such close sympathetic scrutiny and wry humor. Like many of her moral centers, he comes to the book already spiritually advanced, and yet through the aid of flashback and a very active role in the plot, he is presented before us in all his "ire and and his egoism" (132), his foibles and his eccentricities and—in this case, his circumlocutions. After Mr. Irwine, he is the first fully developed character

we see in Eliot to attain anonymous heroism and then pass it on
to someone whose inner dynamic is also open to us.

A few critics[4] have taken an interest in Mr. Lyon, but none has
tried, directly, to explain why he is the first character in Eliot's
fiction to have both the words *heroic* and *heroism* directly applied
to him. Continually, Eliot's narrator is reminding us how small of
stature he is and yet how great of heart. The comments finally
culminate in the credolike statement quoted in the Introduction
to this study. The dismantling of the "cynical sprite"'s perspective
almost foreshadows the end of *Middlemarch,* whereby the apparently forgotten Dorothea is resurrected out of the ashes of her
obscure life. Like the townspeople of Middlemarch and Treby
Magna, we might pass over the efficacy of such characters as
Dorothea and Rufus because they still assume Eliot's world is run
by politics, rather than by faith. In his article *"Felix Holt:* Language, the Bible, and the Problematic of Meaning," Robin Sheets,
for example, speaks not only of Mr. Lyon but also of Felix and
Esther as being "eventually undermined: either their rhetoric is
flawed or their speeches have little impact" (149). But we must
ask the same question here as we do when Dorothea's life is assessed and adjudged inefficacious, particularly from several skep-
tical perspectives—that is, what is "impact"? For Eliot, "impact"
frequently occurs when no impact can be noted at all. It arises
from faith in the unseen and is not necessarily registered by outward recognition. To quote one of Eliot's favorites, Milton: "Fame
is no plant that grows on mortal soil, / Nor in the glistering foil /
Set off to the world nor in broad rumour lies" ("Lycidas" 78–81).[5]
And it is Milton with whom Mr. Lyon is sympathetically compared,
for chapter 6 of the novel introduces the minister this way:

> Even at that time of comparative youth, his unworldliness and simplic-
> ity in small matters (for he was keenly awake to the larger affairs of
> this world) gave a certain oddity to his manners and appearance; and
> though his sensitive face had much beauty, his person altogether
> seemed so irrelevant to a fashionable view of things, that well-dressed
> ladies and gentlemen usually laughed at him, as they probably did at
> Mr. John Milton after the Restoration and ribbons had come in, and
> still more at that apostle, of weak bodily presence, who preached in
> the back streets of Ephesus and elsewhere, a new view of a new
> religion that hardly anybody believed in. (163)

Thus, the passage acknowledges Mr. Lyon on the road to Emmaus
by praising him and all those he represents. In using what I will
later call "the reaffirmed heroic voice," Eliot in showing him to

be, in many ways, at one with Milton. In keeping with this idea, Alison Booth writes, "*Utterly* unsung heroism is a contradiction in terms, just as greatness must be named in at least *one* narrative to be known as such. The favored compromise in realistic fiction is that the protagonist's public fortunes not be great, and that recognition come from readers more than from the community within the narrative" (*Greatness*, 139).

Just after those sentences in *Felix Holt* that raise "a monument to the faithful who were not famous" (ch. 16, 277) and create another vast road to Emmaus, Mr. Lyon is immediately contrasted with Harold Transome, who believes in exteriors. For Harold, along with his mother, lacks the faith necessary to brook disasters and attend to his responsibilities despite them. Rufus emerges as the male hero of the novel—although he is the least "chivalrous"—precisely because his faith enables him to transcend the "male" order and nurture his family. In contrast, the whole Transome circle—Harold, Mrs. Transome, and Jermyn—know very little of nurture and thus are swept into tragedy. As Eliot writes later and quite simply, "Yet the minister, as we have seen, found in his Christian faith a reason for clinging the more to one who had not a large party to back him. That little man's heart was heroic" (ch. 37, 466), in response to his willingness to stand beside another obscure man, Felix Holt. While the Transomes, on the other hand, confine themselves to those who possess grand names, Mr. Lyon is the mother who attends to the downtrodden and thus anticipates Daniel Deronda who, on an even more extended scale, becomes heroic by attending faithfully to an unnoticed political prophet.

Much confusion, then, is disspelled when we stop seeing Esther as Felix's adopted daughter but rather as Mr. Lyon's. Although Bonnie Zimmerman writes that "Esther's education/courtship, in accordance with the novel's main theme, is resolved in terms of mastery, conquest, revolt, and submission" (445), Esther's conversion does not occur because Felix took issue with her Byronic readings, but because she eventually becomes ready, through the catalyst of Felix's asides, to accept the nurturing legacy of her father. In this sense, just as her father is a first in Eliot's novels, so is she. She is the first to break through the paradigm initiated by Eliot's earliest fiction, which, as Barbara Hardy points out, predominates much of what was to follow (*Novels*, 81), the two hamadryads who spend their time gazing into a lake, one of them focused on her own reflection, the other on the reflections of clouds and sky. Up until this time, Eliot's heroines have been divided between the narcissist and the seer—or more particularly,

Hetty and Dinah. But now, because of her father's example, Esther will bridge the two worlds and become the narcissist-turned-seer and thereby clear the way for the even larger-scale transformations of Dorothea Brooke and Gwendolen Harleth.

The chapter that prepares for this change is chapter 6, which could just as well be titled "Mr. Lyon's Love Story." Like Mr. Gilfil, Mr. Lyon is an unlikely candidate for such a tale, and the bracketed tale is an attempt to change our suppositions about romance and the nondescript men and women who pass us in the street. With apparent irony, the epigraph compares him to Tamburlaine the Great, but through the double force characteristic of Eliot's preference of present heroes over past ones, Rufus is given ironic and moral precedence over the ruthless and egoistic emperor. The chapter is also an attempt to present the novel's first case of mutuality between men and women. Initially, when Annette and her baby appear on the sidebank, Rufus is in the rescuer and nurturer role. Like Silas, who "instantly offers hushing tenderness," Rufus instinctively "took the baby in his arms" (164), even when nothing in his past has prepared him for this gesture. Later, however, when Annette is nurtured back to health and he becomes seriously ill, a power shift occurs and she becomes the one to nurse him and eventually hasten their marriage: "[he] was struck with a new expression in her face, quite distinct from the merely passive sweetness which usually characterised it. . . . Mr. Lyon trembled. This illness—something else, perhaps—made a great change in Annette" (172–73). Like Silas, Rufus has had the experience of depending upon a woman to revitalize him, but unlike Silas, he has had the benefit of witnessing a transformation as well, which occasions and parallels a change of psychic politics within himself. A promising ministry is exchanged for love, and "the only satisfaction he had was the satisfaction of his tenderness—which meant untiring work, untiring patience, untiring wakefulness" (174). Perhaps this quote serves as the best possible definition of what in Eliot anonymous heroism is, for "Mr. Lyon will perhaps seem a very simple personage, with pitiably narrow theories; but none of our theories are quite large enough for all the disclosures of time, and to the end of men's struggles a penalty will remain for those who sink from the ranks of the heroes into the crowd for whom the heroes fight and die" (171–72). Mr. Lyon does not have to pay that penalty. Ironically, he is in the front ranks.

The first translation of Mr. Lyon's powers into Esther's life occurs with the subtlety characteristic of Eliot, after the momentous visit from Mr. Christian. One is initially struck, first off, not only with Mr. Lyon's highly sensitized response to the situation but with his complete lack of vindictiveness. After all, if he believed Mr. Christian to be Esther's father, would he have not felt some of Silas's anger over having been a stand-in for so many years? The emotion, however, never touches him, and, in being conspicuous by its absence, serves to intensify the later contrast between the Lyons and the vengeance-driven Transomes. There is a contrast, also, with the angry Oedipus of Colonus, although the emblematic tableau at the close of chapter 13 (of mutual support and succor) is parallel to the one of Antigone serving as a prop for Oedipus and ushers in its sister allusion—King Lear and Cordelia at the end of act 4:

> The tears came and relieved him, while Esther, who had stooped to lift the porridge from the fender, paused on one knee and looked up at him.
> "She was very good to you?" asked Esther, softly.
> "Yes, dear. She did not reject my affection. She thought not scorn of my love. She would have forgiven me, if I had erred against her, from very tenderness. Could you forgive me, child?"
> "Father, I have not been good to you; but I will be, I will be," said Esther, laying her head on his knee.
> He kissed her head. "Go to bed, my dear; I would be alone."
> When Esther was lying down that night, she felt as if the little incidents between herself and her father on this Sunday had made it an epoch. Very slight words and deeds may have a sacramental efficacy, if we can cast our self-love behind us, in order to say or do them. And it has been well believed through many ages that the beginning of compunction is the beginning of a new life. (246)

In recognizing her father on the road to Emmaus, Esther is essentially repeating Cordelia's "No cause! No cause!"—which, as Marianne Novy points out in *Love's Argument: Gender Relations in Shakespeare,* is a sign of the newly emerging mutuality between daughter and father (159); one seeks forgiveness, the other benediction.

One must also remember that no further back than the beginning of chapter 6, Esther was presented as sharing Romola's initial malaise of seeming "to herself to be surrounded with ignoble, uninteresting conditions, from which there was no issue" (159). Thus her change in the "revelation book" of chapter 36—just a little past the exact center of the novel—is all the more remarkable, even while it remains altogether convincing. As in all of

Eliot's fiction, recovery from ennui begins with the concession that a person's immediate context might be heroic, if only he or she would look hard enough and muster the imaginative and prophetic energy to create a transforming vision. In Esther's case—as is true in Eppie's and Romola's—the transference of power is distinctly nonpatriarchal because the father's example, far from carrying certain sexist restrictions, actually encourages the heroine to discover her own potential. This change involves some chastening, but contrary to what some critics observe, "light-footed, sweet-voiced Queen Esther" does not so much lose her tiara and gain household domestic wings as lose her tiara and gain a crown.

Quite interestingly, Eliot's book or chapter of revelation begins with a deliberate misquotation from *King Henry the Fifth*,[6] giving it a startling sex change:

> Consideration like an angel came
> And whipped the offending Adam out of her;
> Leaving her body as a paradise
> To envelop and contain celestial spirits.
>
> (1, i, 29–32)

The alteration of *him* and *his* to *her*, as well as the comparison between Esther and Prince Hal, is both ironic and sympathetic. Esther's regalness has arisen largely from her self-absorbed presence; however, as we shall see in *Daniel Deronda,* the mock-heroic in Eliot frequently has a way of turning back on itself, suggesting continuity rather than sharp disparity. Both Esther and Prince Hal have the potential of becoming powerful leaders, through a tempering of their high spirits, and it must be immediately added that the epigraph's image of Hal, and its very glaring gender change, precludes our seeing Esther as being educated through "simplistic"[7] submission. Like Hal, she must learn the ways of the world and the pitfalls of her own ego—above all, she must learn from the example of the father's psychological prowess and foibles before she can become of full use to the "wide world."

Chapter 26 is only a few pages long; however, it is "wide enough" to encompass the change because for virtually half the novel Eliot has been preparing Esther for the moment when she will become aware of her father's total indifference to "possession." Once Esther recognizes that for years Mr. Lyon never enjoyed the patriarchal advantage of calling himself her father but like an unacknowledged mother performed the tasks anyway, she begins moving in that direction which will give her her full power:

And in the act of unfolding to her that he was not her real father, but had only striven to cherish her as a father, had only longed to be loved as a father, the odd, wayworn, unworldly man became the object of a new sympathy in which Esther felt herself exalted. Perhaps this knowledge would have been less powerful within her, but for the mental preparation that had come during the last two months from her acquaintance with Felix Holt. (354)

Felix Holt's connection with this experience comes, however, not so much from his role as chastiser as his role as nurturer. Previously we have already witnessed the crucial chapter 22, which involves the scene with Job, Felix's "son," as well as the two potential lovers. Some of the "old Adam" begins to leave Esther even there, because the passing of the child—back and forth between them—awakens their vulnerability and serves as a lead to lowering their mutual pride and developing their sexual interest. It is only then that the Byronic heroes begin to fade for her. Thus, in this revelation scene, Esther comes to recognize her father's legacy of anonymous heroism, because she has already witnessed it from a romantic perspective in another male nurturer, Felix:

> Mr. Lyon regarded his narrative as a confession—as a revelation to this beloved child of his own miserable weakness and error. But to her it seemed a revelation of another sort: her mind seemed suddenly enlarged by a vision of passion and struggle, of delight and reununciation, in the lot of beings who had hitherto been a dull enigma to her. (354)

As Esther loses her ennui and recognizes the heroism around her, she becomes a candidate for androgynous balance. As was true of Mr. Irwine, Silas, and Romola, a loss of self occurs for her when she "becomes" the opposite gender. Appreciation and gratitude are the avenues to androgyny and anonymity. Applicable here is Rachel Trubowitz's article "Androgyny in *Macbeth* and *Paradise Lost*," which shows how "Milton's idealization of Adam and Eve as perfect pair informs his depiction of the couple's mutual sexual desire, shared work, and, perhaps most importantly, perfectly conjoined discourse" (324). In the speeches that follow Mr. Lyon's confession, surely this is what we have—"circular and reciprocating patterns of dialogue" (Trubowitz, 324), suggesting not so much that Esther and her father are Adam and Eve, but that her body has become a pre-Fall "paradise / To envelop and contain celestial spirits" because she and her father have obtained a mutual sense of forgiveness. The tableau at the close of the chapter perfectly connects with the one previously mentioned and serves as a reminder of a whole host of balances achieved between classical Renaissance heroes, heroines, and their fathers—starting with Antigone and Oedipus, passing through Cordelia and Lear, and ending, certainly, with Prince Hal and King Henry, at just the moment final accord has been reached between monarch and son and the crown is passed. The words that are pertinent to Esther are not *depression* and *subjugation* but *expansion* and *exultation*.

From the center of the book on, we discover that we have an "Esther Part One" and "Esther Part Two," as well as a "Rufus Before Annette" and "Rufus After." Initially Esther is depicted as completely conventionally feminine—in particular through the allusions to the Calypso of *Télémaque* (ch. 10, 207), a goddess who, according to Fénelon's version, has the intriguing power of making Telemachus effeminate—so much so that Mentor has to warn him that "the Youth who loves to deck himself and vainly trim his Person like a Woman, is unworthy both of Wisdom and of Honour" (1, 7). In other words, the allusion is perfectly consistent with Felix's suspicion that Esther, like all women, has the capacity to "unman" and ensnare him so that eventually his quest will be lost. By chapter 38, however, as Esther's education draws toward its denouement, the allusion is turned around and she is presented as asking herself "Mentor-like questions" (ch. 38, 484). If Mentor is decidedly and conventionally male, Esther has begun to address that component in herself and has owned up to the responsibility and attendant power of making her own choices—in this case, between Harold and Felix.

Esther's ultimate choice has a great deal to do with Harold's shocking attitude towards women. In chapter 36, we learn privately that "Western women were not to his taste; they showed a transition from the feebly animal to the thinking being, which was simply troublesome" (454). As her *bildungsroman* draws to a close, then, much of the major suspense concerns how Esther will penetrate Harold's seeming gentlemanliness and learn that terminal subjugation and slavery lie at the bottom of his plans, just as they do in all the back closets of Transome Court. The discovery occurs through Harold's casual admission in chapter 43 that his wife was, literally, a slave, and also through her close observation of the tragedy of Mrs. Transome, whose life shows the poisonous connection between female subordination and a categorical hatred of men—what has been recently termed "misandrony":

"Men are selfish. They are selfish and cruel. What they care for is their own pleasure and their own pride."

"Not all," said Esther, on whom these words fell with a painful jar. . . .

Esther found it difficult to speak. The dimly-suggested tragedy of this woman's life, the dreary waste of years empty of sweet trust and affection, afflicted her even to horror. It seemed to have come as a last vision to urge her towards the life where the draughts of joy spring from the unchanging fountains of reverence and devout love. (ch. 50, 597)

Because of her father, as well as Felix, Esther can never accept this sweeping dismissal of men. Esther's major lesson will be that hatred for those men who are subtly or openly tyrannical only gives them more power and simply leads a woman to an embittering sense of minor imperiousness which never ventures beyond the parlor anyway. The example of Mrs. Transome's private empire of negative acceptance reminds one of Eliot's aside in her sympathetic review of the work of Margaret Fuller and Mary Wollstonecraft—namely, that "a woman quite innocent of an opinion in philosophy, is as likely as not to have an indomitable opinion about the kitchen" (Byatt and Warren, *Selected Essays,* 335). In Mrs. Transome's case, all of Transome Court is her kitchen.

What alternative exists beyond Mrs. Transome? Gillian Beer writes, "the connection between the *uselessness* of Mrs. Transome's growing rage and the deafness of all political parties to what is meant by change, remains the radical insight of the book" (145). What remains, then, one might ask, for Esther besides anger and the kitchen? The answer lies in *Oedipus at Colonus* and Esther's role as rescuer at Felix's trial. As Esther's forerunner, Antigone, at the end of the Colonus tragedy, speaks lovingly how

> Life was not sweet, yet I found it so
> When I could put my arms around my father.
> Oh father! My dear!
> Now you are enshrouded in darkness,
> Even in that absence
> You shall not lack our love.
>
> (1698–1703)[8]

Just prior to Esther's decision to visit Felix and later to defend him, the heroine also revisits her father (in this case, in the flesh), embraces the old man, and "sob[s] like a child" (549). At the conclusion of the chapter, the narrator says:

It is only in that freshness of our time that the choice is possible which gives unity to life, and makes the memory a temple where all relics and all votive offerings, all worship and all grateful joy, are an unbroken history sanctified by one religion. (ch. 44, 551)

As in *Romola,* the embrace of the old gives a young woman fresh and "regenerating" power; through her return visit to her father, Esther realizes her anonymous place in the growing good of the world, and prepares herself, certainly unconsciously, to act on Felix's behalf. Thus Antigone, while embracing her father in memory during the epode, anticipates Esther when she says:

> If this was our father's cherished wish
> We must be satisfied.
> Send us back, then, to ancient Thebes,
> And we may stop the bloody war
> From coming between our brothers!
>
> (1768–1772)

Stop comes from διακωλύσωμεν, which more literally means *avert* (Campbell 440). Both Esther and Antigone serve the function of carrying on their fathers' peacemaking powers by entering predominantly male contexts and insisting on an ethic of nurturance and love. The point is, they have to appropriate certain male qualities in order to venture into the arena in the first place, and they have to lose themselves in order to rise to the highest occasion of their lives. After Esther has spoken in Felix's defense, the narrator says:

> There was something so naive and beautiful in this action of Esther's, that it conquered every low or petty suggestion even in the commonest minds. The three men in that assembly who knew her best—even her father and Felix Holt—felt a thrill of surprise mingled with their admiration. This bright, delicate, beautiful shaped thing that seemed most like a toy or ornament—some hand had touched the chords, and there came forth music that brought tears. Half a year before, Esther's dread of being ridiculous spread over the surface of her life; but the depth below was sleeping. (ch. 46, 573)

Esther has taken precedence over her father. Dramatically, her speech is presented in full; Rufus's is largely summarized. And by allying herself with Felix Holt at the trial, Esther in fact escapes being an angel of the house and stops being a toy; she had been these when she had been nothing but a fixture in her father's residence, reading Byron and thinking about her clothes. By forgetting herself and her appearance, she surprises rather than courts all male opinion and commands instantaneous respect just when she is least conscious of pursuing it. Truly she is her father's daughter in her self-forgetting, and thus, ironically, is most herself. By averting the harsher sentence and reducing Felix's prison time, Esther actually unlocks her own prison; the decisive action gives her the momentum to free herself from Transome Court. Like Antigone, she remembers her father, and that gives her the power to act on her "religion."

The alternative open to Esther at the end of the novel is Edenic, but it does not exist in Felix anymore than Elizabeth Bennet's alternative exists simply in Darcy or Portia's in Bassanio. Although Jennifer Uglow sums up the romantic ending by saying that "Felix, Esther and their son are banished to a good life in some nameless town" (192), the good life that is imagined is not static but suggests a relationship full of repartee and balance, a continual state of readjustment. Even the proposal scene does not allow itself to be taken too seriously:

> When their hands fell again, their eyes were bright with tears. Felix laid his hand on her shoulder.
> "Could you share the life of a poor man, then, Esther?"
> "If I thought well enough of him," she said, the smile coming again, with the pretty saucy movement of her head.
> "Have you considered well what it would be?—that it will be a very bare and simple life?"
> "Yes—without atta of roses." (ch. 51, 601)

Felix, like Bassanio and Darcy, plays "straight man" to a wife who is simultaneously softening and sportive. While Ruth Yeazell has called Esther Eliot's "most conventional heroine" (142), the fact is, Esther cannot be so, because she has, like Portia, a history of having donned a male role and spoken in court—and a history, through Eliot's motto, of being crowned prince rather than queen.

Her manner, though not as "lively" and "sportive" as Elizabeth Bennet's, extends into the final pages of the novel, because like Elizabeth, she has appropriated certain conventionally male characteristics which make her the right counterpoise to her husband. Like her father, who cautions Felix that the "caustic which you handle in order to scorch others may happen to sear your own fingers and make them dead to the quality of things" (ch. 13, 242), Esther knows when to give a self-righteous and sometimes stuffy man the right "bright and sparkling" correctives. "If you take me in that way," Felix tells her in the final chapter, "I shall

be forced to be a much better fellow than I ever thought of being."
"I call that retribution," Esther answers (ch. 51, 602).

In both Austen and Eliot, the heroines' closing Edenic worlds
are seen to incorporate the fathers as well as the marriages, suggesting, as in *Silas Marner* as well, the balance between male and
female has become internalized, and thus Esther can embrace
her father's wider view:

> And even as each has the joy of contributing to a whole whereby he
> is ravished and lifted up into the courts of heaven so will it be in that
> crowning time of the millennial reign, when our daily prayer will be
> fulfilled, and one law shall be written on all hearts, and be the very
> structure of all thought, and be the principle of all action. (ch. 13, 242)

7

Lydgate's Note and Dorothea's Tomb:
The Quest for Anonymity in *Middlemarch*

THE uncanny impact of the final sentence of Eliot's most celebrated novel perhaps can best be explained by the surprise and
admiration the reader feels in seeing, perhaps for the first time,
that the landscape of *Middlemarch* has been that of "Elegy Written
in a Country Churchyard," advanced to a global scale. The events
of Eliot's life which surrounded the novel's composition could perhaps explain not only the preoccupation with death but also its
emphasis on its transcendence. The overall rhythm of Gray's poem
is the same, with loss and obscurity giving rise to the resurrection
of the reader and of the scribe of anonymous heroism. For Dorothea and Eliot alike are "mindful of th'unhonored Dead" and find
an appropriate resting place in the ultimate phrase, "unvisited
tombs." In November 1872, Eliot could write to Alexander Main
that "I have finished my book ('Middlemarch') and am thoroughly
at peace about it,—not because I am convinced of its perfection,
but because I have lived to give out what it was in me to give, and
have not been hindered by illness or death from making my work
a whole, such as it is" (Cross 3: 142).

One is particularly aware of how much distance Eliot must have
traveled in arriving at an intense and elegaic solution when, in
view of the novel's composition process, all of the author's previous
doubts, griefs, and struggles are taken into account, particularly
her anguish over the loss of her beloved stepson, whose death
"seems to me the beginning of our own" (3: 79). In a letter to Mrs.
Richard Congreve on the very same day that her journal noted
her experimentation with a story called "Miss Brooke," Eliot re-
marked that "my strong egoism has caused me so much melan-
choly, which is traceable simply to a fastidious yet hungry
ambition, that I am relieved by the comparative quietude of personal cravings which age is bringing" (3: 97). If we are to consult
again Eliot's notes on tragedy, such a quietude could only be con-

veyed artistically through a Promethean heroism and the development of a landscape where the unhonored dead are honored, and
their observer is given the lesson of freedom from ambition.

Through Eliot's vast novel, the message could be articulated as
follows: the immortalized dead have no particular advantage over
the obscure; that is, in the graveyard, the concept of a lionizing
copyright is ludicrous. To illustrate, we might say that to be "spoken to" by an author whose work has "lived on" is very much like
receiving a postcard, long delayed in the mails, from a vacationing
friend whose plane disappeared on the return flight home. The
postcard, complete with seascape and sunlit beach, says, "Wish
you were here." But the receiver, alive and holding the card, says
silently to himself, herself, "Wish *you* were here." "Life in print,"
or "life in prestige," is only the illusion of the sunlit beach; the
sender is really dead, despite the mirage of fame. Eliot, in writing
of the quest for immortalization in her essay "Liszt, Wagner and
Weimar," also says that fame

> is but another word for the sympathy of mankind with individual ge-
> nius, and the great poet or the great composer is sure that that sympa-
> thy will be given some day, though his Paradise Lost will fetch only five
> pounds, and his symphony is received with contemptuous laughter, so
> he can transport himself from the present and live by anticipating in
> that future time when he will be thrilling men's minds and ravishing
> their ears. (99)

But what if someone might not be a Lizst, not a Milton and still
have a "Paradise Lost" ongoing in his or her mind? In *Middlemarch,* Eliot proves to be even more concerned with this issue
than ever before. In the extensive character study of chapter 17,
she writes: "Does it seem incongruous to you that a Middlemarch
surgeon should dream of himself as a discoverer? Most of us,
indeed, know little of the great originators until they have been
lifted up among the constellations and already rule our fates"
(175). Here the narrator puts the emphasis not so much on the
distinction between eventual greatness and eventual obscurity as
on the limits on the human ability to recognize what a "star" is.
In this observation, not only is Casaubon's script already written,
but also those quests of a whole populace of Middlemarchers who
might be defined as "subterranean intellectuals." They attempt to
pursue their "genius," whatever it may be, while perceiving, with
varying degrees of success, the total mirage that fame is. And
because fame is illusory for all parties, these characters are seen
to be at one with the distinguished yet extinguished "Shining

Ones." This overarching process is the major context of what many consider to be Eliot's "greatest" novel, because all subterranean intellectuals, whether, from a standpoint of fame, they form eventual constellations or eddies of dust, are required to have faith in themselves, despite overwhelming odds. Such faith, in Eliot, is the central point concerning anonymous or Promethean heroism.

The parallels come to mind quickly. Casaubon, the most prominent example, struggles to find the key to all mythologies; Lydgate travels in pursuit of the primitive tissue; Farebrother makes his small, bemused advances in natural history; Mrs. Garth sustains her small peripatetic school in her kitchen—her daughter, Mary, living on to write "a little book for her boys, called *Stories of Great Men, taken from Plutarch*" (finale, 890); while Mr. Brooke creates conversational compendiums.

Surrounding this community of underground scholars who may or may not understand fame is the grand world of Vesalius, Aquinas, and Milton, which the omniscient narrator is careful to introduce via allusion. How we respond to Lydgate when he is placed side by side with Vesalius or to Casaubon when the figure of Aquinas frequently overshadows him, or—to make the comparison more complicated—to Caleb Garth when his household says he is like Cincinnatus, has a great deal of bearing on our total reaction to the vast novel. The constant comparisons of "apparently big" with "apparently little" challenge the reader with what the real distinction is, and ultimately close the gap, because commitment, a central component of anonymous heroism, exists in either case.

Dorothea, in some respects, might be considered a subterreanean intellectual, too, and the impact of her mind on the outer world raises central issues, when she is placed alongside Saint Theresa or the Virgin Mary. In this context, she serves as a touchstone for understanding how heroic perception redeems and heals all the rest, since her sympathetic understanding is presented as an alternative to the competitive self-evaluation which despairs over the Greats, who always seem to have the advantage. Whatever sympathy fame cannot supply, Dorothea does.

In his article "The Intellectual Background of the Novel: Casaubon and Lydgate," W. J. Harvey concludes that "while the irony of Casaubon is that he is in ignorance of the real work already done by German scholars in the near-past, the irony of Lydgate is that he is just too soon for the real work to be done, again by German scholars, in the near future" (Hardy, *Approaches*, 36). At first, Eliot deliberately teases us with the possibility of a universal law of irony governing their actions, relative to those who were

grander or more "successful." Harvey also says that "George Eliot
does not wish us to think of Lydgate's endeavors as futile in the
same way as Casaubon's." This distinction is quite the case, but
it has less to do with the efficacy of their actions than the way
they perceive themselves. If we invoke the faith Dorothea lives by,
it would be impossible for the actions of either man to be perceived
as totally futile, for "by desiring what is perfectly good, even when
we don't quite know what it is and cannot do what we would, we
are part of the divine power against evil—widening the skirts of
light and making the struggle with darkness narrower" (ch. 39,
427). Dorothea's heart "burns" for the entire Middlemarch community—in other words, the world—and therefore all are valued.
At the same time, her saving vision is thrown into bold relief by
the attitude of Casaubon and others because while Dorothea has
embraced anonymity and sees her own importance and unimportance within the cosmic scheme, Casaubon has embraced prestige—a contrast much greater than the one between youth and
age.[1]

Middlemarch's narrator, particularly in the early sections in
Rome, is careful to point out that Casaubon, even in the midst of
intellectual disaster, could have been a "success" had his nature
not been narrower, "if he would have held her hands between his
and listened with the delight of tenderness and understanding to
all the little histories which made up her experience, and would
have given her the same sort of intimacy in return, so that the
past life of each could be included in their mutual knowledge and
affection" (ch. 20, 230). The point is not so much that Casaubon
is a "complete anachronism, lost in the labyrinth of an exploded
pseudo-science" (*Approaches*, 35), as that he is a complete moral
coward when the awareness of his anonymity approaches; convinced it means futility, he is driven inward toward his own self-
deluded and desperate search for minor immortality,[2] rather than
outward toward Dorothea's pity and tenderness. Part of the binding force of mutual knowledge and affection could have been the
awareness of his mortal limits, as is certainly true in the case of
the Garths, and later in the case of Fred and Mary Vincy. As it is,
he shows the connection, as Neil Hertz points out, between "the
written word" and "the narcissistic imagination" (32) and "to conceive Mr. Casaubon as different from oneself, and to do so 'with
that distinctness which is no longer reflection but feeling' sounds
like a display of the same imaginative power that created the character of Casaubon in the first place" (30–31). Precisely—because
we, like Dorothea, can recognize his value within the scheme of

Middlemarch, or the march of time, even when the pursuit of prestige keeps him from doing so himself.

We can hear a great deal of the author's autobiographical fears in the depiction of Casaubon, for his resistance to anonymous heroism typifies the "egoism" the newly famous Eliot accused herself of some ten years prior, as mentioned in the Introduction. Thus the celebrated incident is not so surprising—"when a young friend put the question direct: 'But from whom, then, did you draw Casaubon?' George Eliot, with a humorous solemnity, which was quite in earnest, nevertheless, pointed to her own heart" (Haight, *Biography*, 450). If the "growing good of the world is partly dependent on unhistorical acts" and the reduction of our ills "is half owing to the number who lived faithfully a hidden life, and rest in unvisited tombs," then Eliot and Casaubon both showed bad faith—one temporarily, one interminably—by affirming what Sara Hennell defined as a sphere of glory, which closes out intimate companions, who can only look back at their lost friends "wistfully and very lonely" (3: 95–96).

It seems that Eliot ultimately distrusted the ability of words, whether written or spoken, to bring happiness, and that is why, in this novel, signed relics frequently offer nothing but psychic death and, ironically, a threat to being remembered: "But he had come at last to create a trust for himself out of Dorothea's nature: she could do what she resolved to do: and he willingly imagined her toiling under fetters of promise to erect a tomb with his name upon it (Not that Mr. Casaubon called the future volumes a tomb; he called them the Key to all Mythologies.)" (ch. 50, 535).[3] Ironically, Dorothea, as the potential choral figure, could have preserved her husband's memory—as she does, in a sense, preserve Lydgate's—had he abandoned his obsession with immortality. If he allowed her to love him, she could have become his living memorial, just as Janet Dempster becomes Mr. Tryan's. To underscore the self-created irony of Casaubon's life, the narrator describes his work both as "shattered mummies" (ch. 48, 519) and "withered in the birth like an elfin child" (ch. 48, 519). In the end, his postmortem attempts to manipulate the living and resurrect his name (as represented also by the codicil to his will) actually serve to cover it; Casaubon's ghost is slain by his own dead hand.

Mr. Brooke, who, particularly during the earlier sections of the novel, offers relief from the darker story of Casaubon, also participates in a polite scholarship befitting his class and undergoes, just after Casaubon's death, an intellectual disaster.[4] An important difference, however, resides in Brooke's willingness to admit defeat, and in his own comic way, to affirm his own existence. Although he shares many of Casaubon's muddles, along with his pedantry, and above all his inability to bring his intellectual life into the world of action, his humorous resiliency places him apart. He does, in essence, acknowledge his own unimportance. Just as Casaubon's self-serving quotation of "Who with repentance is not satisfied, is not of heaven nor earth" (ch. 21, 242) forecasts his final inner descent, so Brooke's "I assure you it was rather comic: Fielding would have made something of it—or Scott, now—might have worked it up" (ch. 39, 428) forecasts his own starlike reascension even when he cannot offer "the forces of his mind honestly to the nation" (ch. 49, 528).

As an "intellect," of course, Brooke occupies himself mainly with stitching together random ideas taken from literature and history, a process which culminates in his support for moral reform in general and the Reform Bill in particular. Taken together, chapters 39 and 51 form a relentless five-act comedy, whereby Brooke's lack of moral reform on his own land is so obvious that he is first driven from his own property and then from his own lofty oration. Further, the illogic of his jump from "ideas" to action is dramatized by the intellectual diffusion which overcomes him the moment he must address someone else, whether it be Dagley or the crowd:

> This was a bold figure of speech, but not exactly the right thing; for, unhappily, the pat opening had slipped away—even couplets from Pope may be but "fallings from us, vanishings," when fear clutches us, and a glass of sherry is hurrying like smoke among our ideas. Ladislaw, who stood at the window behind the speaker, thought, "It's all up now." (ch. 51, 547)

Eliot, in a sense, turns the allusions in on Mr. Brooke at this moment, since the passage, complete with literary quotation, imitates the drift of Brooke's cluttered mind. As in the case of Casaubon, a fragmentation of intellectual purpose spells disaster, but because we are in a comic world, the nightmare images of dim anterooms and "the dark river-brink" of Acheron change into the Punch-voiced effigy of Mr. Brooke himself. In Neil Hertz's terms, we "recognize" Mr. Brooke also, but the creative energy spills over into the man himself, because this time the irony works its way through the sherry into his own ideas. At first consistent with his unconscious hypocrisy, he proves unable to "see himself," and thus, when the crowd laughs at his own caricature, he laughs with them. When the voice ultimately calls for the Bill, Mr. Brooke is placed in the rather painful position shared by Mrs. Arrowpoint, who, in *Daniel Deronda*, is forced to live up to her own words, which have been stylishly and safely developed within a basement intellect. Certainly the aristocratic lady and "authoress of 'Tasso'" parallels Mr. Brooke when she proves unable to "see herself" "when what she had safely demanded of the dead Leonora was enacted by her own Catherine" (ch. 22, 288). The result, in both cases, is a comic collapse of a pretentious wall between word and deed.

The laughter, however, is soon over, and what strikes the reader the moment the humiliated Mr. Brooke enters the committee room is not his silliness but his indestructible good humor. His compromise, in the face of defeat, takes two forms, one minor and one major. The first is altogether expected, his bowing out of the race. The second, however, involves his surprising willingness to follow the progress or retrogression of political reform at a humble distance and to defer, where his own land is concerned, to the anonymous hero, Caleb Garth. Thus, in the finale, Mr. Brooke and his anthropomorphic pen are presented in a wholly sympathetic light, the pen not representing, as it did in the case of Casaubon, the stillborn elfin child but instead the baby boy brought into being by the union of Will and Dorothea, which his note unconsciously blesses. For once word and deed are brought into accord. In the end, Brooke participates in "the growing good" of the world, because, with the apparent failure of his ideas, his benevolent nature—the wellspring of his muddled good intentions—reasserts itself and invisibly advances the forces of light.[5]

When one turns to the final three underground scholars, Lydgate, Farebrother, and Mrs. Garth—those whose scholarship issues into more readily "visible" activity—one must first look at their external "failures." Lydgate ends up marrying an egoist and gradually loses hold of his original scientific pursuit; Farebrother's interest in natural history hardly advances beyond the pickled animals in his study; and Mrs. Garth's peripatetic school is only a further reminder to her neighbors that she had been a teacher once and had to make her own way. Their willingness, however, to create a compromise—or in Mrs. Garth's case, sustain a coexistence—once their academic pursuits recede from them is largely responsible for their growth in character and, together with Dorothea's "sacrifice," instrumental in building the "network" of good which laces the novel.

Lydgate is never entirely fulfilled, either morally or intellectually, yet critics have tended to overemphasize the irony of his life,

accepting too readily his final view of himself as the correct one.[6]
Within the body of the novel itself, Lydgate moves from a "benevo-
lently contemptuous" conceit (ch. 15, 79) to "that twice-blessed
mercy [which] was always with Lydgate in his work at the Hospital
or in private houses, serving better than any opiate to quiet and
sustain him under anxieties and his sense of mental degeneracy"
(ch. 61, 720). One cannot deny that he interprets his life as a
steady intellectual decline, but this fact, taken in the context of
the larger vision of the novel, acquires only secondary importance,
especially when Lydgate is seen as entering more and more the
role of the compassionate healer within the novel proper and—
as will be true of Dorothea—eventually finding self-healing in
the process.

One may look at him in relation to one man alone, Farebrother,
in order to see the change. In chapter 17, which subtly contrasts
them, Lydgate is presented as having strong reservations about a
man who does not share his fixity of purpose or high sense of
vocational commitment; he is reading Farebrother's life the way
he will later read his own. Yet, ironically, as the chapters progress,
Lydgate proves able to achieve the wider view only in relation to
his friend's life and work, even when he cannot in relation to his
own. Once he has come to reflect on his mistake of voting for
Tyke over and against Farebrother—as well as to reflect on his
own struggles to obtain medical reform in Middlemarch—Lydgate
advances to a clear perception of Farebrother's true worth, to the
point that he intercedes on his friend's behalf. In effect he comes
to assert anonymous heroism by separating the man out from
the rest:

> "Instead of telling you anything about Mr. Tyke," he said, "I should
> like to speak of another brother, the Vicar of St. Botolph's. His living
> is a poor one, and gives him a stinted provision for himself and his
> family. His mother, aunt, and sister all live with him, and depend upon
> him. I believe he has never married because of them. I never heard
> such good preaching as his—such plain, easy eloquence. He would
> have done to preach at St. Paul's after old Latimer. His talk is just as
> good about all subjects: original, clear. I think him a remarkable fel-
> low; he ought to have done more than he has done."
> "Why has he not done more?" said Dorothea, interested now in all
> who had slipped below their own intention.
> "That's a hard question," said Lydgate. "I find myself that it's un-
> commonly difficult to make the right thing work: there are so many
> strings pulling at once." (ch. 50, 536–37)

Lydgate, in rejecting the rigid standard of judgment of his earlier days, serves as a model for the reader, who will later have a more ameliorative view of Lydgate himself as one who "slipped below [his] intention" but is still valued. Because of this conversation, Farebrother is given the Lowick living two chapters later. Lydgate's reference to his own failure is crucial, since in Eliot, sympathy is possible only through a keen recollection of one's own losses. The "many strings pulling at once" anticipate the channels of the finale, and in this instance, Lydgate is speaking to the right person, since Dorothea, eleven chapters earlier, has also anticipated the wider standard of the final pages.

The perception of Lydgate's true worth then, over and beyond his intellectual failure, must rest with Dorothea, in a manner parallel to Lydgate's perception of Farebrother's innermost talents. In the midst of the Bulstrode scandal, coupled with the collapse of his marriage, Lydgate is snatched back from total dishonor and self-hatred by Dorothea's belief in him, which is symbolic of his having adopted a more androgynous view of what heroism is. There is a telling moment in chapter 69, when Eliot writes, "The strong man had had too much to bear that day. He let his head fall beside hers [Rosamond's] and sobbed" (755). Here the narrator seems to give Lydgate an almost motherly word of consolation, acknowledging his right to be heroic in what, by conventional standards, would be considered an "unmanly" way. In chapter 76, as we shall see, Dorothea offers the same sort of balance, tempering Lydgate's masculine sense that his life is a failure because prestige and reputation have told him so. "The presence of a noble nature, generous as its wishes, ardent in its charity, changes the lights for us: we begin to see things again in their larger, quieter masses, and to believe that we too can be seen and judged in the wholeness of our character" (819). This is the charge that Eliot brings to bear upon the reader: we cannot allow ourselves to share Lydgate's narrow view of himself, as a man who began with great intellectual dreams, and ended up paralyzed. Rather, the wholeness of his character testifies to his active participation in anonymous achievements that are not ironically undercut. Dorothea can save Lydgate's memory in a way she cannot her former husband's, because in the face of intellectual loss he has become concerned with the care of others rather than the minor immortalization of his achievements. When he says, "Yet you have made a great difference in my courage by believing in me" (825), we are forced to think of him not as a man who started in pursuit of the primitive tissue and concluded with a treatise on gout but as a man who, facing up to the pressure of external circumstances as well as his misguided decisions, fell short of epic or tragic grandeur but was remembered anyway. Once again, we have to think of Romola's statement to her uncle, "You shall help me—always—because I shall remember you."

Farebrother, as a subterranean intellectual, thus escapes a sense of ironic frustration, and does not have as far to travel in his moral education; moreover, several others have seen his value: his simplicity of speech and his sureness of touch with people of all stations and in all situations. In contrast to Lydgate, Farebrother has passed through his "failure" by the time the novel opens, so that he is perceived as a consistently humble and compassionate man, who has only a self-amused struggle of feeding "a weakness or two lest they should get clamorous" (ch. 17, 202) to undergo. If he had a calling in the field of natural history, it is surely gone by the time Lydgate meets him. This fact does a great deal to explain why, in chapter 17, Farebrother is so understanding toward their mutual friend Trawley and Lydgate is so harsh. Farebrother knows "what it is to want spiritual tobacco" (202), whereas Lydgate has never tried out his intellectual endeavors—at least to the point that he could understand why someone could fail. Farebrother is keenly aware of this problem and tries to give him a warning cast in simple scriptural terms:

> "Your scheme is a good deal more difficult to carry out than the Pythagorean community, though. You have not only got the old Adam in yourself against you, but you have got all those descendants of the original Adam who form the society around you. You see, I have paid twelve or thirteen years more than you for my knowledge of difficulties." (203)

Since this warning, as well as others, goes unheeded, Lydgate must be the one to repeat Trawley's example.

In addition, Farebrother stands in contrast to his friend—and indeed to Casaubon and Mr. Brooke as well—by being the first to reconcile his basement studies with the "upperworld"—the realm of social relationships. It is very important that, symbolically speaking, Farebrother can move smoothly and comfortably from his mother's drawing room to his study and back again—as distinct from Casaubon, whose mind often goes "too deep during the day to be able to get to the surface again" (ch. 20, 231–32). The success of Farebrother's transition can be explained in a variety of ways: the relative smallness of his intellectual commitment, his perception of his own limitations, and, above all, the significance he assigns to his want of "spiritual tobacco." Unlike Casaubon and Lydgate, who are driven toward desperation once their intellectual failings have become apparent, Farebrother uses his "study" as a fixed and self-satiric symbol of what he cannot achieve, how far he cannot go.

Ironically, then, he travels a great deal further, both vocationally and spiritually. Like Mrs. Garth, he is aware of his moral limits. As has already been seen, he does not find it difficult to unite his deep scriptural learning with the world of action like Mr. Irwine; he knows which *exempla* apply and which do not. In participating in the invisible channels of good in the novel, he imitates Lydgate but goes beyond him in selflessness, by sacrificing himself so that Fred Vincy's self-respect can survive. Characteristically and symbolically, during the middle stages of his intercessions with Mary, he leaves the couple alone in his study so that they can speak freely, transforming his place of cogitation into a theater for romance at his own expense. Because of the vicar's efforts, Fred Vincy's courtship—and therefore his vocation—is saved, and, ironically, by renouncing himself, Farebrother seals his commitment to the clerical profession, where one's own desires must frequently be qualified. Earlier in the novel, when he is led to dismiss Prodicus's story of Herculean virtue as a "pretty tale" (ch. 18, 218), he shows a fully conscious understanding of the modern-day heroism of anonymity, which could only imbue his actions later.

Like Farebrother, Mrs. Garth closes the gap between the worlds of learning and activity, but in her case the closure is more complete: what could be more direct than firing out questions on Roman history while doing the baking? There is little, if any, of the mock-heroic here, since the juxtaposition of Roman agrarian virtue and the lives of the Garths points to continuity rather than difference. Like the Farebrother household, the family lives amidst a lovingly heaped accumulation of past and present, which becomes a metaphor for the ease with which the wisdom of the past, both personal and historical, is infused into their daily existence. Implicit is an acceptance of one's mortality, which, paradoxically, issues in images of vitality, in contrast to Casaubon, whose attempts to head off death only take him further and further into anterooms and the tombs of "shattered mummies," where daylight has been banished. With death acknowledged and not feared, the Garths can live in a vital coexistence where Livy may be discussed or Walter Scott read aloud over and above the clatter of dishes or the sound of children's voices. All in all, the atmosphere sounds very much like the state of mind that the younger Marian Evans embodied when, in her early life, she was learning about so many things at once:

> My mind presents just such an assemblage of disjointed specimens of history, ancient and modern, scraps of poetry picked up from Shakespeare, Cowper, Wordsworth and Milton, newspaper topics, morsels of Addison and Bacon, Latin verbs, geometry, entomology and chemistry, reviews and metaphysics, all arrested and petrified and smothered by the fast thickening every day accession of actual events, relative anxieties and household cares and vexations. (*Letters* 1:28)

Jennifer Uglow, in her biographical outline (20), highlights this letter as central to our understanding of Eliot's growth of mind, at its initially most creative, and I would add that it is the hallmark of what Eliot considered to be creativity—the dynamic hodgepodge, alluded to in the Introduction. Thus, Mrs. Garth, like Piero di Cosimo and indeed the exhilarated narrators of the novels before *Middlemarch*, becomes a kind of vortex of transferable culture.

It does not seem, then, that as a subterranean intellectual Mrs. Garth has reached a state of self-eclipse. Although Gilbert and Gubar point out that she is the one to stylize herself as being an advocate of female subordination (531), it is quite clear that Eliot's humor is alive when Mrs. Garth, while insisting on the old-style hierarchy, is never subordinate herself, since she mixes life and intellect at least as well if not better than her husband or any other man in the novel. There is little self-eclipse in her life, little of what would be called hidden—which is exactly the point; from her point of view, it is "good for them to see that she could make an excellent lather while she corrected their blunders 'without looking',—that a woman with her sleeves tucked up above her elbows might know all about the Subjunctive Mood or the Torrid Zone" (ch. 24, 275). Thus, she undergoes a transition that is even smoother than Farebrother's; there is not even the small separation between drawing room and study: all occurs in her kitchen, and, it could be added, without the domination of others, whether male or female. To Ben's question concerning the relevancy of grammar, she has an immediate and simple answer; and the concept of a useless or cloistered education does not exist for her, anymore than a concept of "failure" or "compromise" exists in the aftermath of her past teaching life.

Thus, unlike Casaubon and Brooke, Mrs. Garth does not find it

difficult to live up to the virtue extolled in her favorite *exempla*.
When Fred Vincy interrupts the Roman history lesson with news
that the Garth family is going to be even harder pressed, she
asserts the rare quality of *gravitas,* so cherished in the remote
early republic: "Like the eccentric woman she was, she was at
present absorbed in considering what was to be done, and did not
fancy that the end could be better achieved by bitter remarks or
explosions" (ch. 24, 281). And it is important to note here that the
ability to meet the challenges of the situation does not come from
a sense of female subordination but from the capacity to avoid
losing all power by doing what Marianne Novy describes as sub-
mitting first and attacking in the midst of vulnerability later.[7] Just
as there is no division between learning and the workaday world,
so there is little hypocritical division between word and deed.

Eliot's use of literary allusion in this episode is very telling,
especially in light of these consistencies. In the Casaubon and
Brooke sections, the mock-heroism is frequently heavy, but as the
gap between intellectual and practical activity narrows, so does
the potential for mockery. Casaubon, for all the special pleading
the narrator offers, is momentarily laughed at when placed alongside the shade of Aquinas. When, however, Mrs. Garth is indirectly
compared to a Roman matron, or Caleb Garth directly called Cincinnatus, there is no laughter, because there is little disparity. As
a quick reference will show, Mr. Garth, for his part, is like the
historical personage in at least four ways: his devoted love of the
land, associated with strength of purpose, his intense hatred of
petty talk, and his strong belief that one should leave a task if it
cannot be completed on one's own terms. Thus when, in a later
chapter, Mrs. Garth says, "Here is an honour to your father, children. . . . He is asked to take a post again by those who dismissed
him long ago," the parallel is nearly exact, since Cincinnatus was
called back as well, thus showing "That he did his work well, so
that they feel the want of him" (ch. 40, 437). She has found an
anonymous hero in her husband, and thus, in her recognitions,
has become one herself.

Such continuities, as represented by Mrs. Garth and by extension, her husband, belong to an even larger one—that of past and
present—and through all of them we may return to the universal
perspective of the finale. At the conclusion we find that both Fred
and Mary live to produce works of minor research and scholarship,
Fred's being the *Cultivation of Green Crops and the Economy of
Cattle-Feeding,* consistent with what he learned from his father-
in-law, and Mary's being *Stories of Great Men, taken from Plu-*

tarch, consistent with what she learned from her mother. Thus even the life of intellect in the case of the Garths is cyclical: belonging to the links between generations rather than the rise and fall of individual endeavor. Frequently the concerns of the novel have been divided between the cyclical and the linear, between the "middle," which moves but stays constant like the twelve-month year, and the "march," which is progressive. Within these divisions, the separation between anonymous heroism and the pursuit of prestige is highly apparent. Anonymous heroism occurs through the sort of parenthood that Silas Marner, along with the Garths, makes clear. The pursuit of prestige, as embodied in Casaubon, comes from a linear sense of annotating, criticizing, and "improving" on what has come before. The point of Mary's book is not so much that her subject was men, borrowed from men's history, as that she wrote it from a tradition initiated by her mother, for the living, immediate audience of her own children and did it without taking quibbling issue and without signing her name. We know from George Eliot herself that names frequently kill, and she positions this statement in the exact center of the novel when she has her heroine articulate the novel's overall vision: "'Please not to call it by any name,' said Dorothea, putting out her hands entreatingly. 'You will say it is Persian, or something else geographical. It is my life'" (ch. 39, 427). Dorothea prefers to keep her religion anonymous, and when it is, it becomes life itself. Thus, taken together, the Garth chapters develop the most clearly epic pattern in the novel, culminating in communal celebration and forming the affirmative note that the novel proper ends on, since they are the most consistently aware of the "fine issues" that can result though they are "not widely visible."

As a group, all the subterranean intellectuals in *Middlemarch* take part in the growing good of the world and constitute the nucleus of a theme, reasserted with widening emphasis, that to fail to achieve acclaim is not to fail at all. Those who begin furthest from this fact suffer the bitterest anguish; those who start with it as a given achieve the greatest personal sense of fulfillment. In between we find Dorothea, who, approaching the roar on the other side of silence and driven by a "keen memory of her own life" (ch. 76, 823), achieves through hard work that finely tuned consciousness that perceives "that element of tragedy which lies in the very fact of frequency" and even heroism in efforts that are at best only partially fulfilled and at worst ironically undercut.

Because of this vision, it is not too much to say that all points of the novel meet in her, and further illumination can be given to this theme, if we look through the novel again, in light of "her story." Judging from Eliot's composition process, as described by Jerome Beaty (Hardy, *Approaches,* 41–42), we can see that the author had the goal of creating a narrative center in Dorothea quite early. While all the subterranean intellectuals could be said to attain anonymous heroism, no one perceives it quite so clearly as Dorothea. It is for this reason, of course, that the novel must end, so perfectly, with its focus on her, since her consciousness must shade into the reader's.

Relatively early in the book—and consistent with the role of a classical heroine—Dorothea passes through the Roman nightmare of "ruins and basilicas [and] . . . the dimmer but yet eager Titanic life gazing and struggling on walls and ceilings; the long vistas of white forms whose marble eyes seemed to hold the monotonous light of an alien world" (ch. 20, 225), and undergoes rites of passage reminiscent of Antigone, Ariadne, and Goethe's Iphigenia. In speaking of the Ariadne statue associated with Dorothea during her painful epiphany, Jennifer Uglow writes, "Dorothea had wanted to help her husband out of the labyrinths of his scholarship (as Ariadne helped Theseus)" (211). Goethe's Iphigenia (whom Eliot studied in 1854 while Lewes was writing his celebrated biography of the poet) has strong applicability in that both heroines see themselves as caught in a fearful matrix of the past, which must be transcended, through an identification with all who feel themselves to be outsiders. (See McCobb, 176, for an indication of Eliot's having read the play.) Dorothea's role of redeeming the value of Lydgate's struggles, as well as Farebrother's, thus becomes parallel with the sublime Iphigenia's healing of her lost and temporarily insane brother. She emerges from the described nightmare of her lineage as well as her own near-death (act 1) into the capacity to charm insanity out of the minds of others.

To be released from nightmares that continue into the center of the present is a complex process for any heroine, no matter what her model, and Uglow, in writing of the book as a whole, says

> *Middlemarch* is imbued with the idea of sisterhood, but it is a sisterhood where women lead the way and it is often combined with a lover-like tension. Ariadne and Antigone mingle. The idea of the sister is there in the slow growing love of Fred and Mary Garth; in the way Dorothea, like the sister who remains at home, directs Will's passage in the wider world, and in the bond between Dorothea and Lydgate, alike and yet separate. (213)

The concept of Dorothea's role as a loving and healing sister becomes especially resonant when one adds Goethe's Iphigenia to the list of classical models. When Iphigenia prays for the restoration of Orestes' sanity, she prays to "You brother-sister pair" (1317) and speaks of how "Thou dost, Diana, love thy gracious brother / Above all else that earth and sky can offer" (1321–22). The binary form of these entreaties foreshadows the actual family ritual where Orestes is shown breaking through to sanity while being "clasped in my sister's arms / And at my dear friend's heart" (1355–56), in a crisis which is compared to the formation of a rainbow, where "Iris of the lovely hues with light / Hand parts the grey veils of the final clouds" (1353–54). At the end of this highly charged scene which closes the third act, Goethe's joint theory of color and personality is made manifest—of sanity in diversity and of the soul being like light; that is, it forms a prism when subject to stress. The character grouping—Orestes, as flanked by his sister Iphigenia and his soulmate Pylades—represents an androgynous balance and represents the redemption of the soul through sympathy. To borrow one of Eliot's terms, which was indeed borrowed from Goethe, his soul—and his sister's—becomes iridescent in this scene.

Thus, like Antigone (particularly the Antigone of *Oedipus at Colonus*), Ariadne, and finally Iphigenia, Dorothea is able to lead men out of nightmare because she has been through one herself. She heals through sympathy. Her relationship with authority, having gone through many tests, and her resistance to deceit make it possible for her to perceive the unacknowledged heroism of others. We can see the further formation of this ability at almost the exact center of the book, in the celebrated dialogue with Will, where, as mentioned before, Dorothea affirms that "by desiring what is perfectly good, even when we don't quite know what it is and cannot do what we would, we are part of the divine power against evil—widening the skirts of light and making the struggle with darkness narrower" (ch. 39, 427). Desire for what is perfectly good is enough, since, for the heroine as for Eliot, people must be judged by their good intentions rather than the visible effects of their actions. For this reason, I think, the famous chapter 39 is capped with a quotation from Donne's "The Undertaking," which speaks of daring to "forget the He and She," since anonymous heroism causes exactly this transcendence.

The clustering of the four heroines, classical and Victorian alike, also suggests that the solution is found in the acceptance of apparent loss, so that room can be made for the actual gain.

The Antigone of Colonus accepts the fact of her father's death and wins the return to her final confrontation in Thebes. Ariadne offers help to Theseus, and, Uglow points out, is eventually rescued by Cupid. Iphigenia offers herself as a sacrifice, and in so doing, wins Thoas over to her higher law and gains safe passage for her brother, now newly restored to sanity. Dorothea, in being prepared to submit to her husband's tyrannical request, is later able to perceive and act on a distinction between "that devotion to the living, and that indefinite promise of devotion to the dead" (ch. 48, 521). Dorothea thus affirms her desire to see Will Ladislaw and the truth that "Life would be no better than candle-light tinsel and daylight rubbish if our spirits were not touched by what has been, to issues of longing and constancy" (ch. 54, 583). For all four women, longing and constancy are initially at odds, and it is their willingness to ride through to difficult solutions that gives them their healing powers.

It is important at this stage to single out Eliot's model of Iphigenia, since she most accentuates the theme of healing which comes at the end of the novel. In fact, Eliot mentions her archetypal story in her earlier notes on tragedy (Cross 3: 32, 35), and Lewes, in agreeing with Schiller, comments that Goethe's version "must for ever remain the delight and wonderment of mankind" (272). In the instance quoted earlier in this chapter, where Dorothea gives Lydgate the one hearing he needs to make him whole again, surely Lydgate plays Orestes, returning to sanity, to Dorothea's Iphigenia, when she shows her healing touch: "The presence of a noble nature, generous in its wishes, ardent in its charity, changes the lights for us: we begin to see things again in their larger, quieter masses, and to believe that we too can be seen and judged in the wholeness of our character" (ch. 76, 819). There is something of Goethe's prism here, although, characteristic of Eliot, it is more subtle. There is an emphasis on the diversity within Lydgate's character; the "lights" are changed; he is not the bad man that society would have him be, any more than Orestes is the simple, lunatic matricide that the Furies would have him be. Thus what, in their edition of the German drama, Lewis A. Rhoades and Carl Selmer say of the healing relation between Goethe's Orestes and Iphigenia could equally be said of Lydgate and Dorothea:

> At the same time his soul responds to the deep impression of her purity and love going out in tenderness and sympathy to him in his

guilt, and because she can still believe in him and love him instead of avenging upon him his crime, he believes in himself again. (xx)

It is important to emphasize, however, that in Eliot, healings of this kind are frequently symbiotic. While Dorothea perceives and articulates Lydgate's anonymous heroism, so does Lydgate perceive hers. "As Lydgate rode away, he thought, 'This young creature has a heart large enough for the Virgin Mary'" (826). The two major protagonists on the road to Emmaus recognize each other with burning hearts, affording Dorothea the greater honor of being compared silently to the Virgin Mary by an ultimately unknown kindred spirit, who cries "soul to soul," a glory greater than the one owned by the widely celebrated Saint Theresa, who can only speak "down"—from more saintly to less saintly, rather than from soul to soul, in the "same embroiled medium." Dorothea only has a heart "large enough for the Virgin Mary" and becomes so only for a moment in Lydgate's private thoughts, when he recognizes her the way Orestes does Iphigenia. She is not a disembodied goddess or divinity; she is better. She is, in Feuerbach's terms, "the essence of Christianity." When Dorothea says to Lydgate, "There is no sorrow I have thought more about than that— to love what is great, and try to reach it, and yet to fail" (ch. 76, 821), she is speaking with "a keen memory of her own life" (823), and is said, in an earlier chapter, to have spoken of her first marriage "looking through the prism of her tears" (ch. 72, 792). Of course she has the privilege of applying the same balm to herself; her feminine side joins with the doctor's masculine side and she becomes whole in the process. When Lydgate speaks of his regrets about misleading Rosamond, she answers, "I know, I know— you could not give her pain, if you were not obliged to do it," speaking for herself as well. When he says, later, "Yet you have made a great difference in my courage by believing in me," one must say the difference, although "not widely visible," is still critically significant, not only in the life of Lydgate but in her own as well.

The acclaimed chapter 81, where Dorothea visits Rosamond, has an epigraph from *Faust, Part Two* and provides another key to Eliot's concept of anonymous hero as healer. In the context of the literary allusion, Faust, transported to a "Pleasing Landscape" after the Gretchen nightmare, is found to be recovering, affirming life again and "*constantly to strive for the utmost of life*" (Hornback, *Middlemarch*, 545, italics Eliot's). The end of his speech, not quoted by Eliot, but implicit in the allusion, raises once again the concept of sanity and recovery as "prism":

> Out of this thunder rises, iridescent,
> Enduring through all change the motley bow,
> Now painted clearly, and now evanescent,
> Spreading a fragrant, cooling spray below.
> The rainbow mirrors human love and strife;
> Consider it and you will better know:
> In many-hued reflection we have life.
>
> (4721–27, Kaufmann, trans.)

With such a heavy allusion, indeed it is impossible not to see healing as the principal theme in this extraordinary chapter. These German lines are part of a scene that assures the audience that Faust has survived his tragedy and is now ready for an epic life. Likewise Dorothea, having gone through her dark night of the soul over thinking Will unfaithful, and having embraced magnanimity and affirming the "pearly light" of chapter 80, now moves forward into helping Lydgate and Rosamond, even though she is "as dangerously responsive as a bit of finest Venetian crystal" (851). Close, in her "nervous exaltation," to the "roar which is on the other side of silence," she embraces her alter ego and "the two women clasped each other as if they had been in a shipwreck" (856). Thus, a few chapters before the finale, we witness anonymous heroism ramifying outward into the growing good of the world. The symbiosis is also clear as well, since Rosamond, while not converted, is refreshed in spirit, and Dorothea is given the information that will release her from the past and from the false surmises concerning the man she will eventually choose.

Other changes exist in this chapter, as illuminated by the Goethean allusion of healing. Anonymous heroism, in being transferrable, appears in Lydgate as well, even before Dorothea approaches Rosamond. He has written her a note of thanks, which he hands her directly as tangible evidence that he has learned what it is to appreciate another person in her wholeness. "When one is grateful for something too good for common thanks," he says, "writing is less unsatisfactory than speech—one does not at least *hear* how inadequate the words are" (849). These are virtually the last words he speaks in the novel, emphasizing the point that his life in *Middlemarch* proper is not a failure, only one that grew anonymously toward the understanding the narrator had prepared for him. The healer ultimately experiences the healing of recognizing another for who she is.

The other illumination in the chapter has to do with the biographical note mentioned in the Introduction. The scene between Rosamond and Dorothea was the one which, according to Cross, Eliot used to illustrate the "not herself" that visited when she composed. While speculations are sometimes idle, it is gratifying and perhaps even thrilling to wonder what sorts of healing Eliot herself experienced when the two antipoles of her psyche—which had pursued her originally in the form of the two hamadryads in her juvenilia—were finally united in the clasp of the two women. "Then abandoning herself," Cross writes, "to the inspiration of the moment, she wrote the whole scene exactly as it stands, without alteration or erasure, in an intense state of excitement and agitation, feeling herself entirely possessed by the feelings of the two women" (3: 344).

The finale itself presses forward the questions of healing and redemption, questioning again whether prominence, visibility, and fame are necessary for vindication. Frequently, in the criticism of the past two decades, the quiet achievements of Dorothea, like those of Lydgate, have been seen as something of a failure, because, in her case, she started with lofty spiritual aims and ended in a state where "many who knew her, thought it a pity that so substantive and rare a creature should have been absorbed into the life of another, and be only known in a certain circle as a wife and mother" (894). Gilbert and Gubar, for example, actually assume that Dorothea is absorbed into Will (530), when really it is only social opinion which says so. In another study, "*Middlemarch: A Feminist Perspective*," Ellen Ringler writes that

> the web of connections she [Eliot] has carefully traced in *Middlemarch* is, as the author often acknowledges, significantly ruptured because the public roles of women are in no way commensurate with their personal force. It is when Eliot offers to mend the rupture, with rationalizations about the 'good' perpetrated by 'unhistoric acts' and the efficacy of 'hidden lives,' that feminists must demur. The disjunctures between male and female social power illustrated throughout the novel simply cannot be adequately patched by those weak threads. (59)

The novel ultimately, however, is not concerned with power such as this form of feminism would pursue. We do not know, in fact, from the finale that Dorothea did *not* advance the causes of the Woman's Movement in some form. Indeed from the cosmological standpoint of *Middlemarch,* we do, in some ways, have every reason to believe she did, the way 99 percent of all reformers, whether devoted to the Women's Movement or others, did—anonymously and without historical credit. To say Dorothea's life was lost because her acts received "no great name" on earth would be to miss the overall vision of the novel and apply Casaubon's shortsightedness instead—a code of prestige that, ironically, has been perceived from the onset as highly masculine by the narrator.

Another critic, Lee R. Edwards, laments that Eliot never dramatized the world "she forced into existence when she stopped being Mary Ann Evans and became George Eliot" (Hornback, *Middlemarch*, 690). But this is exactly the point. When Mary Anne Evans became George Eliot, she embraced exactly what Dorothea and Mary Garth did and indeed what every "hero," whether male or female, in the novel embraces—anonymity. Dorothea's history has "no great name on earth," but the namelessness only serves to emphasize the greatness the specially privileged narrator and reader perceive. One way of looking at Dorothea's life is to say that she started out a high-minded potential reformer and ended a wife and mother; another is to say she started out in search of "a certain spiritual grandeur ill-matched with the meanness of opportunity; perhaps a tragic failure which found no sacred poet and sank unwept into oblivion" (prelude, 25) and became that sacred poet herself by acquiring the widest view of her community's anonymous heroism and embodying, more fully than any other character, the novel's cosmic alternative to prestige.

In order to show the individual's proportionate position in her great community of being, Eliot, like her disciple Tolstoy,[8] had to create characters of towering psychology and then, by way of contrast, suddenly back up and present them in context—in this case, in a world of subterranean intellectuals. Jerome Beaty (Hardy, *Approaches*, 61–62) and Susan Meikle (Smith, *George Eliot*, 186) have pointed out the difference in nuance between the final sentence of Eliot's manuscript and what finally arrived in print. Originally she wrote, "for the growing life of the world is after all chiefly dependent on unhistoric acts, and that things are not so ill with you and me as they might have been is owing to many of those who sleep in unvisited tombs, having lived a hidden life nobly" (Smith, 183). Although Meikle concludes that "the conviction of, or even desire to believe in, the 'good' of the world being affected by the acts of its individual members has been reduced to an almost reluctant acknowledgement of possibility" (186), it is clear that the real emphasis is on "rest" and on "faithfully," for "nobly" would suggest some external recognition and end the novel offkey. Death renders all audiences one or nothing at all. For Dorothea they are "one"; for Casaubon they are nothing. Dorothea is the one who lives "faithfully a hidden life"; Casaubon lives distrustfully, and therefore they are a universe apart. In between is Lydgate, who, like Casaubon, "regarded himself as a failure" but who, like Dorothea, still knows exaltation because he believes, as shown in his final note, in her more compelling generosity, which encompasses him along with Middlemarch. Anonymous heroes are aware of this double perspective and enjoy the advantage that, while they celebrate themselves and each other in all their psychological magnitude, they transcend those superficial mirrors of external honor, which only cause their invaluably complex egos to become bigger than they need be and therefore to suffer. In the words of Sir Thomas Browne, whom Eliot assiduously studied during the composition of *Middlemarch*,[9] "the man of God lives longer without a tomb than any by one, invisibly interred by angels" (*Hydriotaphia*, 46). For Eliot, there are two kinds of immortality—the frozen prestige of a name and the resurrection that comes from a death delivering over individual consciousness to the growing collective consciousness of the world. As in her poem, "O May I Join the Choir Invisible," the dead "live again in minds made better by their presence" (Pinion, 131).

That is why the narrator speaks of the "many Dorotheas" in the second-to-last paragraph of the novel; for it is here that the principal character enters fully into anonymity, an anonymity that is shared with the unnamed narrator and reader, who are in turn bridged by the sentence "But we insignificant people with our daily words and acts are preparing the lives of many Dorotheas" (896), an experience which the novel's eighty-six chapters have been gently and subtly pushing us toward. We become the heroine's "interring angels" as well as our own. Thus Dorothea is not so different from Saint Theresa—and certainly not Iphigenia— after all, because anonymous heroism becomes the Key to All Mythologies. The "unvisited tombs" that includes "us" as the novel closes does not mean so much oblivion as it means and provides freedom through resignation to one's ultimate anonymity, if not in the here and now, certainly in the eventual graveyard of Gray's and Eliot's elegies. That is why the heroes "rest" instead of "sleep," for "sleep" implies oblivion while "rest," ironically, still suggests a resigned consciousness and immortality—actually life itself—but of another order, for heroine, community, narrator, and reader. Thus, in *Middlemarch*, whose elegiac nature may perhaps be traced to Eliot's own loss of her beloved stepson and her own doubts and fears about her own ambition, death becomes the illness from which we eventually do recover through the extraordinary nature of the novel's carefully defined heroism.

8

Celebrity, Anonymity, and the Heroic Voices of *Daniel Deronda*

In her essay, "Three Months in Weimar," Eliot writes of visiting Goethe's house and says:

> One of the most fitting tributes a nation can pay to its great dead, is to make their habitation, like their works, a public possession, a shrine where affectionate reverence may be more vividly reminded that the being who has bequeathed to us immortal thoughts or immortal deeds, had to endure the daily struggle with the petty details, perhaps with the sordid cares, of this working-day world." (*Essays*, 92)[1]

Such reminding takes dramatic form in both *Middlemarch* and *Daniel Deronda*, where the great dead are ushered in and asked to become human again, so that a continuity between past and present might be restored. Conversely, the petty, anonymous associates of our "working-day" lives are given a measure of greatness, through the linkages with the "Shining Ones," and through the use of what I call the reaffirmed heroic voice. That is, Eliot approaches us with a presumed disparity between past and present, with apparently mock-heroic and laughable differences between the great "gone-by" and the small "at hand," and then undercuts that presumption by having us recognize the once living pettiness of those who are now conveniently and grandly dead and the greatness of those who are our contemporary companions and who are perhaps inconveniently close.

To begin with, we might consider a very simple example of the mock-heroic when Mrs. Cadwallader refers to Mr. Casaubon as "our Lowick Cicero." Here the past certainly diminishes the present, and, in fact, on the same page, she herself is said to be "a lady of immeasurably high birth, descended, as it were, from unknown earls, dim as the crowd of heroic shades" (ch. 6, 76), showing that the narrator is capable of sharing Mrs. Cadwallader's edge. Later, however, this voice itself is mocked when Mr. Casaubon is presented as feeling "as if he suddenly found himself on the dark river-brink and heard the plash of the oncoming oar, not discerning the forms, but expecting the summons" (ch. 42, 462), where the underworld is invoked not to create derision but sympathy, and where, with the aid of the reaffirmed heroic voice, Mr. Casaubon becomes a man of flesh and blood and physical fear.

Both methods are alive in another, apparently characteristic section of *Middlemarch*, where Eliot develops a familiar comedy of comparing contemporary smallness with past grandeur:

> In fact much the same sort of movement and mixture went on in old England as we find in older Herodotus, who also, in telling what had been, thought it well to take a woman's lot for his starting point; though Io, as a maiden apparently beguiled by attractive merchandise, was the reverse of Miss Brooke, and in this respect perhaps bore more resemblance to Rosamond Vincy, who had excellent taste in costume, with the nymph-like figure and pure blindness which gave the largest range to choice in the flow and colour of drapery. (ch. 11, 122–23)

The effects of dimunition and perspective are clear; one sees Rosamond (and Dorothea) better by having her compared, laughingly, to Io; one sees Lydgate (and his overweening pride) better by having him compared to the lustful Jove. The immediate effects of the mock-heroic characterization are very much like those of "The Rape of the Lock." But there is more here than meets the "eye." The narrator has a chatty familiarity with his or her source, who seems, in some ways, to be exhumed in a most friendly way. While the mock-heroic depends on a shadow effect where the past broods diminishingly over the present, some of the present here is brooding back: "as we find in older Herodotus, who also, in telling what had been, thought it well. . ." (123). Herodotus appears as a character, a living man, rather than the dead author of a classical text. The effect comes from Eliot having him think beyond the actual text of his history; he belongs to a vital world, a world connected with that of the more immediate Middlemarch, a sphere of motion and process. And it is as though this reaffirmed heroic voice, capable of making the past as well as the present alive, has not only exhumed but resuscitated him.

A clearer and yet more complex example comes in her famous invocation of Fielding, who arrives as the novel's epic muse instead of Calliope:

> A great historian, as he insisted on calling himself, who had the happiness to be dead a hundred and twenty years ago, and so to take his place among the colossi whose huge legs our living pettiness is observed to walk under, glories in his copious remarks and digressions as the least imitable part of his work, and especially in those initial chapters to the successive books of his history, where he seems to bring his armchair to the proscenium and chat with us in all the lusty ease of his fine English. (ch. 15, 170)

Here what I would call the "compensatory shadow" of the present is even more evident. Fielding may be a colossus and dwarf our lives the way the amours of Olympus dwarfed those of Middlemarch, but Fielding is also dead. It is as though all the doubts Eliot had about words, whether written or spoken, are coming out again in a subtle attack on the idea of prestige and "life in print." Paradoxically, however, the moment this attack occurs, Fielding springs to life; the historical man acquires the present tense of the literary one, with the addition that, the chatty and familiar narrator supplies some of the furniture—a "proscenium" as well as an "arm-chair." Saying we have a reaffirmed heroic voice in our ears is to say we have playfulness and intimacy, since the original mock-heroic always brings laughter and dimunition through accentuated disparity and a sense that the past is grand but dead. Although Fielding was a colossus in the first sentence, his "huge legs" fall like those of Ozymandias in the second, and he ends up on a "camp-stool in a parrot-house," which is presumably located somewhere in and around Middlemarch.

But there is compensatory light as well as shadow. We have already seen how Fielding gains some postmortem breath by being brought into the "particular web" of the novel, and it is also clear that the thunderous roll of this paragraph gains (along with its inhabitants) some special grandeur by echoing the prestigious Fielding, a Fielding mocked and brought down to size—not only by the deflating picture but also by the parody in the slightly circumlocutory sentences. The particular web would seem less important, had not Fielding, unlucky fly (see Spenser's "Muiopotmos"), been caught in it.

To illustrate the reaffirmed voice further, let us also consider chapter 3 of *Middlemarch*, which pictures the pedagogic Casaubon standing before the adoring Dorothea:

> For he had been as instructive as Milton's "affable archangel"; and with something of the archangelic manner he told her how he had undertaken to show that all the mythical systems or erratic mythical

fragments in the world were corruptions of a tradition originally re-
vealed. (46)

As we read further into the scene, we also discover that Mr. Casaubon's memory is "a volume where a *vide supra* could serve instead
of repetitions" (49). The *vide supra* cues us back to the top of the
chapter, its epigraph, which, somewhat devilishly and like a wall-
hung engraving of a *Paradise Lost* tableau, has angel and human
slightly breaking character; their smiles are just perceptibly imp-
ish and a bit urbane. Certainly the past overshadows the present
in a mock-heroic way; Casaubon and Dorothea are put into their
proper perspective, but at the same time, Eve and Raphael, who,
in another sense, have the happiness to be extinct, gain new life
by rubbing shoulders with the living characters. This effect, in
plainer form, comes up again when Dorothea is presented juxta-
posed to the reclining marble Ariadne, "a breathing blooming girl,
whose form, not shamed by the Ariadne, was clad in Quakerish
grey drapery" (ch. 19, 220). The reclining Ariadne becomes more
alive, too, just by Dorothea's proximity, and Dorothea is made
more grand by her nonsatirical connection with the classical
heroine.

Another example of the reaffirmed heroic voice arrives when,
quite startlingly, Casaubon is presented at Milton's expense rather
than vice-versa:

> . . . and even Milton, looking for his portrait in a spoon, must submit
> to have the facial angle of a bumpkin. Moreover, if Mr. Casaubon,
> speaking for himself, has rather chilling rhetoric, it is not therefore
> certain that there is no good work or fine feeling in him. (ch. 10, 110)

It seems here that Milton, as created by the overly familiar, slightly
irreverent narrator, is becoming as much a character in the novel
as the inhabitants of nineteenth-century provincial society. The
present, in overshadowing the past, has also spread its light and
brought Milton to rise from the grave and to be ushered immediately—as is appropriate in a "home epic"—into the kitchen. Because the colossal image of Milton is embroidered with laughable
particulars, with the compensation that his dead image is brought
back into preposterous life, so Casaubon, originally preposterous,
is given more vitality and depth by acquiring some of the Miltonic
shine. As Felicia Bonaparte writes, "The surprising inversion in
the angle of vision assures us that 'superlative' and ludicrous characteristics inhere not in men but in the point of view" (*Will*, 168).

And this inversion arises because Milton has been restored to his proper state of anonymity. We see him as he "is" or was, stripped of his state of "celebrity."

What, Eliot seems to ask, is self-importance? If the "great divide" of prestige is pushed aside as insignificant, then the prophet, the seer, and the genius join in the dangerous company of the fanatic, the crank, and the dilettante. Anonymity causes us to redefine, continually, what we mean by living a hidden life faithfully, even those of us who became famous after we passed from this life. In a work as early as "Mr. Gilfil's Love Story," the narrator speaks of the eccentric Sir Christopher, who created his Gothic mansion, much to the dismay of his neighbors, and offers this tribute:

> But I, who have seen Cheverel Manor, as he bequeathed it to his heirs, rather attribute that unswerving architectural purpose of his, conceived and carried out through long years of systematic personal exertion, to something of the fervour of genius, as well as inflexibility of will; and in walking through those rooms, with their splendid ceilings and their meagre furniture, which tell how all the spare money had been absorbed before personal comfort was thought of, I have felt that there dwelt in this old English baronet some of that sublime spirit which distinguished art from luxury, and worships beauty apart from self-indulgence. (ch. 4, 159)

Detecting this fervour of genius is at the heart of *Middlemarch* with all its subterranean intellects, and it forms the heart of the fascination one feels for many of the characters in *Daniel Deronda*. Frequently we must ask ourselves if Klesmer, Mordecai, Mab, Gwendolen, and Deronda himself are fools, geniuses, dilettantes, seers, or all four, since instead of being enshrined in a Legion of Honor, they are placed on one of the most sustained roads to Emmaus which Eliot created. The epigraphs to the chapters and the allusions within them only serve to accentuate what *Middlemarch* began earlier: the development of both the mock- and the reaffirmed heroic voices, whereby the contemporary populace is elevated to Parnassus as well as laughed at and the Shining Ones are invited into the gambling spa and stable as well as the Pantheon.

Quite early in the Deronda story, when Mirah "rescues"[2] the hero and leads him, via destiny, to his friends the Meyricks, the narrator backs up and describes the household this way:

Outside, the house looked very narrow and shabby, the bright light through the holland blind showing the heavy old-fashioned window-frame; but it is pleasant to know that many such grim-walled slices of space in our foggy London have been, and still are the homes of a culture the more spotlessly free from vulgarity, because poverty has rendered everything like display an impersonal question, and all the grand shows of the world simply a spectacle which rouses no petty rivalry or vain effort after possession. (ch. 18, 237)

It is interesting that Eliot, in her very last novel and her only one with a contemporary setting, would finally create the scene promised in the manifesto chapter of *Adam Bede* seventeen years earlier, where "an old woman bend[s] over her flower-pot, or eating her solitary dinner, while the noonday light, softened perhaps by a screen of leaves, falls on her mob-cap" is extolled. As the manifesto implies, in *Daniel Deronda* the light of recognition transforms, redeems all; we have a plain matron reading aloud to her daughters by candlelight, a tableau enclosed by a rough exterior but still made beautiful within, through the selection of detail. But surprisingly enough, the narrator of *Adam Bede* had extolled this picture at the expense of "cloud-borne angels . . . prophets, sibyls, and heroic warriors" (152), and here in *Daniel Deronda*, we find hung on Mrs. Meyrick's wall the very things the narrator had thrown out a decade and a half before: "the Virgin soaring amid her cherubic escort, grand Melancholia with her solemn universe; the Prophets and Sibyls; the School of Athens; the Last Supper; mystic groups where far-off ages made one moment; grave Holbein and Rembrandt heads; the Tragic Muse; last-century children at their musings or their play; Italian poets,—all were there through the medium of a little black and white" (ch. 20, 249–50). As suggested earlier in the Introduction, we are as close as we will ever be to Eliot's creative center. The literary corollary to this erudite parlor can be found in the very chapters of Eliot's later novels themselves: an erudite ornament or epigraph followed by a homey, more immediate context. In line with the example of Mrs. Meyrick and her literary compatriot Mrs. Garth, we are asked to embrace the petty medium of the present, to accept our anonymity and then to bring the greatness of the past back anyway by recognizing continuity. In this context, even the ardently romantic Meyrick sisters seem right, when they ask their brother to paint Deronda as a Prince Camaralzaman, and thus we can only conclude that Eliot's esthetics had sufficiently expanded, between

Adam Bede and *Daniel Deronda,* so as to bridge the immediate with the heroic.

The painting—not the engravings by themselves—but the entire aggregate portrait Eliot has created seems altogether "postmodern." In an age where the protagonist has only "bas-reliefs of Milton and Dante" (ch. 43, 606) in his study, and the second-hand bookshop he passes presents "the literature of the ages . . . in judicious mixture, from the immortal verse of Homer to the mortal prose of the railway novel" (ch. 33, 435), the resonance of past heroism can only be reclaimed by mocking the present through ludicrous juxtaposition and then affirm what is continuous just the same. On a broader scale, this is what Eliot does, in the counterpoint structure, by advancing Grandcourt as the failed and obsolete romantic hero first and then offering a redemption of that image in the form of Deronda. When—to draw from our own age—Umberto Eco defines what postmodernism is, he arrives at this same double movement: "I think of the postmodern attitude as that of a man who loves a very cultivated woman and knows he cannot say to her 'I love you madly', because he knows that she knows (and that she knows that he knows) that these words have already been written by Barbara Cartland. Still there is a solution. He can say 'As Barbara Cartland would put it, I love you madly'" (67). In the chapter where Deronda begins to affirm Mordecai's significance, the narrator says:

> In the heroic drama, great recognitions are not encumbered with these details; and certainly Deronda had as reverential an interest in Mordecai and Mirah as he could have had in the offspring of Agamemnon; but he was caring for destinies still moving in the dim streets of our earthly life, not yet lifted among the constellations, and his task presented itself to him as difficult and delicate, especially in persuading Mordecai to change his abode and habits. (ch. 43, 604)

This is a strong "but"; of course we cannot see the world the way Homer saw it, and yet of course we can if we laugh first and revere later—that is, move on ahead, on the road to Emmaus, to recognize the greatness of our associates anyway—in this case by making living arrangements for the ailing Mordecai. It is no accident that Hans Meyrick, the mouthpiece for mock-heroism in the story, is the son of Mrs. Meyrick and is also a painter. And indeed in his long letter of chapter 52, one which F. R. Leavis dismisses for its "utterly routing Shakespearean sprightliness" (83), he adopts the perfect mocking tone, calling Gwendolen a "fair Supralapsarian," which she is and isn't, and calling the now married

Klesmers luminaries who shine forth as "might be expected from the planets of genius and fortune in conjunction" (709). Hans supplies the distance, and his mother's vision—and those of his sisters—supply the romance which closes it.

In *Daniel Deronda*, life's mystery is—we do not know who the heroes of the future will be, even though they are presently walking at our side. Suppose indeed they are ourselves? Thus, we must develop those voices that help shape the proper attitude of sympathetic detection. The mystery case put to Deronda is not so much his identity as a Jewish man as it is the question of his Hebraic background as it emerges through the anonymous heroism of a man perceived to be a fanatic. Will Deronda, the narrator eventually asks, have the greatness to recognize greatness in his own time—or to cast it in *Middlemarch* terms, to recognize "tragedy in the very fact of frequency"? How convenient it would be if all that were happening now were in the past, among immediately recognizable heroes, and prestige and fame could do the work for him. This is a pressure and a longing which even the grand Romola feels. How convenient if Mordecai, or Ezra Cohen, had the name of Agamemnon. At once the dramatic role of the reaffirmed heroic voice becomes clear; the narrator is returning the Shining Ones to their proper state of mystery, that is, to their original anonymity among their peers, so that the reader can share in Deronda's detective work rather than patronizing it by borrowing on the perspective of time.

Almost all of chapter 41 is given as an explanation of this drama. Heading the pivotal book 6, entitled "Revelations," the chapter offers a rational critique of the predominance of reason:

> Reduce the grandest type of man hitherto known to an abstract statement of his qualities and efforts and he appears in dangerous company: say that, like Copernicus and Galileo, he was immovably convinced in the face of hissing incredulity; but so is the contriver of perpetual motion. We cannot fairly try the spirits by this sort of test. If we want to avoid giving the dose of hemlock or the sentence of banishment in the wrong case, nothing will do but a capacity to understand the subject-matter on which the immovable man is convinced, and fellowship with human travail, both near and afar, to hinder us from scanning any deep experience lightly. Shall we say, "let the ages try the spirits, and see what they are worth"? Why, we are the beginning of the ages, which can only be just by virtue of just judgments in separate human breasts, separate yet combined. (569)

Here is a new key to Eliot's mythology. We achieve immortality, for ourselves and others, in our detective work—which raises both them and ourselves to the level of myth. We become the present-day makers of heroes the moment we take the leap of faith required to acknowledge them. Thus, the most important moment in Deronda's life is not his marriage to Mirah, his journey to the East, his confessing of Gwendolen, or even his discovery of Mordecai, but rather, his inward cry of "yes, greatness" when he gives up "reason" in chapter 43 and privately affirms "this consumptive Jewish workman in threadbare clothing" (604) as his mentor—but only after the heroic voices have invoked, disspelled, and reaffirmed the names of Agamemnon, Orestes, and Iphigenia alongside the man.

In an illuminating article, Marianne Novy has pointed out that Deronda is the closest personal link we can find with Eliot's narrators and her own autobiographical life (*Women's Re-Visions*, 101). This is true not only because out of all of her novels, Deronda is the character who adopts the most points of view but also because he occupies the unusual position of "protagonist as chorus." While we would expect him to have a more subordinate role, since his mission is, primarily, to observe the lives of Mordecai and Gwendolen, Eliot, much to the dismay of some critics[3], assigns him a full narrative life. The generous attention given to his quest allows the full steps of his detective work to become "widely visible," so that no finale will be necessary; the elegy is ongoing rather than cumulative and final.

Such detective work changes our understanding of what literary forms are, tragedy in particular, and in another "engraving" of an epigraph, the one, in fact, quoted in my Introduction, the highly erudite narrator, somewhat in the manner of another favorite painter, Piero di Cosimo[4], says:

> There be who hold that the deeper tragedy were a Prometheus Bound not *after* but *before* he had well got the celestial fire into the νάρθηξ whereby it might be conveyed to mortals: thrust by Kratos and Bix of instituted methods into a solitude of despised ideas, fastened in throbbing helplessness by the fatal pressure of poverty and disease— a solitude where many pass by, but none regard. (ch.38, 527)

Prometheus is an excellent case in point, because he throws the *agons* of both Mordecai and Gwendolen into bold relief. On the one hand, we can say that before the fire incident, Prometheus had to deal with his own anonymity; such are the tragedies of Mordecai and Gwendolen, who have mute patience as the major part of their emotional challenges. In a recent edition of *Prometh-*

eus Bound, Mark Griffith characterizes Kratos and Bia as having "ugly manners" (6). Surely there could be no better description of what the anonymous hero and heroine must abide—in this case, in the form of Grandcourt and Mirah's father.

On the other hand, we can also say that Prometheus Bound—that is, after the theft of fire—is indeed another perfect iconographic symbol of anonymous heroism, since pinioned to his Caucausian rock, he finds again that all honor and glory are lost to him and he must depend on a chorus of apparently insignificant sea nymphs to give his life shape and meaning. To offer another allusion, like the Dantean trees summoned in the prologue to *Felix Holt,* these characters arrest our attention precisely because they cannot move even within the confines of their own tragedies. Thus, little separates the presumably passive Deronda from the two people he observes, and thus little separates the necessarily passive reader from them or him, or the narrator who hangs the iconographic symbol on the wall. As Gillian Beer writes, "In this book, the surge of anger, vengeance and compassion keeps freezing into tableaux," and the collection of silences issues in an extraordinary sense of intimacy between reader and character, where "the process of reading is assimilated very tightly to the silent movement of thought within us" (214).

In the *Prometheus* epigraph of *Daniel Deronda,* it is also important to note that the overall tone, while not exactly playful, is not strictly somber, either. The Greek symbols and the antiquated diction are deliberately ornate and obtrusive, and the change of typeface has the effect of a misprint; like the *vide supra,* it reminds us, heavily, that we are reading a book.[5] Overall, the scholastic prose bristles like a heavily carved baroque chair, and it slightly satirizes the classical erudition that would be associated with the Promethean story, so that, freed of pretense, it can apply directly to the modern-day prophet depicted in the ensuing chapter. The Greek characters form a contrast with their English associates, just as the dusty story forms a contrast with the contemporary one. But all is born anew when the narrator, with a degree of scholastic sportiveness, revises the original tragedy, breaks the spell of prestigious myth, returns Prometheus to his state of anonymous heroism and develops a bridge to the prophet at hand. Would a reader even completely ignorant of Greek be unable to guess what νάρθηξ really means, once the life of the myth becomes clear?

The epigraphs and the asides are not all that bring the sense of reaffirmed heroism to the novel. A number of critics have pointed out that Herr Klesmer is one of the few portraits of true genius in Eliot—and indeed in all of English fiction.[6] If he is a "true" genius, one modeled perhaps on Liszt or Mendelssohn, then he is here with the expressed ironic purpose of mocking celebrity and affirming anonymity as a way of life. "Klesmer was not yet a Liszt" (ch. 22, 280) is a very important statement; like her fashioned composer, Eliot is only interested in those artistic quests that precede recognition by the outer world, if indeed it ever arrives, and like Deronda, who "had often made stories about Pericles or Columbus, just to fill up the blanks before they became famous" (ch. 15, 206–7), she focuses on that time of life when prestige does not blur the question of faith. In terms of her earlier essay on Liszt, Eliot centers on that Promethean courage that gambles on supporting mankind, rather than on any actual "cashing in" on any gratitude forthcoming from the minute beings. Klesmer may, in some ways, be genuinely like Ulysses or Milton, but if he is, he must also hold up Milton's spoon and stare into it, sharing the same awkwardness and anonymity while he plays the country bumpkin in a superficially refined and small-minded society:

> Draped in a loose garment with a Florentine *berretta* on his head, he would have been fit to stand by the side of Leonardo da Vinci; but how when he presented himself in trousers which were not what English feeling demanded about the knees?—and when the fire that showed itself in his glances and the movements of his head, as he looked round him with curiosity, was turned into comedy by a hat which ruled that mankind should have well-cropped hair and a staid demeanour, such, for example, as Mr. Arrowpoint's, whose nullity of face and perfect tailoring might pass everywhere without ridicule? One sees why it is often better for greatness to be dead, and to have got rid of the outward man. (ch. 10, 136)

Klesmer is assigned the task of assessing Gwendolen's potential for accepting her own anonymity, and his mission parallels the detective work which Deronda, with apparently much greater success, directs toward Mordecai. One might immediately say, however, that while Gwendolen apparently fails the test, by refusing the artist's lot of "unsung" heroism, the "audition" of chapter 23 sets in motion all the elements that constitute Gwendolen's paradoxical growth and recognition by the end of the novel. Although Jennifer Uglow argues that "the musicians and poetic visionaries in *Daniel Deronda* are the equivalent of the 'great souls' in *Middlemarch* . . . [and] Gwendolen is excluded from this vocation just as certainly as she is excluded from Daniel's Jewish destiny" (234), we will see how the heroine does become a "great soul" and surely an artist but in the context of the novel's extraordinary conclusion.

To begin with, one might say that Gwendolen's education is also a way of allowing us to see the Promethean myth and "heroic Promethean effort" anew. In the early chapters of the novel, she is mocked by the narrator, and yet this mockery is later undercut by the editorial asides and by the complex structure of the story, so that we can view her with sympathy. For example, in chapter 3, Gwendolen strikes an attitude and stands by an organ, posing as St. Cecilia, the saint of song and music. While one might smile thinking of Dryden's ode or sharing in Witemeyer's belief that "every time we are invited to admire her in a picturesque attitude, our response is qualified by our peripheral awareness that she has calculated the visual effect and admires it too" (63–64), Gwendolen's consciousness can be seen as at least partially right, as well, if one allows one irony to cancel out another. The whole scene occurs as flashback, whose "return" will present us once again with Gwendolen stripped of Offendene and truly solicitous of her mother. Eliot's earlier statement in "Notes on Form in Art," that "in the later development of poetic fable the αναγνωρισις tends to consist in the discernment of a previously unrecognized *character*" is already applicable here, even though we are no further than the third chapter. Gwendolen's future self, whom we have already met in chapter 1, stands just behind the woman posing as the saint at the organ, and the mock-heroic statement is mocked back; Gwendolen is much deeper than our immediate ridiculing might allow.

On a broader scale, part of the anagnorisis of the entire novel has to do with the "rejected Gwendolen" who imbues every page. Frequently we have the disturbing feeling that we are reading a book that is even more mistitled than *Felix Holt* or that we are curiously examining the intricacies of a young woman's history in a subsection called "Mordecai." The eclipse is everywhere, and in one reading, Bonnie Zimmerman has traced the problem to Eliot's goal of offering us an androgynous male hero in tandem with his patriarchal mentor, as a means of avoiding the political implications of Gwendolen's eventual psychological imprisonment as a woman (Nathan, 231–36). This is a hard argument to resist, and one might push it even a step further by saying that the Deronda-Gwendolen-Mordecai triangle is just that, an undisclosed menage à trois, with Deronda "throwing over" Gwendolen for the man with whom he feels "as intense a consciousness as if they had been two undeclared lovers" (ch. 40, 552). (Also see Zimmerman, "George Eliot's Sacred Chest," Booth, 165). The effect of this rejection, whether foreshadowed or at hand, is to reject the ridicule, whether from the narrator or the characters, which settles in on "the spoiled child." Gwendolen's chastened character is before us virtually from the first sentence of the novel; it is the anagnorisis that provides the light and shadow needed to cause our hearts to "burn" for her. The presence of Mirah only heightens this effect, for what Zimmerman says of the final Gwendolen—that she arrives at a state of "tired, spiritless, self-sacrificing femininity" (235)—really applies more to her rival. The difference between Mirah and Gwendolen at the close of book has to do with the difference, crucial in Eliot, between facelessness and anonymity, paralysis and serenity of mind.

The journey toward this final state begins just when the flashback ends, and the focus on Herr Klesmer helps to clarify how Eliot sees "significance" and "insignificance." In the chapter just prior to the audition, Mrs. Arrowpoint, in a manner parallel, as mentioned earlier, to Mr. Brooke, is suddenly confronted with the unreality of her literary life, "when what she had safely demanded of the dead Leonora was enacted by her own Catherine" (ch. 22, 288), and Klesmer is suddenly presented to her as a prospective son-in-law. In other words, the plot has taken a reaffirmed heroic turn.

> Mrs. Arrowpoint's state of mind was pitiable. Imagine Jean Jacques, after his essay on the corrupting influence of the arts, waking up among children of nature who had no idea of grilling the raw bone they offered him for breakfast with the primitive *couvert* of a flint; or Saint Just, after fervidly denouncing all recognition of pre-eminence, receiving a vote of thanks for the unbroken mediocrity of his speech. (288)

Suddenly the living reality of humanized genius is pushed into the pathway of the aristocratic subterranean intellectual, the way Milton and Fielding, Columbus and Copernicus have been or will be pushed into the pathway of the reader. Up until this point, Klesmer, prematurely apotheosized, had been as conveniently distant from Mrs. Arrowpoint's life as a dead and canonized author on a shelf. Now he is taking up a growing corner of her life that will encompass her own daughter.

Thus, the threat that Klesmer poses—that of the lessons of anonymous heroism—is established even before it intrudes on

Gwendolen's life. One might also say, however, that the previous episode involving Mrs. Arrowpoint and her historical companions Jean Jacques and Saint Just deflects a great deal of the mockery away from Gwendolen, so that we might be inclined to see our heroine more as the vulnerable Marian Evans, faced with the terrorism of literary critics. Indeed, we would have to extend the corollary and say she is a young Marian Evans, had Marian shown her early sketches to a sympathetic male mentor, without confidence and without yet the protection of a persona. In addition, the previous example of Catherine Arrowpoint's defiance of polite society plays a surprisingly softening function in our perceptions of the apparently inflated Gwendolen. Although Catherine might be taken as a morally chastening contrast to Gwendolen's self-doubt and fear of artistic exile, as Gillian Beer certainly insists (220), she proves to be more like the Greek characters in the Promethean epigraph—that is, showing acute similarity once the glaring contrast has been admitted. The light and shade of her character promise what Gwendolen will be at the end of the novel: "but she was one of those satisfactory creatures whose intercourse has the charm of discovery; whose integrity of faculty and expression begets a wish to know what they will say on all subjects, or how they will perform whatever they undertake; so that they end up raising not only a continual expectation but a continual sense of fulfilment" (ch. 22, 282). The continuity with Catherine Arrowpoint also comes from the anagnorisis of seeing Gwendolen before and after Offendene; in a sense we have seen her in exile already.

During Klesmer's audition, Gwendolen is, then, perfectly positioned to hear the statement that Eliot has been making implicitly throughout her first seven books of fiction but has waited until now to voice directly: "you must not be thinking of celebrity:-put that candle out of your eyes and look only at excellence" (299). The pose, mocked earlier, of Gwendolen-as-Hermione, is brought back, and through a dismissal of the apparent disparity, it is now a truly pathetic analogy. When Klesmer informs her, "You would at first only be accepted on trial. You would have to bear what I may call a glaring insignificance" (303), she is the dethroned queen facing a life of anonymity—the only life, in Klesmer's and Eliot's terms, worthy of a true artist, of a hidden life "lived faithfully," where "you will hardly achieve more than mediocrity" (303). Gwendolen's flight to the imprisonment of Gadsmere and eventually Grandcourt's yacht arises from her unwillingness to be a subterranean intellectual.

Having said all of this, however, we need to acknowledge what is becoming enormously apparent—the wide disparity of sympathy between Gwendolen on the one hand and almost everybody else on the other, a disparity that at least one reading of this novel brings.[7] This may arise, in fact, from the paradox that the spokesmen for anonymity in the book—Klesmer and Deronda, in particular—lose some of it in speaking in its behalf. In the audition, particularly towards its conclusion, Klesmer teeters on the edge of self-inflation, as does Deronda, during the New Year's celebration at the Abbey, when he gives Gwendolen directions on making her fear a safeguard: "Deronda, too was under that sense of pressure which is apt to come when our own winged words seem to be hovering around us" (ch. 36, 508). Of all the characters in the vast dramatis personae, Gwendolen is, ultimately and ironically, the one we will expect never to act in bad faith once the novel is over, since her education unrelentingly divests her of ego, never leading her to full illumination until virtually the last paragraph. In other words, she never has the chance to feel she has art (as does Klesmer) or religion (as does Deronda) at her back. In a novel that so closely links esthetics and morality through a sense of anonymity, this means that the Gwendolen of the very last sentences is to be the greater soul: a status that causes the reader to reevaluate her capacity for art and artistic receptivity itself.

To illustrate, we might say that during the audition, Gwendolen answers Klesmer's criticisms with "I did not pretend to genius," a statement that ironically opens her up to the beauties of Mirah's and Klesmer's music later on and to sympathies that neither Deronda nor Klesmer can attract, because her ego is, from henceforth, peculiarly vulnerable. Moreover, some of the moments of sublimest esthetic perception come from the "Vandyke duchess," because her dethronement is an ongoing process and because anonymity is a goal for her rather than—as it is for her mentors—something nearly or already achieved. Although Eliot could have easily narrated the wonderfully orchestrated chapel epiphany through Deronda's eyes,[8] Eliot gives Gwendolen's point of view one of the longest sentences in the novel, in an attempt to explain her heroine's "Oh, this is glorious!" immediately afterwards, as well as her "forgetfulness of everything but the immediate impression" (ch. 35, 473).

In this sense, Gwendolen is a better vessel of poetry than even Mordecai, since "the chief poetic energy" is earlier defined as "the force of imagination that pierces or exalts the solid fact, instead of floating among cloud-pictures. To glory in a prophetic vision of knowledge covering the earth is an easier exercise of believing imagination than to see its beginning in newspaper placards, staring at you from a bridge beyond the cornfields" (ch. 33, 431). By this definition, what is more poetic than seeing the beauty of a chapel-as-stable? Although Hans Meyrick may refer to Gwendolen as the "Vandyke duchess," the mock-heroism bows to our other impression that in some ways Gwendolen shares some of the properties of Vandyke, while providing a dynamism that goes beyond the allusion. Her resting point is not yet achieved and never will be. Partly because anonymity arrives late for Gwendolen, she holds the singular position of always being in a process of becoming, a role that makes her more artistic and attractive than the three male protagonists, who, lacking spontaneity at least, become fixed relatively early, even though they say the right things about yielding up one's ego to higher concerns. In this sense, she fulfills Eliot's early model of an artist, as defined by her description of her friend Macarthy, who makes an elegaic appearance in her very early "Poetry and Prose, from the Notebook of an Eccentric," and whose soul "was of exquisite structure . . . a bird endowed with rich and varied notes" but "the poor bird ceased to sing, save in the depths of the forest or the silence of the night" (Pinney, 14–15).

To put it a different way, Gwendolen begins by turning away from the opportunity to be schooled in anonymous heroism and yet ends up on the road to anonymity anyway by making the wrong marriage decision and finding the education of her supersensitive nature in a highly tragic quarter. Her eventual willingness to be schooled—and in particular by the opposite sex—in matters utterly foreign to her causes her to share an apparently unlikely kinship with Silas Marner. As she gives up recognition from the outside world, she also opens herself to the masculine side of her psyche. She acquires aspects of Deronda's male and patriarchal character, just as Silas acquires female and matriarchal components from Dolly. Key moments in both novels come when the education issues in a defense of the beloved against male domination. Gwendolen rising up against Grandcourt's disparagement of Deronda as a shameless lord with a satellite mistress (ch. 48)[9] is parallel to Silas's refusal to bow, unquestioningly, to Godfrey's claims to counteradoption.

The sense of unsettledness of the end of *Daniel Deronda* may stem at least in part from the fact that, contrary to the usual patterns of anonymous heroism, Mordecai and Deronda do not open themselves to schooling by the opposite sex and stand firmly planted on the patriarchal premises of Judaism. Thus, they seem to shadow over Gwendolen at the novel's conclusion and cause a questioning of her triumph. The androgynous evolution that we have seen in Lydgate—as a direct response to his personal suffering—we simply cannot find in Deronda in the final scene of the novel that bears his name. Mirah has learned from him, but what has he learned from Mirah, or indeed from any other woman in the book—his mother included?

In fact, earlier in the book, just at the moment when Deronda's all-dominant presence should command more of our attention and cause us to rejoice in his emerging visions of the Holy Land, one of Eliot's most striking uses of the reaffirmed heroic voice turns our sympathies squarely in Gwendolen's favor, leaving Deronda behind. Just prior to the drowning, the narrator compares the heroine to Madonna Pia of the *Purgatory*, all at the former epic's expense:

> And thus, without any hardness to the poor Tuscan lady who had her deliverance long ago, one may feel warranted in thinking of her with a less sympathetic interest than of the better known Gwendolen who, instead of being delivered from her errors on earth and cleansed from their effect in purgatory, is at the very height of her entanglement in those fatal meshes which are woven within more closely than without, and often make the inward torture disproportionate to what is discernible as outward cause. (ch. 54, 731–32)

The quote thus provides a pivot. Because "she had a root of conscience in her and the process of purgatory had begun for her on the green earth" (733), Gwendolen overshadows the celebrated Tuscan lady, and her triumph becomes clear. After the jaunty reference to the Siennese husband having "got rid of her there," the narrator works to put Gwendolen one level above even *The Divine Comedy*, because while Gwendolen is lesser known to the outer world, she is better known to the reader.

Also paradoxically, at the end of the novel, when Gwendolen is "reduced to a mere speck," her identity becomes huge, because her anonymity has outstripped that of any other character. Mary Wilson Carpenter has noted that

> whereas Daniel has recently been given the key to his father's chest, suggesting a restoration of history for him, Gwendolen seems to have received no inheritance but that of a penitential existence at Offendene. . . . the union of the narratives in a history of humanity in exile

still suggests a romantic fulfillment only from the Jewish perspective. (140)

Yet her absence from the last chapter is grandly, sublimely conspicuous; her renunciation larger than any in the Jewish parts of the book because her name has been spectacularly missing from her own story. While Mordecai dies in an orchestrated apotheosis, she is only granted a note much like Lydgate's at the end of her own story. Thus, the superiority of her education is made abundantly manifest not only by her absence but because of it. As in the case of her narrator, her anonymity yields to omnipresence. Mordecai is given the novel's tragic and Miltonic epitaph, but because Gwendolen is the unnamed heroine behind it, she receives the greater glory. And again she parallels her narrator. As the narrator of the novel is subsumed in the final chorus of Milton's last major work, so is Gwendolen, reminding us, in the reaffirmed heroic voice, that the book has had little to do with killing whole multitudes by pulling down Philistine pillars, but everything to do with a young woman who was afraid of criticism at first but ended up most nobly accepting her anonymity.

This is a turn towards a new age, when the apparent pastness of heroism is a given. "I have been reading—after Fielding," Vladimir Nabokov once wrote to Edmund Wilson, "a very curious fat book, with incredible Victorian coils of coyness about it—*Daniel Deronda* by G. Eliot" (283). One wonders, if, as a predecessor of postmodernism and as one fascinated by the "neo-Homeric metaphor" (*Transparent Things,* 156), he was referring to the reaffirmed heroic voice. Perhaps he also meant the way the book coyly attacks our sense of canon—although we would have to add that her revisionist outlook is quite different from what is being done today. Eliot does not change our assumptions about tradition by painting a new Mona Lisa or disparaging the old one—as some twentieth century artists were known to do—by painting on a moustache or changing her smile into a leer. Rather, it is done by having Mona Lisa sit down, perhaps, to dinner after three steady days of riding by rail and by coach, and by having her get slightly irritated with the delay of dinner or nonplussed with the crumbs in her lap. "Hamlet, Prince of Denmark," the narrator writes in a similarly irreverent vein in *The Mill on the Floss,* "was speculative and irresolute, and we have a great tragedy in consequence. But if his father had lived to a good old age, and his uncle had died an early death, we can conceive Hamlet's having married Ophelia, and got through life with a reputation of sanity, notwithstanding many soliloquies, and some moody sarcasm towards the fair daughter of Polonius, to say nothing of the frankest incivility to his father-in-law" (351, book 6, 6). Nonetheless, our final impression of Mona Lisa, like that of Hamlet in the version just quoted, would be all the more luminous, because the fun-making always would bring new vitality to the dignity of the original. Leonardo's magic mountains behind his celebrated subject would be restored again in our minds, right along with her smile, all in the beauty of unabashed pigments and joyous artifice. And in looking again, we might even see some subtle but surprising additions of lamps in a few contemporary cottages—a writers' or artists' colony perhaps—adorning the lakefront and backdrop of our mental recollection of the classic painting. And all because Eliot went beyond the mock-heroic to the reaffirmed.

If postmodernism dances in its "pastness," is joyously reconstructive, in every sense of that word, resisting the formulaic downward spirals of modernism, reaffirming the anonymous heroics of the unknown artist, and yet accentuating its artiness by flourishing the pen or paintbrush in the audience's face, then *Daniel Deronda* is an important ancestor. Virginia Woolf perhaps caught her mistress's influence most acutely when, at the conclusion of *To the Lighthouse*, she had Lily Briscoe accept her anonymity and then move on to finish her painting just the same:

> Quickly, as if she were recalled by something over there, she turned to her canvas. There it was—her picture. Yes, with all its greens and blues, its lines running up and across, its attempt at something. It would be hung in the attics, she thought; it would be destroyed. But what did that matter? she asked herself, taking up her brush again. (310)

Is there anyone, even Herr Klesmer himself, who better pursued excellence, better transcended "celebrity" in its behalf, than did Gwendolen and her compatriot Lily Briscoe?[10] Although this transcendence might seem like a negation of identity, really it is a plenitude, a dramatic one, from which all the other characters of the novel spring—as indeed all the novels, according to Eliot, sprang from the author's "not herself." Without Gwendolen's education towards anonymity, we would have none of the other "characters" who take their form against her extraordinary background.

It is telling that Eliot chose the story of Prometheus for her last book. It harkens back to a grand allusion in *Middlemarch*, which admiringly compares Lydgate to the heroes of the Renaissance and then says "but the sense of a stupendous self and an insignificant world may have its consolations. Lydgate's content was much harder to bear; it was the sense that there was a grand existence in thought and effective action lying around him" (ch. 64, 698). How far we are from the other Eliot's "No! I am not Prince Hamlet," where the Renaissance only serves to belittle. Gwendolen's case, like Lydgate's, also insists that the burden of finding grandeur in the world is not so large, if we look around and do some detective work, reaffirm some heroism, in estimating ourselves and each other. Prometheus is not far from Gwendolen, anymore than Hamlet is from Lydgate. While living in the pre–νάρθηξ state, Prometheus brought human beings into existence, just as Gwendolen's unknown existence rushes the entire dramatic cast into the sixty-nine chapter novel. And just as Lydgate finds peace and healing by stepping into the "analogical matrix"[11] of Middlemarch, discovering the "twice-blessed mercy [of healing . . . which served] better than any opiate to quiet and sustain him under anxieties and his sense of mental degeneracy" (ch. 66, 720), so Gwendolen achieves anagnorisis and catharsis by freeing her ego from contemplating itself and entering a life held in relation to others. In the same way, by contemplating Gwendolen's increasingly anonymous lot, held in the shifting continuum of Eliot's mimetic fiction, the reader is also freed from a pursuit of one view into a multiple recognition of others. He or she becomes an anonymous hero as well. "The greatest benefit we owe to the artist, whether painter, poet, or novelist, is the extension of our sympathies" (Pinney, 270). Of all Eliot's characters, Gwendolen Harleth requires the greatest extension, both of herself and of us. It is fittest that as an artist of a special sort, she was the last and most extraordinary creation of the greatest novelist in English, who nevertheless, like her heroine, maintained her anonymity during the whole of her literary life, through the medium of words, and in her own case, as "George Eliot."

Notes

CHAPTER ONE. *SCENES OF CLERICAL LIFE* AND THE ART OF INDIRECT IDEALIZATION

1. In a review written close to the inception of *Scenes of Clerical Life,* Eliot speaks of "the days of Greek glory" and the "two great schools of Phidias and Praxiteles" (*Notebook* 244). When writing of Phidias, Eliot was singling out an artist who, by tradition, had become a symbol of the art which transcends imitation. Of Phidias's statue of Zeus, Plotinus has written, "[the sculptor] did not ponder over any sensible thing or cast his gaze on anything on which he might model his work but elevated his imagination above the sensibilia and loveliness of the beautiful forms" (*Opera,* 377). Through a series of literary echoes, with Proclus as intermediary (*In Platonis Timaeum* 1: 265), Cicero arrives at the same conclusion, "Surely the great sculptor while making the image of Jupiter or Minerva, did not look at any person whom he used as a model, but in his own mind there dwelt a surpassing vision of beauty" (311). Again, through the intermediary of Junius Franscisus, whose *Painting of the Ancients* discusses both Proclus and Cicero (21), the Phidian statue reached Sir Joshua Reynolds and therefore the short novel. Junius quotes both Cicero and Proclus in order to analyze what he calls the "Imaginative facultie": "for the exercise of this same facultie doth more properly belong unto such Artificers as labour to be perfect, studying alwayes by a continuall practise to enrich their Phantasie with all kinde of perfect Images, and desiring to have them in such a readinesse, that by them they might represent and resemble things absent" (21).

Also see A. J. Festugière's edition of Proclus, *Commentaire sur le Timée,* for the original tracing to Plato. Translated, the passage from the *Timaeus* reads: "Now whenever the maker of anything looks to that which is always unchanging and uses a model of that description in fashioning the form and quality of his work, all that he thus accomplishes must be good. If he looks to something that has come to be and uses a generated model, it will not be good" (16).

2. U. C. Knoepflmacher has pointed out that sometimes the narrator is erudite and literary, sometimes "commonsensical" and anti-intellectual (*George Eliot's,* 57). Although he sees these changes as an inconsistency, it can also be said the slippage serves to reinforce the nonphotographic nature of the scenes the narrator seeks to represent. In addition, it presents a challenge, effectively although perhaps unintentionally, to the reader's powers of identification.

3. See Praz, *Hero in Eclipse* 319.

4. Hardy writes, "This is the tragedy of the little soul. Unlike Oedipus and Lear, who commit themselves to tragedy with giant fury and endurance, Amos and Hetty hardly recognize tragedy when they meet it" (*Novels,* 26).

5. In reply, Henry Auster in his *Local Habitations: Regionalism in the Early Novels of George Eliot,* agrees with these same divisions, but then offers the

emphatic qualification that the treatment is not really ironic: "Under the crust of half-enlightened, comically quaint provincialism of the group characters, there is usually a sure grasp of what is essentially important, true, and right" (82). However, we have yet to find who, beyond the narrator and reader, can truly assess Mr. Gilfil.

6. In "'Scenes of Clerical Life': The Diagram and the Picture," Derek and Sybil Oldfield conclude that the story is "little more than a sentimental melodrama" (Hardy, *Critical*, 7). This conclusion does not take into account, however, how the melodramatic elements serve to heighten the thematic distance between past and present, the apparent Mr. Gilfil and the inner man.

Chapter Two. Heroic Perception in *Adam Bede*

1. In *The Art of George Eliot*, W. J. Harvey writes, "the reader is repelled by having his reactions determined for him; he feels himself, and not the character, to be a puppet manipulated by the author" (70). He later qualifies this criticism by saying that the "infuriating" intrusion becomes a device which "bridges" the worlds of the novel and the reader.

2. See Barbara Hardy, *The Novels of George Eliot*, 32–46; Felicia Bonaparte, *Will and Destiny*, 180–89; and Dorothee Supp, *Tragik bei George Eliot*, 28–37, 74–86.

3. For a treatment of the difficulties surrounding the Hetty story, see George R. Creeger, "An Interpretation of *Adam Bede*," 86–106; U. C. Knoepflmacher, *George Eliot's Early Novels*, 116–27; also Murray Kreiger, who writes, "the loss of Hetty is absolute, and remains naggingly present to the end—and beyond" (219); and Dorothea Barrett, who calls Hetty "a kind of Frankenstein's monster for George Eliot. Created for a specific and limited purpose, Hetty breaks her confines and threatens to take over the novel" (43). Knoepflmacher concludes that Hetty's "'lower nature' remains an obstacle in the way of the novelist's desire to demonstrate the rationality of universal love in a universe no longer ordered by a providential dispensation" (124).

4. For an analysis of Arthur as tragic hero, with Mr. Irwine serving as commentator, see Supp, *Tragik bei George Eliot*, 33–36.

5. In her essay "Three Months in Weimar" (Pinney 86–93), Eliot begins to formulate her concept of modern heroism when criticizing the false idealization of Goethe in a "colossal statue" (86) and referring later to his being a part of "this working-day world" (92). As Suzanne Graver demonstrates (82), "working-day" is central to our understanding of George Eliot—indeed the novelist, she points out, brought the phrase into the mainstream of English prose—and here it serves to remind us that heroism is alive and well and working still among us. See final chapter on *Daniel Deronda*.

6. Krieger writes: "It is the element of secrecy and isolation which defeats the healthy, if routine, efforts of the natural human community and which, consequently, makes Irwine no longer an adequate pastor to meet such exigencies" (206). Herbert softens the criticism somewhat and yet in the end, it is just as all-encompassing: "it is his very virtues—his tolerance, his tenderness, his trust in human nature—that cripple him for dealing effectively with Arthur and thus help to precipitate the tragedy. Had he shared Dinah's anxious consciousness of lust and guilt, he would surely have been a more aggressive confessor to

Arthur at the crucial moment" (426). Jerome Thale sees Mr. Irwine as ineffectual throughout (20–21).

7. Wiesenfarth also speaks of Adam as "the risen Christ" (90), and Knoepfl-macher writes that "Adam Bede eventually becomes a personification of Feuer-bach's Suffering Jesus" (*George Eliot's*, 90). These comparisons, however, seem to advance the idealization too far, making Adam susceptible to James's criticism that "he is too good" (Carroll, *Critical*, 45). For a close discussion of both the Miltonic and Wordsworthian influence on *Adam Bede*, see Knoepflmacher, *Religious Humanism and the Victorian Novel: George Eliot, Walter Pater, and Samuel Butler*, 89–127.

Chapter Three. The Narrative One-Room Schoolhouse of *The Mill on the Floss*

1. In particular, see Jerome Buckley, *Season of Youth: The Bildungsroman from Dickens to Golding*. Buckley concludes that "*The Mill on the Floss* describes the beginning of a life necessarily still incomplete; and its interest and power lie in the unfolding of that life rather than in the end imposed upon it" (115). The unfolding, however, also involves various forms of incompleteness.

2. A. W. Bellringer, in "Education in *The Mill on the Floss*," explores the correlation between Eliot's own personal views on education and educational reform and what is borne out in the novel.

3. David Leon Higdon, for example, sees a disparity between the rhythms of the first two volumes and those of the final one: "In Volumes I and II, Maggie and Tom are brought to a point of awareness and then left. Volume III violates this design in presenting the event (the flood) and the perception (Tom's recognition) and then following these with yet another event (the drowning) which neither resolves an action nor contributes to the thematic development" (189).

4. In "A Reinterpretation of *The Mill on the Floss*," John Hagan views this recognition as Eliot's way of emphasizing Tom's former narrowness. Although this interpretation is most workable in light of the overall educative plan, Hagan denies the major fact of mutual victimization when he presents Tom's "fanaticism" (60) as virtually the sole source of Maggie's suffering. This denial is partially the result of an overly enthusiastic reading of Thomas à Kempis's words and therefore an overly positive view of Maggie's role as martyr.

5. For an extensive treatment, see William J. Sullivan, "Music and Musical Allusion in *The Mill on the Floss*."

6. In the childhood scenes as well as the final rescue, a great deal is suggested as to what an active, fully adult Maggie would have been like—and even the implications of what Tom could have been are made clear. If we enlarge the momentarily enlightened Tom of the conclusion into a wholly sustained character, we end up with something like the young Tom Brangwen of *The Rainbow*. In *D. H. Lawrence: The Man and His Work: The Formative Years: 1885–1919*, Emile Delavenay writes, "[Brangwen's] unsuccessful venture in the paths of learning is not unlike that of Tom Tulliver in *The Mill on the Floss*: both Toms have the same generous character, the same natural sensitivity" (360). Indeed, the parallel is made even clearer by Lawrence's own description of the academic tortures that the acutely nonacademic and highly physical Tom undergoes: "When he got to school, he made a violent struggle against his physical inability to study. He sat gripped, making himself pale and ghastly in his effort to concen-

trate on the book, to take in what he had to learn. . . . In feeling he was developed, sensitive to the atmosphere around him, brutal perhaps, but at the same time delicate, very delicate" (10). This experience is quite close to that of Tom Tulliver, who finds the abstractions "hideously symbolized." The crucial difference, however, lies in their varying responses to the impending crisis of delicacy: Brangwen grows in sensitivity and survives to a more advanced age (although killed in a flood); Tulliver fights off his sensitivity, numbs his spirit at an early age, only to enter a premature death.

7. See Knoepflmacher, *George Eliot's Early Novels*, 184, as well as Martin's *The Mill on the Floss* and The Unreliable Narrator" (Smith, 36–54) and A. Robert Lee's "*The Mill on the Floss:* 'Memory' and the Reading Experience." Martin sees a conflict between the musing narrator and the one who instructs. Lee shows how there are consistent lessons in memory throughout.

Chapter Four. *Silas Marner* and the Anonymous Heroism of Parenthood

1. In his characteristically approving-disapproving manner, James writes, "To a certain extent, I think *Silas Marner* holds a higher place than any of the author's works. It is more nearly a masterpiece; it has more that simple, rounded, consummate aspect, that absence of loose ends and gaping issues, which marks a classical work" (46). F. R. Leavis, clearly following up on James's observation, presents *Silas Marner* as closing "the first phase of George Eliot's creative life" (47).

2. I am indebted to Donald F. Stone, who, in *The Romantic Impulse in Victorian Fiction* (218–20), points out the strong applicability of Schiller's definition.

3. Of this word. Q. D. Leavis writes, "a Midlands and northern dialect word meaning 'broken into very small flakes,' used of breaking up curds and whey if the flakes are small, and hence metaphorically, to mean 'worried', 'bewildered', but with a vivid particularity these words lack, of course" (*Silas*, 262, note 2).

4. U. C. Knoepflmacher tells how, in view of its tensions, *The Mill on the Floss* ends where *Silas Marner* begins, how "Earth and water, fixity and motion, tradition and change, at odds in *The Mill on the Floss*, coalesce with this wanderer's return to the lands denied to Tom and Maggie" (*George Eliot's*, 233).

5. In writing of George Eliot's conception of sympathy, Elizabeth Ermarth notes that it is "Silas's 'trusting simplicity' [that] likewise makes him vulnerable to a rapacious friend" (100).

6. See *Letters* 3: 382.

7. As Brian Swann writes in another study, "Silas Marner and the New Mythus," "Eppie is that striven-for particle Silas lost in his mother and little sister, the feminine part of him" (108).

8. In her article "The Question of Vocation: From *Romola* to *Middlemarch*," Susan M. Greenstein writes, "*Silas Marner* makes clear that not all work is worthy of the sacrifice of the affections or leads to the salvation predicated in the motion of a secular vocation. Silas's labor had to be redeemed and transformed through a service to which it could be subordinated. And the primary form of service in George Eliot is maternal" (502). Although Greenstein goes on to show how Silas's love for Eppie leads "him to stretch his understanding in order to make every maternal effort for her well-being" (502–3), her main point is that the maternal life, in Eliot, is usually at odds with the "nurture of one's

genius" (503). *Silas Marner,* however, supplies the appropriate counterexample, as long as "genius" is seen as having certain anonymous properties.

9. See Schiller, *Naive and Sentimental Poetry,* 146.

10. For the artistic comparison, see Knoepflmacher (*George Eliot's,* 257) and Swann, *Silas Marner* (103). The storyteller is suggested in the sentence "he worked far into the night to finish the tale of Mrs. Osgood's tablelinen" (64, pun surely intended).

11. In *George Eliot and Community,* Suzanne Graver writes, "Because Silas begins as an outcast and has a 'strange history,' the narrator carefully solicits our sympathy for uncommon experience but maintains a certain distance between the author and the reader lest the overture become too overbearing" (286–87).

12. Carroll, in his analysis of the parallels between the two men, writes, "George Eliot wants us to locate the crucial difference, to discover for ourselves the razoredge between potential salvation and damnation" (*Silas Marner,* 178). This statement, which makes Godfrey overly culpable, finds its reply in Bruce K. Martin's "Similarity Within Dissimilarity: The Dual Structure of *Silas Marner*" (479–89), which presents him as a victim. In addition, as an interesting twist, Alexander Welsh, in *George Eliot and Blackmail,* observes, "For those tempted to scorn someone who has been unable to make the two halves of his life meet, Godfrey Cass suffices as a target. To yield to this response, however, is curiously to side with the much more despicable Dunstan Cass" (165–66).

13. As John R. Reed and Jerry Herron have shown, this particular kind of tension fascinated and absorbed Eliot throughout her career as a novelist.

CHAPTER FIVE. *ROMOLA* AND THE PRESERVATION OF HOUSEHOLD GODS

1. It is clear that George Eliot was thinking repeatedly of this play close to the time of *Romola's* creation, not only from her references in *The Mill on the Floss* but also from an entry in her *Writer's Notebook* (19, entry 43).

2. A number of critics have noted a parallel. Felicia Bonaparte sees a similarity in that both scholars possess very incomplete knowledge (43), and Andrew Sanders ("Waking," 191) links them through the implied or stated allusions to Milton's blindness. Susan Greenstein finds them united through a mutual desire to enslave: "her father's request imposes a task on her as onerous and pointless as the one Casaubon tries to force upon Dorothea, although Romola dearly wishes to discharge it in devotion to his memory" (500).

3. In "*Romola* and the Myth of Apocalypse" (Smith, 83–84), Janet Gezari points out that, historically, Savonarola did not have the opportunity to influence the Bernardo verdict. This fact highlights, even more, Eliot's determination to oppose the two worlds and to undermine, ultimately, her heroine's worship of the Frate. Andrew Sanders sees an interesting parallel between the "pleading" scene and the great debate between Angelo and Isabella in the second act of *Measure for Measure* ("Waking," 179).

4. The history of Piero's rise in critical stature in the Eliot critical canon is a rather dramatic one. Initially taken as a fictional embodiment of Vasari's cranky hermit, he is given one of his first serious treatments in Barbara Hardy's *The Novels of George Eliot: A Study in Form* (170–76), where his visionary qualities are brought to the fore. Edward T. Hurley's "Piero di Cosimo: An Alternate

Analogy for George Eliot's Realism" works to establish Piero's "insight into the actual" (54), an ability that best represents Eliot herself and her belief that art must transcend crude realism. William J. Sullivan's crucial articles, "Piero di Cosimo and the Higher Primitivism in *Romola* and his "The Sketch of the Three Masks in *Romola*," show the corollary between Piero's values and those guiding Romola's education. As a further development of Hardy, Gezari's "*Romola* and the Myth of Apocalypse" (Smith, 93–94) stresses Piero's ability to see through the externals of characters, Tito especially.

5. See Mina Bacci, ed., *L'opera Completa di Piero di Cosimo*. Many of the mythological paintings may be grouped together as stories, and several of the religious ones narrate sacred legends through their background figures. In general, the secular works are flamboyant, sometimes garishly so, and are probably responsible for the term *primitivism* being applied so often. R. Langton Douglas, in his study *Piero di Cosimo*, argues, however, that this vision changed toward the end of the historical Piero's life, as shown by his largescale work, *The Story of Prometheus* panels: "The men that he now represents are no longer in a state that was but little above that of the animals: they are 'as Gods knowing good and evil': they have to bear the inevitable penalty that the gift of such knowledge brought with it" (81).

6. Barbara Hardy writes that the sources of the triptych may have been found in "aspects of several of Piero's paintings that she would either have seen or read about in Vasari's detailed descriptions. Possible sources in the paintings themselves are the *Ariadne*, though there is no resemblance except in the character of Ariadne, and also the *Mars and Venus and her Loves and Vulcan* and *Perseus Frees Andromeda*, both of which might give the suggestion for the loves and the strange sea-monster" (*Novels*, 173). Although Hugh Witemeyer argues that "there is no evidence that George Eliot knew any of his work at first hand, beyond what she learned from the *ecphrases* of Vasari" (200), it seems highly improbable that such a thorough researcher as Eliot would create an entire character without familiarizing herself with at least some of her historical model's *opus*. The *Oedipus and Antigone at Colonus* that her character proposes is suggested more by his *Prometheus* and the two earlier paintings in the *Vulcan* series than it is by anything described in Vasari.

7. For a description of the apocryphal *Tèseo e Arianna* and *Bacco e Arianna*, see Mina Bacci, *L'opera Completa*, 122.

8. Boccaccio provided the source for the *Vulcan* and *The Story of Prometheus* paintings (Douglas, 81). For Boccaccio's version of the Oedipus legend, see *Genealogie Deorum Gentilium Libri* 1: 113–14.

9. See G. A. Wittig Davis, "Ruskin's *Modern Painters*," 200.

10. In chapter 5, 102–3, Bardo also refers to having "the *aes triplex* of clear conscience," a reference to the *Odes of Horace* but also, as T. E. Page says, to the *Prometheus Bound* of Aeschylus (*Carminum Libri* 4: 143).

11. As in the case of Tom Tulliver, who creates similar difficulties for *The Mill on the Floss*, the Creon side of the Creon-Antigone duality is editorially defended but rarely evoked. Savonarola really does not arrive center stage until chapter 62; for the rest of the novel he exists as little more than a meandering postscript or admonishing voice. This absence of characterization is perhaps the only significant one in the novel; however, it does qualify our responses to Dino, who is his convert, and to Romola, who agonizes over exhortations that come, as it were, from behind a curtain. When Eliot draws it, it is too late, and just as in those moments when Tom chastises and redirects Maggie, one finds it difficult

to understand why such an empty voice should cause such an intelligent heroine such turmoil.

Chapter Six. Esther and Rufus Lyon: "A More Regenerating Tenderness" in *Felix Holt*

1. In her essay, Florence Howe sees the traditions of Woolf and T. S. Eliot as largely opposed. "Eliot believed in individual genius, including his own. Virginia Woolf believed that 'the experience of the mass is behind the single voice'" (Howe, 5). This is quite true. However, as T. S. Eliot's "Tradition and the Individual Talent" makes clear, the celebration of the experience of the mass is not necessarily in opposition to a belief in talent or great works.

2. In his early and highly influential article "*Felix Holt* as Classic Tragedy," Fred Thomson notes that in the book, "the characters have to keep pace with the story as best they can." He also adds that "if George Eliot was deliberately trying to adapt the functions and techniques of Greek drama to her novel, it must be conceded that she fell short of her aim. The total impression left by *Felix Holt* is rather of Elizabethan luxuriance, with an injection too, one fears of grand opera" (57). Arnold Kettle carries this observation forward by saying, "The plot is excessively tortuous and involves not only two mysteries of parentage, but a most formidable paraphernalia of legal detail over which the author (assisted by the eminent Positivist lawyer, Frederic Harrison) was excessively conscientious" (Hardy, *Critical Essays,* 107), an assessment which was summed up later by Peter Coveney in his Penguin edition of the novel: "The adverse things, the idealization of Felix Holt himself and the largely unrewarding complexity of the plot, have inevitably coloured opinion against it" (7).

3. One might consider Transome Court as the "norm" as far as the hostility of these conditions is concerned, and this postlapsarian condition might be one of the reasons why Eliot focuses on Harold and his mother first and alludes to her as a member of the Dantean suicides in the introduction. This strategy is similar to Milton's in *Paradise Lost,* which presents the more identifiable imperfections of the infernal world first.

4. F. R. Leavis put everyone off the scent by calling Rufus Lyon "incredible and a bore" (52), an assessment probably connected to the frequently sexist premises of his Great Tradition. In an analysis which dismisses Daniel Deronda as "a woman's creation" (82), there could hardly be room to appreciate the subtleties of another man who is an androgynous balance. Later, Jerome Thale has more to say in his behalf and admits that he "comes off much better as a character than Felix because he is better thought out and better presented in terms of the political context." However, his final view is that "we are not asked to esteem him except for the honest simplicity of his nature, and we are not asked to take his ideas seriously simply because he means well" (95).

More recently, in "Unveiling Men: Power and Masculinity in George Eliot's Fiction," U. C. Knoepflmacher, however, describes Rufus more sympathetically as an "avuncular figure," along with Mr. Gilfil, Seth Bede, Mr. Keen, the Reverend Farebrother, "and that asexual male mother, Silas Marner, all of whom are bereft of brides or wives" (139). Finally, Mary Ellen Doyle, in her *The Sympathetic Response: George Eliot's Fictional Rhetoric,* writes, one year later, that "as the small, shortsighted preacher of orotund phrases, dubious exegesis, and unquestionable sincerity and zeal, he is completely credible and a genuinely felt obligation on Esther's and the reader's sympathetic understanding" (104).

5. It is important to emphasize that Milton's elegaic masterpiece was only signed "J. M." when it originally appeared. Also, for a discussion of how the prophet, the eccentric, and the fanatic join in dangerous and troubling company, see the final chapter of this study.

6. It is also known that she was reading *Henry the Fourth, Part One* while writing the novel (see Clarendon edition of the novel, xxviii).

7. Sally Shuttleworth, in *George Eliot and Nineteenth-Century Science: The Make-Believe of a Beginning*, comments pointedly on Felix's demand that Esther change: "Interestingly, George Eliot sees Esther's response to this demand as the confirmation of her femininity; she acquires 'a softened expression to her eyes, a more feminine beseechingness and self-doubt to her manners' (ch. 24, II, 4–5). George Eliot's reduction of her heroine to this stereotype of the feminine is in line with the simplistic political message of the novel" (137). However, Esther develops a great deal more than a beseeching attitude, once her Byronic worship stops.

8. The Campbell edition of Sophocles glosses "even in that absence" (οὐδὲ γέρων) as "Even old as thou wert (or art), and then adds, "It has been observed . . . that the soul in Hades was imagined as having all the characteristics of the person at the time of death: and nothing can be more natural than that Antigone in the first moment of her sorrow should speak of her father as if he still needed tendance and care" (1: 436).

Chapter Seven. Lydgate's Note and Dorothea's Tomb: The Quest for Anonymity in *Middlemarch*

1. For an alternative view of Casaubon's relation to Dorothea, see Greenstein again and Ellmann (in the Norton Critical Edition of *Middlemarch*, ed. Hornback), also Hertz's "Recognizing Casaubon."

2. In Casaubon we can find a surprising and yet compelling corollary to Napoleon in *War and Peace*. In a recent study, *Leo Tolstoy: Resident and Stranger*, Richard Gustafson's remarks concerning "The Emperor of Europe" could equally apply to the little-known, dust-ridden scholar who tried to control from beyond his unvisited grave:

> Napoleon is totally self-enclosed. "Only what was happening in his own soul had interest for him. Everything in the world (*mir*) seemed to him to depend on his will" (III, i, vi). From the point of view of the will, Napoleon stands in opposition to all that exists. He sees the battle for life as a "game of chess" in which he moves the figures (III, ii, xxix). From the point of view of the intellect also, Napoleon stands in opposition to all that exists. He is the subject; everything else is the object. (229)

The only real distinction between Casaubon and Napoleon is that one meets his goal of attaining prestige and the other does not. In both Eliot and Tolstoy, this is a distinction, really, without a difference—Tolstoy concluding that Napoleon was ultimately "the most insignificant tool of history" (1,011) because of his egoism. Casaubon and Napoleon are "authors" trying to put their names to works in worlds which will not allow individual copyright, where Divine Will, or the growing good of the world, belies taking full moral credit for anything. For this reason, both characters stand in landscapes of death.

3. In the Introduction to this study, I mentioned Eliot's doubt, expressed to Sara Hennell, that "we are quite unable to represent ourselves truly" (*Letters* 3: 90), a response, in part, raised by the loss of her anonymity. Even earlier, however, when trying to console Sara over the death of her mother, she had written, "words are very clumsy things—I like less and less to handle my friends' sacred feelings with them" (2: 464). Apart from Casaubon's story, the theme is taken up in the Bulstrode murder case where, on the morning after the crime, the narrator says, "—about six—Mr. Bustrode rose and spent some time in prayer. Does any one suppose that private prayer is necessarily candid—necessarily goes to the roots of action! Private prayer is inaudible speech, and speech is representative: who can represent himself just as he is, even in his own reflections?" (ch. 70, 763).

4. Harvey speaks of how Mr. Brooke's "butterfly mind and cluttered pigeon-holes become a comic analogue" to the intellectual quests of both Casaubon and Lydgate ("Introduction to *Middlemarch*," 12).

5. For a less positive view of Mr. Brooke's role, see Knoepflmacher's "*Middlemarch*: An Avuncular View."

6. See Knoepflmacher's "*Middlemarch*: The Balance of Progress" chapter in *Religious Humanism and the Victorian Novel* (72–84). John Hulcoop (*George Eliot: A Centenary Tribute*) observes, "just as Lydgate relinquishes his sense of the poetry of life, succumbs to the 'petty medium' and writes a treatise on gout, so Dorothea is disillusioned by her short-sighted idealisation of the man she supposes to hold the Key to All Mythologies" (158). Also see chapter 4 of Mintz's *George Eliot and the Novel of Vocation* and Dorothea Barrett's *Vocation and Desire,* which concludes that "in the finale we see Lydgate slaughtered off in his prime, and Rosamond surviving him. It seems almost cruel, especially in a Victorian novelist" (145). Patricia Lundberg sees this death as a plan of the "persona, 'George Eliot,' the Angel of Destruction, to wreak havoc in the lives of her patriarchal characters" (280).

7. In *Love's Argument,* Novy shows how Goneril and Regan of *King Lear* prove to be more stereotypical (as defined by the Western literary tradition) by going "along with the social order" (152) and later "use the power they receive with a coercion like Lear's own" (155).

8. Miriam Berlin ("George Eliot and the Russians" in *A Centenary Tribute,* Haight and VanArsdel, eds.) and Philip Rogers and Shoshanna Knapp have done some extremely interesting studies of Eliot's influence on Tolstoy. Knapp speaks more generally and Rogers writes of the specific part *Felix Holt* played in Tolstoy's writings. It is no surprise that Tolstoy's *What is Art?* celebrated *Adam Bede* as an example of "the highest art flowing from love of God and man" (152), when the book had had such an enormous impact on the writing of *Family Happiness*. Tellingly, Eliot in "The Natural History of German Life" concluded that "the greatest benefit we owe to the artist, whether painter, poet, or novelist, is the extension of our sympathies" (Pinney, 270), while Tolstoy declares four decades later that art "is a means of union among men, joining them together in the same feelings, and indispensable for the life and progress toward well-being of individuals and of humanity" (*What is Art?,* 52).

Also in *War and Peace,* in a manner very similar to Eliot's, Tolstoy directly contrasts Pierre, his new anonymous hero, with Napoleon, the old "great" one. While Napoleon is busy burning up Russia and raising monuments to himself, Pierre learns, in his captivity, a new way of life through the unsung example of the peasant Karataev:

"Karataev!" flashed into Pierre's mind. And all at once there rose up, as vivid as though alive, the image, long forgotten, of the gentle old teacher, who had given Pierre geography lessons in Switzerland. "Wait a minute," the old man was saying. And he was showing Pierre a globe. This globe was a living, quivering ball, with no definite limits. Its whole surface consisted of drops, closely cohering together. And those drops were all in motion, and changing, several passing into one, and then one splitting up again into many. Every drop seemed striving to spread, to take up more space, but the others, pressing upon it, sometimes absorbed it, sometimes melted into it.

"This is life," the old teacher was saying.

"How simple it is and how clear," thought Pierre. "How was it I did not know that before? God is in the midst, and each drop strives to expand, to reflect Him on the largest scale possible. And it grows, and is absorbed and crowded out, and on the surface it disappears, goes back into the depths, and falls not to the surface again. That is how it is with him, with Karataev; he is absorbed and has disappeared." (992–93, 14, ch. 15)

The interweaving of all lots into one whole suggests a great deal of *Middlemarch*'s vision, and also, here, Pierre's memory becomes his road to Emmaus. In becoming the peasant's living memorial, in having his heart burn for him, when apparently the man had been lost to oblivion, he in essence "slays" Napoleon, the old-style hero of the Western world. The answer, then, has not been to take the conqueror's life literally, as had been Pierre's original intent, but to adopt a new heroism instead. Dorothea does the same when she exchanges Edward Causaubon for Will Ladislaw and the movement her new husband represents.

9. The "Brownian motion" of *Middlemarch* is disclosed through a consultation of the *Middlemarch Notebooks* (Pratt, Neufeldt) as well as *Some George Eliot Notebooks* (Baker), which in fact contains two sections entitled "Browneisms." A phrase from *Pseudodoxica Epidemica* that Eliot was apparently fond of was "pyramidally happy" (Baker, 67), which would describe the condition that ever eludes Casuabon. In addition, the vision of the last judgment in *Urn Burial* seems to capture, after modern translation, the judged condition of Eliot's egotists in *Middlemarch* along with the "saved" condition of those who transcend their own selfish ends:

If in the decretory term of the world we shall not all die but be changed, according to received translation, the last day will make but few graves, at least quick resurrections will anticipate lasting sepultures, some graves will be opened before they be quite closed, and Lazarus be no wonder, when many that feared to die shall groan that they can die but once. The dismal state is the second and living death when life puts despair on the damned, when men shall wish the coverings of mountains, not of monuments, and annihilation shall be courted. (46)

CHAPTER EIGHT. CELEBRITY, ANONYMITY, AND THE HEROIC VOICES OF *DANIEL DERONDA*

1. It is important to note how, at least according to Lewes's account, Goethe entered Italy under a pseudonym and the guise of a merchant and how, according to his painter friend Wilhelm Tischbein, the great man lived a simple and sequestered life during the crucial composition stages of the *Iphigenia*. In his *Artist in Chrysalis: A Biographical Study of Goethe in Italy*, H. G. Haile quotes and translates a description of the hard-at-work dramatist that Tischbein passed on to another friend:

"What I like so much about Goethe is his simple life. He desired of me a little room where he could sleep and work undisturbed, and extremely simple food. I was able to give him both very easily, because it takes so little to satisfy him. Now he sits in there and works mornings until nine at finishing his *Iphigenia*. . . . There was the plan of honoring him in the same way other great poets who have been in Rome before were honored. He excused himself, however, on account of the time which would be consumed, thus in a courteous manner avoiding the appearance of vanity. It certainly does him just as much honor as being crowned with laurel at the Capitoline Hill" (82–83).

Also, according to the Cross biography, Eliot wrote to Sara Hennell in August of 1853, that "The landlord of my lodgings is a German, comes from Saxe-Weimar, knows well the Duchess of Orleans, and talked to me this morning of *Mr.* Schiller and *Mr.* Goethe [italics Eliot's]. *A propos* of Goethe, there is a most true, discriminating passage about him in the article on Shakespeare in the *Prospective*. *Mr.* Goethe is one of my companions here, and I had felt some days before reading the passage the truth which it expresses" (1: 224). Cross then includes the article—one that criticizes Goethe's literary works for their scientific detachment, a fault attributed to his being a stranger to life. It is interesting that at this point "Mr." Goethe was truly becoming a man with faults and humanness in Eliot's estimation, for the precise reason that he seemed to resist joining the human race. Perhaps it was because of this changing impression that Eliot was so taken, later in the same month, with the portrait of Goethe painted on a cup. Perhaps she was getting ready for her famed image of Milton gazing into a spoon, another reduction of another luminary—to the level of humanity, or dining room, or kitchen.

2. In "The Decomposition of the Elephants: Double-reading *Daniel Deronda*," Cynthia Chase discusses the way characters can wish events into being, through an interpolation of causes and effects. In this sense, Mirah wishes for a rescuer and thereby "creates" Deronda as one. However, this role is exactly what he needs to save him from the "self-repressed exterior" (ch. 19, 245) which dominates his life. Marianne Novy's comments connecting Deronda with Hamlet (*Women's Re-Visions*, 99–100) are especially helpful here as well, since one could visualize him hesitating and soliloquizing for years had it not been for Mirah.

3. See Henry James, "*Daniel Deronda*: A Conversation" and F. R. Leavis, *The Great Tradition* (79–85), where the argument and even the ridicule are carried forward. Leavis's sexism is evident in his criticism of Deronda as a "woman's creation" (82), perhaps because the protagonist is more a receiver of information than a decided or deciding agent. In a footnote to the "creation" phrase, Leavis gives even more of himself away by saying, "But this about his experience at Cambridge is characteristic of the innumerable things by the way that even in George Eliot's weaker places remind us we are dealing with an extremely vigorous and distinguished mind, and one in no respect disabled by being a woman's" (82). In a very evocative article, "Re-reading the Great Tradition," Catherine Belsey answers with "If in offering a feminist reading of *Daniel Deronda* I concentrate on Leavis' 'good half' of the text, this is not to reinforce his value judgement, but to insist that his partiality is more than simply a preference for one part of the text" (Widdowson, 131).

Other critics who followed Leavis's line of criticism are Bennett (185) and Thale (123), but toward the end of the 1950s and the early 1960s, Hardy and Harvey, by emphasizing formal consistency, began the retrieval of the characterization of Deronda.

4. The two panels of Piero's *Mito di Prometeo* both contrast active, semicon-

temporary figures with a statuesque representation of the ideal man or god, a method not far from Eliot's. It is interesting that in one painting the statue seems modeled after the sculpture of the Greeks, in the other after medieval or Renaissance crucifixions (Bacchi, plates 47 and 48). Also see note 5 to Chapter 6 above.

5. Eliot creates a similar effect in *Romola*, in the chapter "The Black Marks become Magical," where Baldassarre confronts a quoted Greek word, all in capitals, and suddenly Pausanias returns to him: "an hour or two ago he had been looking hopelessly at that page, and it had suggested no more meaning to him than if the letters had been black weather-marks on a wall; but at this moment they were once more the magic signs that conjure up a world" (405). Here the Greek characters ΜΕΣΣΗΝΙΚΑ.'ΚΒ'. are used in order to create an identification with the haunted man's dyslexia and subsequent humiliation. In the Prometheus epigraph, they inculcate, perhaps, a sense of anonymity through our inability to read the text with a feeling of detachment or superiority.

In addition, recently Harold Fisch has written that "character as verbal sign remains with us in spite of the term having been applied to psychology or moral behavior" (593), and it is interesting in both *Romola* and *Daniel Deronda* [and even *The Mill on the Floss* where the plain mock-heroic is used (90; 1, 10)] that the Greek characters serve to underscore the "character" associated with them, just as a single letter is accentuated and indeed made visible by the plain background behind it. While the surprise of the foreign letters breaks the illusion of the narrative reality momentarily, it ultimately serves to deepen the mimesis.

6. W. J. Harvey has called him "one of the few convincing geniuses of fiction" (*Art*, 237). Also see Emily Auerbach's "The Domesticated *Maestro:* George Eliot's Klesmer." Auerbach discusses the suggested historical models and makes the interesting comment "the phrase 'even Genius' takes on new meaning by the end of *Daniel Deronda* as Eliot illustrates that artists, however inspired, must work diligently, earn a living, and accommodate themselves to a society increasingly unreceptive to their vocation" (281). This is backed up by a reaffirmed heroic passage where the narrator takes exactly the same attitude toward Klesmer as the narrator did towards Milton in *Middlemarch*. This one Auerbach also quotes: "Klesmer stood like a statue—if a statue can be imagined to wear spectacles" (ch. 5, 78).

7. In preferring to focus on Gwendolen, James and Leavis show their social-realist assumptions. Belsey, while taking issue with Leavis, also writes, "In reality Leavis's dismissal of the 'bad half' of the text is informative, in that it suggests what many readers have sensed, that the enigma which the title of the novel proposes as central ('who is Daniel Deronda?') is repeatedly displaced by the more insistent question, 'what is Gwendolen Harleth?'" (131). Zimmerman writes, "Nor does Daniel's sympathy with the oppressed sensitize him to the fact that Judaism oppresses its own women. Not only does he ignore his mother's anger, he treats Mirah, his future wife, as an angelic housefrau" (Nathan, 234).

8. See my article on point of view in *Daniel Deronda*, 150.

9. For an analysis of Gwendolen's "rise" against Grandcourt in this chapter, see my article "George Eliot and the Ambiguity of Murder," 68.

10. The rough and final versions of *To the Lighthouse* show exactly the way Woolf revised Lily Brisco into the ultimate anonymous heroine. In the last paragraphs, Mr. Carmichael is at first present, then removed. Then in the final lines, Lily concludes the novel in her own voice, rather than the third-person narrator's, thereby suggesting a complete privacy of vision. See Susan Dick, ed., *To the Lighthouse: The Original Holograph Draft*, 366.

11. See Mark Schorer's "Fiction and the 'Matrix of Analogy'" (*Middlemarch: An Authoritative Text, Backgrounds, Reviews, and Criticism*), 706–14.

Bibliography

Adam, Ian, ed. *This Particular Web: Essays on Middlemarch*. Toronto and Buffalo: University of Toronto Press, 1975.

Adams, Harriet Farwell. "Dorothea and 'Miss Brooke' in *Middlemarch*." *Nineteenth-Century Fiction* 39 (1984): 69–90.

Aeschylus. *Prometheus Bound*. Translated by David Grene, *Aeschylus Two: The Complete Greek Tragedies*. Edited by David Grene and Richmond Lattimore. New York: Washington Square Books, 1967.

———. *Prometheus Bound*. Edited by Mark Griffith. Cambridge: Cambridge University Press, 1983.

Allen, Walter. *George Eliot*. New York: Collier Books, 1964.

Alley, Henry. "George Eliot and the Ambiguity of Murder." *Studies in the Novel* 25 (1993): 59–75.

———. "Gwendolen Harleth, George Eliot's Modernization of Hamlet." *A British Studies Sampler*. Edited by Richard D. Fulton. Vancouver: Cannel Library: 1994. 21–40.

———. "New Year's at the Abbey: Point of View in the Pivotal Chapters of *Daniel Deronda*." *The Journal of Narrative Technique* 9 (1979): 147–59.

Argyle, Gisela. *German Elements in the Fiction of George Eliot, Gissing, and Meredith*. Frankfurt: Peter Lang, 1979.

Aristotle. *The Poetics*. Edited by S. H. Butcher. London: Macmillan and Company, 1902.

Ashton, Rosemary. "George Eliot and Goethe (1854–76)." In *The German Idea: Four English Writers and the Reception of German Thought, 1800–1860*. Cambridge: Cambridge University Press, 1980. 166–73.

Auerbach, Emily. "The Domesticated Maestro: George Eliot's Klesmer." *Papers on Language and Literature* 19 (1983): 280–92.

Auerbach, Eric. *Mimesis: The Representation of Reality in Western Literature*. Translated by Willard R. Trask. Princeton: Princeton University Press, 1953.

———. "'Figura.'" In *Scenes from the Drama of European Literature: Six Essays*. Translated by Ralph Manheim and Catherine Garvin. New York: Meridan Books, 1959. 11–76.

Austen, Zelda. "Why Feminist Critics Are Angry with George Eliot." *College English* 37 (1976): 549–61.

Auster, Henry. *Local Habitations: Regionalism in the Early Novels of George Eliot*. Cambridge: Harvard University Press, 1970.

Bacci, Mina, ed. *L'opera Completa di Piero di Cosimo*. Milan: Rizzoli Editore, 1976.

Baker, William. "George Eliot's Projected Napoleonic War Novel: An Unnoted Reading List." *Nineteenth Century Fiction* 29 (1974): 453–60.

———. "George Eliot's Shakespeare Folio at the Folger Library." *George Eliot-Henry Lewes Newsletter* 1 (1982): 6–7.

———. *Some George Eliot Notebooks: An Edition of the Carl H. Pforzheimer Library's George Eliot Holograph Notebooks*, 2 vols. Salzburg Studies in English Literature 46. Edited by James Hogg. Vol 1. Salzburg: Institut für Englishce Sprache und Literatur, 1976.

Bakhtin, Mikhail. *Problems of Dostoevsky's Poetics*. Edited and translated by Caryl Emerson. Minneapolis: University of Minnesota Press, 1984.

Barrett, Dorothea. *Vocation and Desire: George Eliot's Heroines*. London: Routledge, 1989.

Barth, John. "The Literature of Replenishment: Postmodernist Fiction." *Atlantic Monthly* 245 (1980): 65–71.

Beer, Gillian. *George Eliot*. Bloomington: Indiana University Press, 1986.

Bellringer, A. W. "Education in *The Mill on the Floss*." *Review of English Literature* 7 (1966): 52–61.

Belsey, Catherine. "Re-Reading *The Great Tradition*." In *Re-Reading English*. Edited by Peter Widdowson. London: Methuen, 1982. 121–35.

Bennett, Joan. *George Eliot: Her Mind and Her Art*. Cambridge: University Press, 1948.

Bergman, Ingmar. "Cries and Whispers." *Four Stories by Ingmar Bergman*. Translated by Alan Blair. Garden City, N.J.: Anchor Books, 1977.

Boccaccio. *Genalogie Deorum Gentilium Libri*. Edited by Vincenzo Romano. Bari: G. Laterza and Sons, 1951.

Bonaparte, Felicia. *Will and Destiny: Morality and Tragedy in George Eliot's Novels*. New York: New York University Press, 1975.

Booth, Alison, ed. *Famous Last Words: Changes in Gender and Narrative Closure*. Charlottesville: University Press of Virginia, 1993.

———. *Greatness Engendered: George Eliot and Virginia Woolf*. Ithaca: Cornell University Press, 1992.

Boumelha, Penny. "George Eliot and the End of Realism." *Women Reading Women's Writing*. Edited by Sue Roe. New York: St. Martin's Press, 1987.

Bradley, Anthony G. "Family and Pastoral: The Garths in *Middlemarch*." *Ariel* 6 (1975): 41–51.

Browne, Sir Thomas. *Hydriotaphia (Urn Burial) and The Garden of Cyrus*. Edited by Frank L. Huntley. Northbrook, Ill.: AHM Publishing Corporation, 1966.

Buckler, William E. "Memory, Morality, and the Tragic Vision in the Early Novels of George Eliot." In *The English Novel in the Nineteenth Century: Essays on the Literary Mediation of Human Values*. Edited by George Goodin. Urbana: University of Illinois Press, 1972. 145–63.

Buckley, Jerome. *Season of Youth: The Bildungsroman from Dickens to Golding*. Cambridge: Harvard University Press, 1974.

Buckley, Jerome Hamilton. "George Eliot's Double Life: *The Mill on the Floss* as a *Bildungsroman*." In *From Smollett to James: Studies in the Novel and Other Essays Presented to Edgar Johnson*. Edited by Samuel I. Mintz, Alice Chandler, and Christopher Mulvey. Charlottesville: University Press of Virginia, 1981. 211–36.

Butcher, S. H. *Aristotle's Theory of Poetry and Fine Art.* New York: Dover Publications, 1951.

Byrd, Scott. "The Fractured Crystal in *Middlemarch* and *The Golden Bowl.*" *Modern Fiction Studies* 18 (1972): 551–54.

Caron, James. "The Rhetoric of Magic in *Daniel Deronda.*" *Studies in the Novel* 15 (1983): 1–9.

Carpenter, Mary Wilson. *George Eliot and the Landscape of Time: Narrative Form and Protestant Apocalyptic History.* Chapel Hill and London: University of North Carolina Press, 1986.

Carroll, David. *George Eliot and the Conflict of Interpretations.* New York: Cambridge University Press, 1992.

———. "*Silas Marner:* Reversing the Oracles of Religion." In *Literary Monographs.* Vol. 1. Edited by Eric Rothstein and Thomas K. Dunseath. Madison: University of Wisconsin Press, 1967. 167–201.

Chapman, Raymond, and Eleanora Gottlieb. "A Russian View of George Eliot." *Nineteenth-Century Fiction* 33 (1978): 348–65.

Chase, Cynthia. *Decomposing Figures: Rhetorical Readings in the Romantic Tradition.* Baltimore and London, Johns Hopkins Press, 1986.

Cicero. *Orator.* Edited by H. M. Hubbell. Cambridge: Harvard University Press, 1939.

Cohan, Steven. "Figures Beyond the Text: A Theory of Readable Character in the Novel." *Novel: A Forum on Fiction* 17 (1983): 5–27.

———. "Narrative Form and Death: *The Mill on the Floss* and *Mrs. Dalloway.*" *Genre* 11 (1978): 109–28.

Cook, Ellen Piel. *Psychological Androgyny.* New York: Pergamon Press, 1985.

Creeger, George R. "*An Interpretation of Adam Bede.*" *George Eliot: A Collection of Critical Essays.* Edited by George R. Creeger. Englewood Cliffs, N.J.: Prentice-Hall, 1970. 116–27.

Cross, J. W. *George Eliot's Life as Related in her Letters and Journals.* 3 vols. New York: E. B. Hall, 1884.

Culler, Jonathan. *On Deconstruction: Theory and Criticism After Structuralism.* Ithaca: Cornell University Press, 1982.

Dante. *The Divine Comedy, Purgatorio.* Edited and translated by Charles S. Singleton. Princeton: Princeton University Press, 1973.

Davis, G. A. Wittig. "Ruskin's *Modern Painters* and George Eliot's Concept of Realism." *English Language Notes* 18 (1981): 195–201.

Delavenay, Emile. *D. H. Lawrence: The Man and His Work: The Formative Years: 1885–1919.* Carbondale: Southern Illinois University Press, 1972.

Derrida, Jacques. *Writing and Difference.* Translated by Alan Bass. Chicago: University of Chicago Press, 1978.

DiBattista, Maria. *Virginia Woolf's Major Novels: The Fables of Anon.* New Haven: Yale University Press, 1980.

Douglas, R. Langston. *Piero di Cosimo.* Chicago: University of Chicago Press, 1946.

Doyle, Mary Ellen. *The Sympathetic Response: George Eliot's Fictional Rhetoric.* East Brunswick, N.J., and London: Associated University Presses, 1981.

Eco, Umberto. *Postscript to Name of the Rose.* New York: Harcourt Janovich, 1983.

Eliot, George. *Adam Bede*. Edited by John Patterson. Boston: Houghton Mifflin Company, 1968.

———. *Daniel Deronda*. Edited by Barbara Hardy. Baltimore: Penguin Books, 1967.

———. *Essays*. Edited by Thomas Pinney. New York: Columbia University Press, 1963.

———. *Felix Holt*. Edited by Peter Coveney. Baltimore: Penguin Books, 1972.

———. *Felix Holt*. Edited by Fred C. Thomson. Oxford: Clarendon Press, 1980.

———. *The George Eliot Letters, 1840–1870*. 9 vols. Edited by Gordon S. Haight. New Haven: Yale University Press, 1954–56, 1978.

———. *The Lifted Veil*. New York: Penguin Books—Virago Press, 1985.

———. *Middlemarch*. Edited by W. J. Harvey. Baltimore: Penguin Books, 1965.

———. *Middlemarch: An Authoritative Text, Backgrounds, Reviews and Criticism*. Edited by Bert G. Hornback. New York: W. W. Norton, 1977.

———. *The Mill on the Floss*. Edited by Gordon S. Haight. Boston: Houghton Mifflin, 1961.

———. *Romola*. Edited by Andrew Sanders. New York: Penguin Books, 1980.

———. Review of *Life and Opinions of Milton*. *Westminster Review* 8 (1855): 601–4.

———. *Scenes of Clerical Life*. Edited by David Lodge. Baltimore: Penguin Books, 1973.

———. *Selected Essays, Poems and Other Writings*. Edited by A. S. Byatt and Nicholas Warren. New York: Penguin Books, 1990.

———. *Silas Marner*. Edited by Q. D. Leavis. Baltimore: Penguin Books, 1967.

———. *A Writer's Notebook, 1854–1879, and Uncollected Writings*. Edited by Joseph Wiesenfarth. Charlottesville: University Press of Virginia, 1981.

Eliot, T. S. *Selected Poems*. New York: Harcourt, Brace and World, 1964.

———. *Selected Prose*. Edited by Frank Kermode. New York: Harcourt Brace Jovanovitch, 1975.

Emerson, Caryl. "The Tolstoy Connection in Bakhtin." *PMLA* 97 (1982): 68–79.

Ermarth, Elizabeth Deeds. *George Eliot*. Boston: Twayne Publishers, 1985.

———. "George Eliot's Conception of Sympathy." *Nineteenth-Century Fiction* 40 (1985): 23–42.

Fast, Robin Riley. "Getting to the Ends of *Daniel Deronda*." *Journal of Narrative Technique* 7 (1977): 200–17.

Felperin, Howard. *Beyond Deconstruction: The Uses and Abuses of Literary Theory*. Oxford: Clarendon Press, 1985.

Fénelon, Francois de Salignac. *The Adventures of Telemachus*, 2 vols. rpt; 1720. New York: Garland Publications, 1979.

Feuerbach, Ludwig. *The Essence of Christianity*. Translated by George Eliot. New York: Harper Torchbooks, 1957.

Fisch, Harold. "Character as Linguistic Sign." *New Literary History* 21 (1990): 593–606.

Forster, E. M. "Anonymity: An Enquiry." *Two Cheers for Democracy*. New York: Harcourt, Brace, and World, 1951. 77–87.

———. *Aspects of the Novel*. New York: Harcourt Brace and World, 1927.

Fraser, Hilary. "St. Theresa, St. Dorothea, and Miss Brooke in *Middlemarch.*" *Nineteenth-Century Fiction* 40 (1986): 400–411.

Fricke, Douglas C. "Art and Artists in *Daniel Deronda.*" *Studies in the Novel* 5 (1973): 220–28.

Frye, Northrop. *Anatomy of Criticism: Four Essays.* Princeton: Princeton University Press, 1957.

Fulmer, Constance Marie. *George Eliot: A Reference Guide.* Boston: G. K. Hall and Company, 1977.

Furbank, P. N. *E. M. Forster: A Life.* New York: Harcourt Brace Jovanovich, 1978.

Gallagher, Catherine. "The Failure of Realism: *Felix Holt.*" *Nineteenth Century Fiction* 35 (1980): 372–84.

Genette, Gerard. *Narrative Discourse: An Essay in Method.* Translated by Jane E. Lewin. Ithaca: Cornell University Press, 1980.

Gilbert, Sandra M., and Susan Gubar. *The Madwoman in the Attic.* New Haven and London: Yale University Press, 1979.

Goethe, Johann Wolfgang von. *Essays on Art and Literature.* Edited by John Gearey. Vol. 3 of *Goethe's Collected Works.* New York: Suhrkamp Publishers, 1986.

———. *Goethe's Faust.* Translated by Walter Kaufmann. Garden City: Anchor Books, 1961.

———. *Goethe's Faust: Parts 1 and 2.* Edited by R. M. S. Heffner, Helmut Rehder, and W. F. Twaddell. Boston: D. C. Heath and Company, 1954–55.

———*Iphigenie auf Tauris.* Edited by Lewis A. Rhoades and Carl Selmer. Rev. ed. Boston: D. C. Heath and Company, 1961.

———. *Iphigenia in Tauris.* Translated by Charles E. Passage. New York: Frederick Ungar Publishing Company, 1963.

Gottfried, Leon. "Structure and Genre in *Daniel Deronda.*" In *The English Novel in the Nineteenth Century: Essays on the Literary Mediation of Human Values.* Edited by George Goodin. Urbana: University of Illinois Press, 1972. 164–75.

Graver, Suzanne. *George Eliot and Community: A Study in Social Theory and Fictional Form.* Berkeley: University of California Press, 1984.

Greenstein, Susan M. "A Question of Vocation: From *Romola* to *Middlemarch.*" *Nineteenth-Century Fiction* 35 (1981): 487–505.

Gustafson, Richard. *Leo Tolstoy: Resident and Stranger: A Study in Fiction and Theology.* Princeton: Princeton University Press, 1986.

Guth, Barbara. "Philip: The Tragedy of *The Mill on the Floss.*" *Studies in the Novel* 15 (1983): 356–63.

Hagan, John, "A Reinterpretation of *The Mill on the Floss.*" *PMLA* 87 (1972): 53–63.

Haight, Gordon S. *George Eliot: A Biography.* New York: Oxford University Press, 1968.

———, ed. *A Century of George Eliot Criticism.* Boston: Houghton Mifflin Company, 1965.

———, and Rosemary T. VanArsdel, eds. *George Eliot: A Centenary Tribute.* Totowa, N.J.: Barnes and Noble, 1982.

Haile, H. G. *Artist in Chrysalis: A Biographical Study of Goethe in Italy.* Urbana: University of Illinois Press, 1973.

Hands, Timothy. *A George Eliot Chronology.* London: Macmillan and Company, 1989.

Hardy, Barbara, ed. *"Middlemarch": Critical Approaches to the Novel.* London: Athlone, 1967.

———, ed. *Critical Essays on George Eliot.* London: Routledge and Kegan Paul, 1970.

———. *Particularities: Readings in George Eliot.* London: Peter Owen, 1982.

———. *The Novels of George Eliot: A Study in Form.* London: Athlone Press, 1959.

Harvey, W. J. *Character and the Novel.* Ithaca: Cornell University Press, 1965.

———. *The Art of George Eliot.* London: Chatto and Windus, 1961.

Heilbrun, Carolyn G. *Toward a Recognition of Androgyny.* New York: Harper Colophon Books, 1973.

Herbert, Christopher. "Preachers and the Schemes of Nature in *Adam Bede.*" *Nineteenth-Century Fiction* 29 (1975): 412–27.

Hertz, Neil. "Recognizing Casaubon." *The End of the Line: Essays on Psychoanalysis and the Sublime.* New York: Columbia University Press, 1985. 75–96.

Higdon, David Leon. "Failure of Design in *The Mill on the Floss.*" *The Journal of Narrative Technique* 3 (1973): 183–92.

———. "The Iconographic Backgrounds of *Adam Bede,* Chapter 15." *Nineteenth-Century Fiction* 27 (1972): 155–70.

———. *Time and English Fiction.* Totowa, N.J.: Rowman and Littlefield, 1977.

Hogan, James. *A Commentary on the Plays of Sophocles.* Carbondale, Ill.: Southern University Press, 1991.

Homans, Margaret. "Eliot, Wordsworth, and the Scenes of the Sisters' Instruction." In *Bearing the Word: Language and Female Experience in Nineteenth-Century Women's Writing.* Edited by Catherine R. Stimson. Chicago: University of Chicago Press, 1986. 120–52.

Horace. *Odes.* Edited by T. E. Page. London: Macmillan and Company, 1962.

Howe, Florence. "T. S. Eliot, Virginia Woolf, and the Future of 'Tradition.'" *Traditions and the Talents of Women.* Edited by Florence Howe. Urbana: University of Illinois Press, 1991. 1–33.

Hurley, Edward T. "Piero di Cosimo: An Alternate Analogy for George Eliot's Realism." *The Victorian Newsletter* 31 (1967): 54–56.

Jacobus, Mary. "The Question of Language: Men of Maxims and *The Mill on the Floss.*" *Critical Inquiry* 8 (1981): 207–22.

James, Henry. "*Daniel Deronda:* A Conversation." In *George Eliot: A Collection of Critical Essays.* Edited by George R. Creeger. Englewood Cliffs, N.J.: Prentice-Hall, 1970. 161–76.

———. "The Novels of George Eliot." *Atlantic Monthly* 18 (1866): 479–92.

———. "The Novels of George Eliot." Edited by Gordon S. Haight. *A Century of George Eliot Criticism.* Boston: Houghton Mifflin Company, 1965. 43–65.

———. "Unsigned Review [of *Felix Holt*]." In *George Eliot: The Critical Heritage.* Edited by David Carroll. New York: Barnes and Noble, 1971. 273–77.

Joseph, Gerhard. "The *Antigone* as Cultural Touchstone: Matthew Arnold, Hegel, George Eliot, Virginia Woolf, and Margaret Drabble." *PMLA* 96 (1981): 22–35.

Junius Fransciscus. *The Painting of the Ancients.* 1698. Reprint. Westmead: Gregg International Publishers, 1972.

Karlinsky, Simon. *The Nabokov-Wilson Letters, 1940–1971.* New York: Harper and Row, 1979.

King, Jeannette. *Tragedy in the Victorian Novel: Theory and Practice in the Novels of George Eliot, Thomas Hardy, and Henry James.* Cambridge: Cambridge University Press, 1978.

Knapp, Shoshana. "Tolstoj's Reading of George Eliot: Visions and Revisions." *Slavic and East European Journal* 27 (1983): 318–26.

Knoepflmacher, U. C. "George Eliot's Anti-Romantic Romance: 'Mrs. Gilfil's Love Story.'" *The Victorian Newsletter* 31 (1967): 11–14.

———. "*Middlemarch:* An Avuncular View." *Nineteenth-Century Fiction* 30 (1975): 53–81.

———. "Unveiling Men: Power and Masculinity in George Eliot's Fiction." In *Men by Women.* Edited by Janet Todd. New York: Holmes and Meier Publishers, 1981. 130–46.

———. *George Eliot's Early Novels: The Limits of Realism.* Berkeley: University of California Press, 1968.

———. *Religious Humanism and the Victorian Novel: George Eliot, Walter Pater, and Samuel Butler.* Princeton: Princeton University Press, 1965.

———. "Genre and the Integration of Gender: From Wordsworth to George Eliot to Virginia Woolf." In *Victorian Literature and Society.* Edited by James R. Kincaid and Albert J. Kuhn. Columbus: Ohio State University Press, 1984. 94–118.

Krieger, Murray. *The Classic Vision: The Retreat from Extremity in Modern Literature.* Baltimore: Johns Hopkins Press, 1971.

Laski, Marghanita. *George Eliot and Her World.* New York: Charles Scribner's Sons, 1973.

Lawrence, D. H. *The Rainbow.* New York: Viking Press, 1961.

Leavis, F. R *The Great Tradition: George Eliot, Henry James, Joseph Conrad.* New York: New York University Press, 1973.

Lee, A. Robert. "*The Mill on the Floss:* 'Memory' and the Reading Experience." In *Reading the Victorian Novel: Detail into Form.* Edited by Ian Gregor. New York: Barnes and Noble, 1980. 72–91.

Levine, George. "George Eliot's Hypothesis of Reality." *Nineteenth-Century Fiction* 35 (1980): 1–28.

Levine, Herbert J. "The Marriage of Allegory and Realism in *Daniel Deronda.*" *Genre* 15 (1982): 421–46.

Lewes, George Henry. *The Life of Goethe.* New York: E. P. Dutton, 1908.

Lodge, David. *After Bakhtin.* London: Routledge, 1990.

Lundberg, Patricia Lorimer. "George Eliot: Mary Ann Evans' Subversive Tool in *Middlemarch.*" *Studies in the Novel* 18 (1986): 270–82.

Malmgren, Carl D. "Reading Authorial Narration: The Example of *Mill on the Floss.*" *Poetics Today* 7 (1987): 471–94.

Mansell, Jr., Darrel. "George Eliot's Conception of Tragedy." *Nineteenth-Century Fiction* 22 (1967): 155–71.

Martin, Bruce K. "Similarity within Dissimilarity: The Dual Structure of *Silas Marner.*" *Texas Studies in Literature and Language* 14 (1972): 479–89.

McCobb, Anthony. *George Eliot's Knowledge of German Life and Letters*. Salzburg: Institute für Anglistik und Amerikanistik, Universität Salzburg, 1982.

McColley, Diane Kelsey. *Milton's Eve*. Urbana: University of Illinois Press, 1983.

McKee, Patricia. *Heroic Commitment in Richardson, Eliot, and James*. Princeton: Princeton University Press, 1986.

McKenzie, P. "George Eliot's Nightmare, Proust's Realism." *Modern Language Review* 79 (1984): 810–16.

Melville, Herman. *Moby Dick*. Edited by Harold Beaver. Baltimore: Penguin Books, 1972.

Miller, J. Hillis. *The Ethics of Reading: Kant, De Mann, Eliot, Trollope, James, and Benjamin*. Walleck Library Lectures at the University of California, Irvine. New York: Columbia University Press, 1987.

———. "Narrative and History." *ELH* 41 (1974): 455–73.

———. "Optic and Semiotic in *Middlemarch*." In *The Worlds of Victorian Fiction*. Edited by Jerome Buckley. Cambridge: Harvard University Press, 1975. 125–45.

———. "The Two Rhetorics: George Eliot's Bestiary." *Writing and Reading Differently: Deconstruction and the Teaching of Composition and Literature*. Edited by G. Douglas Atkins and Michael L. Johnson. Lawrence: University Press of Kansas, 1985.

———, Barbara Hardy, and Richard Poirier. "*Middlemarch*, Chapter 85: Three Commentaries." *Nineteenth-Century Fiction* 35 (1980): 432–53.

Milton, John. *Paradise Lost and Other Poems*. Edited by Edward Le Comte. New York: New American Library, 1961.

Mintz, Alan L. *George Eliot and the Novels of Vocation*. Cambridge: Harvard University Press, 1978.

Molstad, David. "Dantean Purgatorial Metaphor in *Daniel Deronda*." *Papers on Language and Literature* 19 (1983): 183–98.

Nabokov, Vladimir. *Transparent Things*. Greenwich, Conn.: Fawcett Crest Books, 1972.

Nathan, Rhoda B., ed. *Nineteenth-Century Women Writers of the English-Speaking World*. New York: Greenwood Press, 1968.

Newton, K. M. *George Eliot, Romantic Humanist: A Study of the Philosophical Structure of Her Novels*. Totowa, N.J.: Barnes and Noble, 1981.

———. "The Role of the Narrator in George Eliot's Novels." *Journal of Narrative Technique* 3 (1973): 97–107.

Norton, Alexandra M. "The Seeds of Fiction: George Eliot's *Scenes of Clerical Life*." *The Journal of Narrative Technique* 19 (1989): 215–32.

Novy, Marianne. *Love's Argument: Gender Relations in Shakespeare*. Chapel Hill: University of North Carolina Press, 1984.

———, ed. *Women's Re-Visions of Shakespeare: On Responses of Dickinson, Woolf, Rich, H.D., George Eliot, and Others*. Urbana: University of Illinois Press, 1990.

Page, Norman. "The Great Tradition Revisited." In *Jane Austen's Achievement: Papers Delivered at the University of Alberta*. Edited by Juliet McMaster. New York: Barnes and Noble, 1976. 44–63.

Pangallo, Karen. *George Eliot: A Reference Guide, 1972–1987*. Boston: G. K. Hall, 1990.

Paris, Bernard J. *Experiments in Life: George Eliot's Quest for Values.* Detroit: Wayne State University Press, 1965.

Pell, Nancy [Anne]. "The Fathers' Daughters in *Daniel Deronda.*" *Nineteenth-Century Fiction* 36 (1982): 424–51.

Pinion, F. B. *A George Eliot Miscellany: A Supplement to Her Novels.* London: Macmillan and Company, 1982.

Plato. *Timaeus.* Translated by Francis M. Cornford. Indianapolis, Ind.: Library of Liberal Arts, 1959.

Plotinus. *Opera.* Edited by Paul Henry and Hans-Rudolf Schwyzer. Paris: Desclee de Brouwever, 1959.

Poovey, Mary. *The Proper Lady and the Woman Writer.* Chicago and London: University of Chicago Press, 1984.

Pratt, John Clark, and Victor A. Neufeldt, eds. *George Eliot's Middlemarch Notebooks: A Transcription.* Berkeley: University of California Press, 1979.

Praz, Mario. *The Hero in Eclipse in Victorian Fiction.* London: Oxford University Press, 1956.

Proclus. *Commentaire sur le Timée.* Translated by A. J. Festugière. Paris: Librairie Philosophique J. Vrin, 1967.

———. *Procli Diadochi in Platonis Timaeum.* Edited by Ernest Diehl. London: B. G. Tevbneri, 1903–6.

———. *The Commentaries on the Timaeus of Plato.* Translated by Thomas Taylor. London: A. J. Valpy, 1820.

Quick, Jonathan R. "Silas Marner as Romance: The Example of Hawthorne." *Nineteenth-Century Fiction* 29 (1974): 287–98.

Raider, Ruth. "'The Flash of Fervour': *Daniel Deronda.*" In *Reading the Victorian Novel: Detail into Form.* Edited by Ian Gregor. New York: Barnes and Noble, 1980. 253–73.

Redinger, Ruby V. *George Eliot: The Emergent Self.* New York: Alfred A. Knopf, 1975.

Reed, John R., and Jerry Herron. "George Eliot's Illegitimate Children." *Nineteenth-Century Fiction* 40 (1985): 175–86.

Reynolds, Sir Joshua. *Discourses on Art.* Edited by Robert R. Wark. New Haven: Yale University Press, 1975.

Ringler, Ellen. "*Middlemarch:* A Feminist Perspective." *Studies in the Novel* 15 (1983): 55–61.

Rogers, Philip. "Lessons for Fine Ladies: Tolstoj and George Eliot's *Felix Holt, the Radical.*" *Slavic and East European Journal* 29 (1985): 379–82.

Ronald, Ann. "George Eliot's Florentine Museum." *Papers on Language and Literature* 13 (1977): 260–69.

Sadoff, Dianne F. *Monsters of Affection: Dickens, Eliot, and Bronte on Fatherhood.* Baltimore: Johns Hopkins University Press, 1982.

Sanders, Andrew. "'Romola's Waking': George Eliot's Historical Novel." In *The Victorian Historical Novel, 1840–1880.* London: Macmillan and Company, 1978. 168–96.

Schiller, Frederich von. *Naive and Sentimental Poetry and On the Sublime: Two Essays.* Translated by Julius A. Elias. New York: Frederick Ungar, 1966.

Shakespeare, William. *King Henry the Fourth, Part Two.* Edited by Louis B. Wright and Virginia A. Lamar. New York: Washington Square Press, 1961.

——. *The Comedies, Histories, Tragedies, and Poems.* Edited by Charles Knight. 12 vols. 2d ed. London: Charles Knight and Company, 1842–44.

Sheets, Robin. "*Felix Holt* Language, the Bible, and the Problematic of Meaning." *Nineteenth-Century Fiction* 37 (1982): 146–69.

Showalter, Elaine. *A Literature of Their Own: British Women Novelists from Bronte to Lessing.* Princeton: Princeton University Press, 1977.

Shuttleworth, Sally. *George Eliot and Nineteenth-Century Science.* Cambridge: Cambridge University Press, 1984.

Smith, Anne, ed. *George Eliot: Centenary Essays and an Unpublished Fragment.* Totowa, N.J.: Barnes and Noble, 1980.

Sophocles. *Oedipus at Colonus.* Translated by Robert Fitzgerald. *Sophocles 1: The Complete Greek Tragedies.* Edited by David Greene and Richard Lattimore. New York: Washington Square Press, 1967.

——. *Philoctetes.* Translated by David Grene. *Sophocles 2: The Complete Greek Tragedies.* Edited by David Grene and Richmond Lattimore. New York: Washington Square Books, 1967.

——. *The Plays and Fragments,* 2 vols. Edited by Lewis Campbell. 1879. Reprint. Hildesheim: Georg Olm, 1969.

——. *The Plays and Fragments. Part Two: The Oedipus Coloneus.* Cambridge: At the University Press, 1907.

Spenser, Edmund. *The Poetical Works of Edmund Spenser.* London: Oxford University Press, 1912.

Stone, Donald F. *The Romantic Impulse in Victorian Fiction.* Cambridge: Harvard University Press, 1966.

Sullivan, William J. "Music and Musical Allusion in *The Mill on the Floss.*" *Criticism* 16 (1974): 232–46.

——. "Piero di Cosimo and the Higher Primitivism in *Romola.*" *Nineteenth-Century Fiction* 26 (1972): 390–405.

——. "The Sketch of the Three Masks in *Romola.*" *Victorian Newsletter* 41 (1972): 9–13.

Supp, Dorothee. *Tragik bei George Eliot.* Heidelberg: Carl Winter, 1969.

Swann, Brian. "*Middlemarch* and Myth." *Nineteenth Century Fiction* 28 (1973): 210–14.

——. "*Silas Marner* and the New Mythus." *Criticism* 18 (1976): 101–21.

Thale, Jerome. *The Novels of George Eliot.* New York: Columbia University Press, 1959.

Thomson, Fred C. "*Felix Holt* as Classic Tragedy." *Nineteenth-Century Fiction* 16 (1961): 47–58.

——. "Politics and Society in *Felix Holt.*" In *The Classic British Novel.* Edited by Howard M. Harper and Charles Edge. Athens: University of Georgia Press, 1972. 103–20.

Tolstoy, Leo. *War and Peace.* Translated by Constance Garrett. New York: Modern Library, 1931.

——. *What is Art?* New York: Bobbs Merrill Company, 1965.

Trevelyan, Humphry. *Goethe and the Greeks.* New York: Octagon Books, 1972.

Trubowitz, Rachel. "'The Single State of Man': Androgyny in *Macbeth* and *Paradise Lost.*" *Papers on Language and Literature* 26 (1990): 305–33.

Uglow, Jennifer. *George Eliot*. New York: Pantheon Books, 1987.

Virgil. *The Aeneid of Virgil*. Translated by Allen Mandelbaum. New York: Bantam Books, 1971.

Weisinger, Kenneth. *The Classical Facade: A Nonclassical Reading of Goethe's Classicism*. University Park: Pennsylvania State University Press, 1988.

Welsh, Alexander. *George Eliot and Blackmail*. Cambridge: Harvard University, 1986.

Wiesenfarth, Joseph. *George Eliot's Mythmaking*. Heidelberg: Carl Winter Universitats-verlag, 1977.

———. "George Eliot's Notes for *Adam Bede*." *Nineteenth-Century Fiction* 32 (1977): 127–65.

———. "*Middlemarch:* The Language of Art." *PMLA* 97 (1982): 363–77.

Wilt, Judith. *Ghosts of the Gothic: Austen, Eliot, and Lawrence*. Princeton: Princeton University Press, 1980.

Winnett, Susan. "Coming Unstrung: Women, Men, Narrative, and Principles of Pleasure." *PMLA* 105 (1990): 505–18.

Witemeyer, Hugh. *George Eliot and the Visual Arts*. New Haven: Yale University Press, 1979.

Wittreich, Joseph. *Feminist Milton*. Ithaca: Cornell University Press, 1987.

Woolf, Virginia. *A Room of One's Own*. New York: Harcourt, Brace, and World, 1957.

———. *To the Lighthouse*. New York: Harcourt, Brace, and World, 1955.

———. *To the Lighthouse: The Original Holograph Draft*. Edited by Susan Dick. Toronto: University of Toronto Press, 1982.

———. *A Writer's Diary*. Edited by Leonard Woolf. New York: Harcourt, Brace, Jovanovitch, 1954.

Wordsworth, William. *Selected Poems and Prefaces*. Edited by Jack Stillinger. Boston: Houghton Mifflin Company, 1965.

Yeazell, Ruth Bernard. "Why Political Novels Have Heroines: *Sybil, Mary Barton,* and *Felix Holt*." *Novel: A Forum on Fiction* 18 (1985): 126–44.

Zimmerman, Bonnie. "*Felix Holt* and the True Power of Womanhood." *ELH* 46 (1979): 432–51.

Index